D1756260

Drafting and Negotiating
Commercial Contracts

Third edition

Drafting and Negotiating Commercial Contracts

Third edition

By

Mark Anderson
Solicitor, Anderson Law LLP

and

Victor Warner
Solicitor, Anderson Law LLP

Bloomsbury Professional

In memory of Irene Warner

Bloomsbury Professional Ltd, Maxwelton House, 41–43 Boltro Road, Haywards Heath, West Sussex, RH16 1BJ

© Bloomsbury Professional Ltd 2012

Bloomsbury Professional Ltd is an imprint of Bloomsbury Publishing plc

A CIP Catalogue record for this book is available from the British Library.

ISBN   978 1 84766 744 1

Typeset by Phoenix Photosetting Ltd, Chatham, Kent
Printed and bound in Great Britain by CPI Group (UK) Ltd., Croydon, CR0 4YY

Preface

Much has changed in the world of drafting since the last edition of this book in 2007. The continued rise of the internet means that the way many people 'experience' a contract is now no longer as a printed document but on a computer screen.

Many of the traditional boundaries have also fallen away as to who can actively participate in the drafting and production of an agreement. It is now no longer solely in the hands of lawyers. Many clients now participate in drafting or commenting on an agreement. They also have access to many template agreements that are available online. These and other changes have led to a change in the relationship between client and lawyer.

In this third edition we have sought to reflect some of the changes by:

- adding a new chapter on the checking of agreements (and some techniques for doing so).

  In the old days, when the physical typing and preparing of an agreement was in the hands of lawyer, it was the lawyer's job to check a document not only for typos but also for consistency (eg that a defined word was used correctly throughout, or that the agreed commercial terms had been included). Nowadays everyone works to much reduced time-scales, and clients sometimes take responsibility for sending out drafts or even the final version of the agreement.

  The aim of this new chapter is set out some of the steps that can be taken to minimise errors.

- adding a new chapter on the specific issues involved in drafting contracts for use with consumers.

  At the time of the first edition of this book, English law already provided some special rules for contracts with consumers, notably the need to use simple and plain language and not to include unfair terms. But the implications of these requirements had not been worked out to the extent that they now have, in official guidance and court decisions. We feel that the time is right to devote a separate chapter to this topic.

- adding a new chapter on more advanced drafting techniques. This chapter describes some 'bigger picture' issues that are separate from the detailed discussion of individual clauses or individual issues which the rest of the book is concerned.

- adding more explanations as to the meaning of legal terms and principles throughout the text to make the book an 'easier read' for readers who are not lawyers.

Like many publications nowadays this book also has its own website at http://www.draftingcommercialcontracts.info. We will add new developments to the material in the book as well as including more information about the practicalities of drafting. Our firm also has its own blog which often includes postings about and on drafting: http://www.ipdraughts.wordpress.com. Please visit it too!

This book is really one half of a larger book. The other (larger) half is our *A-Z Guide to Boilerplate and Commercial Clauses*, which provides more in-depth commentary on individual clauses than we can incorporate in this book, together with examples of wording. As we finish this book we are hard at work on the 3rd edition of *A-Z Guide to Boilerplate and Commercial Clauses*, which is due to appear in 2012.

Although much has changed, the fundamentals still apply: the contract drafter's objectives are to express the commercial intentions of the parties in clear and direct language, and in a legally effective way. The goal of this third edition remains the same as that of the first edition: to provide a practical guide to help the drafter to meet those objectives.

Mark Anderson
Victor Warner

http://www.andlaw.eu

October 2011

Contents

Contents

Contents

Contents

Contents

Table of statutes

Table of statutory instruments

Table of statutory instruments

Table of Cases

Table of cases

Table of cases

Chapter 1

Legal Formalities for a Binding Contract

Key points

- Put all but the simplest agreement in writing *and* have them signed by, or on behalf of, all the parties to the agreement.

- There are no special requirements as to the format of most written commercial agreements made 'under hand'.

- For agreements made by a company, the simplest method of signing the agreement is normally for an authorised representative to do so 'on behalf of' the company.

- If there are doubts over whether the parties are providing consideration (something of value), consider executing the agreement as a deed. If the agreement is made as a deed, comply with the formalities for executing a deed.

- Do not date agreements and deeds prior to signature; if a deed is not to take effect immediately on signature, make this clear in the text of the deed (that it is not 'delivered' on signature or is delivered subject to conditions).

- If the agreement has an informal format, or is described as a Heads of Agreement (or similar), consider including wording as to whether it is to be legally binding (and if not, at a minimum, state that it is 'subject to contract').

- Consider or take legal advice on whether the agreement meets all the requirements for a legally binding contract, particularly in relation to the basic contract law issues listed later in this chapter.

- If the signature page of the contract is signed before the provisions of the contract are finalised, obtain the agreement of all the parties and document that agreement; but never do this where there is a transaction involving land or you are making a contract by deed.

1.1 Introduction

As a preliminary to discussing how contracts are commonly structured and worded, this chapter will mention some formal legal requirements for legally binding contracts. These are requirements for contracts made under English law; the requirements for contracts made under other countries' laws are in some cases significantly different (and are beyond the scope of this book).

1.2   Must the contract be in writing?

It is possible to make many types of contract which will be legally enforceable under English law without any written record or other formality. An example of such a contract is the purchase of a newspaper from a shop; such contracts are normally made orally and without formality. In fact, shop purchases are often made without any words being used by the shop assistant or purchaser, other than a contractually irrelevant 'thank you'. This lack of formality does not mean that the transaction is not a legally binding contract—far from it. The same legal rules which make a contract for the purchase of a newspaper legally binding apply also to commercial contracts of far greater value and importance.

It is necessary for the following types of contract to be in writing (and signed in some cases) for them to be legally binding[1]:

- contracts for the sale or other disposition of an interest in land[2];

- guarantees (ie guaranteeing performance of the obligations of another)[3];

- certain types of negotiable instrument (bills of exchange and cheques)[4];

- absolute assignment of any debt or other legal thing[5];

- certain types of consumer credit agreement[6];

---

[1]   Historically, the Statute of Frauds 1677, ss 4 and 17 required many types of contract to be in writing or supported by written evidence, but most of these categories were abolished in the last century.

[2]   Under the Law of Property (Miscellaneous Provisions) Act 1989, s 2. The contract must be signed by or on behalf of each party to the contract.

[3]   Statute of Frauds 1677, s 4: 'no action shall be brought … whereby to charge the defendant upon any special promise to answer for the debt default or miscarriage of another person … unless the agreement upon which such action shall be brought or some memorandum or note thereof shall be in writing and signed by the party to be charged therewith or some other person thereunto by him lawfully authorised' (*edited to translate into modern English*) (as amended).
    The Statute of Frauds does not apply to indemnities: *Yoeman Credit Ltd v Latter* [1961] 2 All ER 294 at 296.

[4]   For example, bills (Bills of Exchange Act 1882, s 3(1)), cheques (ibid, s 73) and promissory notes (*ibid*, s 83).

[5]   Law of Property Act 1925, s 136(1) (re-enacting Judicature Act 1873, s 25(6)). The assignment must be absolute and not conditional, and express notice must be given to the debtor. Such an assignment can be made without consideration for it to be effective: *Harding v Harding* (1886) 17 QBD 442; *Re Westerton* [1919] 2 Ch 104. Subject to the formalities and conditions of this section being complied with the assignee can pursue the debtor in the assignee's own name and without joining the assignor as a party to any action.

[6]   See Consumer Credit Act 1974, in relation to loans, hire purchase agreements, mortgages, etc.

- certain types of insurance contract[7];

- arbitration agreement (for the Arbitration Act 1996 to apply)[8];

- main terms of a contract of commercial agency[9]; and

- assignments of patents, trade marks, copyright and registered designs[10], and other intellectual property.

Many types of commercial contract do not fall within the above categories, and therefore do not need to be in writing in order to be legally binding. In the United States, it appears that a Statute of Frauds continues to provide that contracts over a certain value must be evidenced in writing[11]. Other countries require certain types of contract to be in writing and/or signed with particular formalities[12]. In practice, most significant commercial contracts (both domestic and international) are in writing; this will generally be essential to avoid uncertainty as to exactly what terms have been agreed.

1.3   Other requirements as to the form of the contract: advantages of deeds

There are two main types of contract:

- contracts which are simply signed by or on behalf of the contracting parties ('executed under hand')[13]; and

---

[7]   For example, under the Marine Insurance Act 1906.

[8]   Arbitration Act 1996, s 5.

[9]   Commercial Agents (Council Directive) Regulations 1993, SI 1993/3053, reg 3. The principal and the agent are each entitled to receive from the other a written document setting out the terms of the contract of agency between them (including any terms subsequently agreed). The party sending their document must sign it.

[10]   Patents Act 1977, s 30(6); Trade Marks Act 1994, s 23(3); Copyright, Designs and Patents Act 1988, s 90(3); and Registered Designs Act 1949, s 15B(3) respectively. In each case, the assignment must be signed by the assignor (or on the assignor's behalf).

[11]   See the Uniform Contract Code, 2–201: 'Formal Requirements; Statute of Frauds. (1) Except as otherwise provided in this section a contract for the sale of goods for the price of $500 or more is not enforceable by way of action or defense unless there is some writing sufficient to indicate that a contract for sale has been made between the parties and signed by the party against whom enforcement is sought or by his authorized agent or broker. A writing is not insufficient because it omits or incorrectly states a term agreed upon but the contract is not enforceable under this paragraph beyond the quantity of goods shown in such writing.' Some aspects of US commercial law appear to share a common origin with English commercial law, eg a Statute of Frauds, and a statutory implied term of merchantability in contracts for the sale of goods, even though the current expression of such laws diverges significantly from English law.

[12]   Under French law, it is understood that certain types of contract affecting *ordre public* must also be in the French language and subject to the jurisdiction of the French courts.

[13]   'Signing' does not require that actual putting of pen to paper, but could be the typing of a name on an electronic version of an agreement, the use of a rubber stamp with a name and so on.

- contracts which are signed as deeds (and comply with the other formalities of deeds) ('executed as deeds').

In most cases the contracting parties are free to choose whether to execute their contract under hand or as a deed. The main practical advantages—or disadvantages, depending on one's view—of executing a contract as a deed are:

- *No need for consideration.* Contracts under hand are generally not legally enforceable if 'consideration' (something of value) does not pass to or from the parties to the contract[14]. Sometimes a nominal amount (eg £1) is inserted into the contract to ensure that the contract does not fail for want of consideration.

- By contrast, contracts executed as deeds, will generally be legally binding even though they lack any consideration (because no amount is stated in the contract, or there is nothing of value which is exchanged between the parties). Parties sometimes execute their contracts as deeds to avoid uncertainty concerning the existence of consideration or the consideration being of the right 'type'[15], particularly where there are doubts over whether:

  - consideration has passed from one party to the other[16];

  - the consideration is past consideration[17];

  - when a contract is amended all the parties are providing consideration[18].

- *Extended limitation period.* Usually it is not possible to bring a case for breach of contract more than six years after the date on which the cause of action accrued. However, for contracts executed as deeds, the limitation period is extended from six to 12 years[19].

---

[14] Taking the example of the newspaper purchase mentioned earlier, the shop provides consideration in the form of the newspaper, and the purchaser provides consideration in the form of the price paid for the newspaper. What needs providing is something of value (whether monetary or non-monetary), but what worth the something has is generally not relevant.

[15] *Johnsey Estates Ltd v Lewis Manley (Engineering) Ltd* (1987) 54 P & CR 296 at 284, CA. Glidewell LJ said that it was the existence of the consideration which is important and not the amount of the consideration.

[16] *Tweddle v Atkinson* (1861) 1 B & S 393. This covers the situation where Party A offers to provide goods or services to Party B, but Party B offers to pay Party C a sum of money.

[17] *Re McArdle* [1951] Ch 669. This covers the situation where Party A provides some services or goods to Party B, and then later after Party A has made her or his offer to provide the goods or services (or has in fact provided them) Party B then decides to pay a sum of money to Party A. A situation where there is no past consideration is where Party A offers to provide services or goods to Party B in return for a promise by Party B to pay for the services or goods.

[18] For example, the parties may amend a contract where a supplier of goods will supply more of the goods, but for the same price as in the original contract. In such a case there is nothing provided which is 'extra' over the original price by the payor. Making the amending document to the contract as a deed avoids any problems or argument over whether the payor has supplied consideration for the extra goods.

[19] Limitation Act 1985, s 5.

1.3.1   Use of seals

It used to be necessary to use a seal to create a valid deed. This is no longer required for individuals or most types of companies[20]. Certain companies or organisations however must continue to use a seal when making a deed (eg corporate bodies which are not formed or regulated by the Companies Act 2006[21]). Examples of the types of organisations and persons subject to this requirement are a large number of 'public' bodies such as local authorities, certain government ministers (and their departments), the Information Commissioner, the British Museum, universities etc. For these types of organisations, issues as to how the seal is used and who has to use it are found in their constitutional documents (or Acts of Parliament)[22].

1.4   No formalities for execution of contracts under hand

There are no special requirements as to the form of a contract under hand— they are simply signed by each of the parties. There is no need for the witnessing of the signature. Where the contracting party is a company, a single authorised signatory commonly signs the agreement 'for and on behalf of the company'. Under English law it is possible to execute a contract by a company, or on behalf of a company, in a number of different ways:

- *By the company.* The contract may be executed by a company *itself*, by writing[23]:

  ○   under its common seal[24]; or

---

[20]   Following the coming into to effect of Law of Property (Miscellaneous Provisions) Act 1989, s 1(1)(b) (for individuals) and Companies Act 1985, s 43 (for companies formed or regulated by the Companies Act 2006).

[21]   For more on this point, see Mark Anderson and Victor Warner, *Execution of Documents—A Practical Guide* (2nd Edn), 2008 Law Society Publishing.

[22]   The default position is normally that one or more member(s) of the governing body must sign the document and/or the seal is applied in their presence. In practice, particularly for larger organisations of this type, there are often policies in place where certain types of document are signed by a senior official or manager of the organisation and the seal does not need to be applied in the presence of the governing body. Unfortunately each organisation's constitution/governing documents and policies should be checked for the precise procedure.

[23]   Companies Act 2006, s 43(1)(a).

[24]   Companies Act 2006, s 44(1). A company no longer needs to have a common seal: Companies Act 2006, s 45(1). The articles of association of a UK company will set out how to use a seal if a company chooses to do so—for example, see the model articles for private companies limited by shares, art 49 (in Companies (Model Articles) Regulations 2008, SI 2008/3229, Sch 1). Here the seal is applied and then the document is signed by a director (in the presence of a witness, who also signs), or two directors, or a director and the company secretary or someone authorised by the directors sign the document (Regulation 49).

  ○ by:

   *   two directors; or

   *   a director and the company secretary; or

   *   a director in the presence of a witness signing;[25] *and*

   *   the contract being expressed to be executed by the company[26].

- *On behalf of a company.* Alternatively the contract may be executed *on behalf of* a company, by any person acting under its authority, express or implied[27]. Other than for the most important contracts (or in a small company), this is the way contracts are usually executed by companies. In this way, a main board director of the contracting party is not required to sign. Particularly in the case of larger companies (where non-directors have authority to sign even important contracts on behalf of the company), by preference this method of executing contracts is used rather than having the contract signed *by* the company (as described above).

In addition, a contracting party may appoint someone to act as its agent to enter into contracts on its behalf. It is sometimes understood that where a contract is signed *for* another party, this refers to acting in an agency capacity. However, it would be unwise to rely on this assumption, and better to state specifically the nature of any agency relationship[28].

Hence, the different usages of the terms *by*, *for* and *on behalf of.* Practical examples of execution clauses are given in Chapter 2 of this book.

Some additional permitted methods of execution of an English law contract by a foreign company are referred to later in this chapter, in the discussion of execution of deeds by a foreign company.

It is possible to contrast the relative lack of formality in executing an English law contract under hand with the position under the laws of other countries. For example, in some countries it is necessary for two representatives of a corporate party to sign the contract, or a notary must witness the signing.

In contrast to the signing of a contract under hand, the signing of a contract

---

[25]   Companies Act 2006, s 44(1), (2) and (3). A document is validly executed by a company if it is signed on behalf of the company by (i) two authorised signatories or (ii) a director in the presence of a witness. An authorised signatory is a director of the company, and, if the company has one, a company secretary.

[26]   Companies Act 2006, s 44(4).

[27]   Companies Act 2006, s 43(1)(b).

[28]   In *Southern Water Authority v Carey* [1985] 2 All ER 1077 it was held that for someone to be regarded as acting as an agent, they must be at least within the contemplation of the main contractors at the time the document was signed. Thus for a 'third party' to have the authority to sign a contract as an agent of one of the main contractors there has to be something *expressly* conferring authority on that third party—a mere contemplation is not sufficient. The most obvious way to achieve this is in the document/contract itself.

(or other type of document) as a deed must comply with the formal, legal requirements for execution of deeds under English law. The requirements[29] are different in the case of deeds executed by individuals, UK companies[30], and non-UK companies respectively, and are summarised as follows.

1.5   Formalities for execution of deeds by individuals

- *Use of a seal no longer required.* It is no longer necessary for a deed executed by an individual to be sealed[31]. The traditional phrase 'signed, sealed and delivered' summarised the former legal requirements for execution of a deed by an individual.

- *A document must state clearly that it is to be a deed.* It must be made clear on the face of the document that it is intended to be a deed by the person or parties making the deed[32].

- *A document must be 'validly executed' as a deed.* It is possible for the document to be executed by:

    o   the person or a person authorised to execute it in the name, or on behalf of, that person; or

    o   by one or more of those parties or a person authorised to execute it in the name, or on behalf of, one or more those parties[33].

- *Meaning of 'validly executed'.* To be a deed the document must be signed either:

    o   by the individual in the presence of a witness who attests the signature; or

    o   (if the individual does not or cannot sign the document) by another person at the direction of the individual, and that other person must sign in the presence of the individual and also in the presence of two witnesses who must each attest the signature)[34].

---

[29] See the Law of Property (Miscellaneous Provisions) Act 1989, s 1 and the Companies Act 2006; and in the case of companies incorporated outside the UK, see Overseas Companies (Execution of Documents and Registration of Charges) Regulations 2009, SI 2009/1917 from 1 October 2009.

[30] See definition in the Companies Act 2006, ss 1, 2, 3 and 1171.

[31] It has now been made clear by statute that the use of a seal alone will not make a document a deed: Law of Property (Miscellaneous Provisions) Act 1989, s 1(2A).

[32] It is possible to do this in a number of ways, such as stating at the beginning of the document: 'this deed dated …' or at its end that it is being executed or signed as a deed.

[33] Law of Property (Miscellaneous Provisions) Act 1989, s 1(2)(b).

[34] Law of Property (Miscellaneous Provisions) Act 1989, s 1(3).

- *A document must be delivered.* The document must be 'delivered as a deed'[35] by the individual or someone who is authorised to do so on his behalf (eg his solicitor). In practice, deeds are either stated to be (automatically) delivered upon signature, or the parties or their solicitors will agree a different date for delivery or specify conditions in order for a deed to be delivered. Commercial parties who are unfamiliar with this practice of agreeing the date of the document (and who have the draft document on their word processor) will sometimes type in the date of the contract prior to signature, and they may need to be discouraged from doing so. Sometimes deeds are signed by a party and then, by arrangement, held in escrow by the party's solicitor, so that the deed only takes effect when the solicitor states that the deed is released from escrow and delivered (usually when some condition has been met, for example, in a contract of sale, when the contract price reaches the bank account of the seller).

1.6   Formalities for execution of deeds by UK companies formed or regulated by the Companies Act 2006[36]

- *A document must clearly state that it is to be a deed.* It must be made clear on the face of the document that it is intended to be a deed by the person or parties making the deed[37].

- *There is a choice as to whether to use the common seal of the company.*

  - *Choosing to use the seal.* A company can choose to execute a deed by applying its common seal to the document. If it does, it will need to do so in the way described in its articles of association. The current default position for a private limited company is that the seal is applied to a document[38]. Then a director (or the company secretary

---

[35]   Law of Property (Miscellaneous Provisions) Act 1989, s 1(3)(b).

[36]   As to the definition of a UK company for these purposes, see the Companies Act 2006, ss 1, 2, 3 and 1171. It includes a public or private company limited by shares or guarantee. This section also covers the execution of a deed by limited liability partnerships (see Limited Liability Partnerships (Application of Companies Act 2006) Regulations 2009, SI 2009/1804), but references to two directors or a director and secretary are replaced by references to two members of the limited liability partnership executing a document.
  This definition would not include a body incorporated by Royal Charter or statute (eg many UK universities, local authorities, some charities, NHS trusts and other public bodies). They must continue to execute deeds in the way specified in their constitutional documents or Act of Parliament (which will normally mean applying their common seals to deeds).

[37]   Typically by words at the beginning of the contract stating 'THIS DEED is made on _____ 201[ ] BETWEEN:' and/or stating at the place where the parties sign that it is being executed or signed as a deed.

[38]   It does not appear that the seal itself needs applying in the presence of the director etc who signs the document.

or someone authorised by the directors) signs the document in the presence of a witness[39]. This was the traditional method of execution of deeds by a company.

    ○ *Choosing not to use the seal.* As was stated earlier in relation to contracts under hand, it is no longer necessary for a company to have a common seal. A document signed by a director (in the presence of a witness), two directors or a director and a company secretary, and stated to be executed *by* the company (ie wording in the document which says this specifically), has the same effect as if it were executed under the common seal of the company[40].

• *Presumption that a deed is delivered upon signature.* A document which is executed by a company is presumed to be delivered upon its being executed, unless the contrary is proved[41].

• *Presumption in favour of purchaser.* In favour of a purchaser, a document is deemed to have been duly executed by a company if it purports to be signed by a director in the presence of a witness, a director and a company secretary, or by two directors[42].

1.7   Formalities for execution of deeds and contracts under hand (made under English law) by foreign companies

In the case of companies incorporated outside the UK, the rules relating to UK companies are modified[43]:

---

[39] See the Model articles for private companies limited by shares, art 49 (in Companies (Model Articles) Regulations 2008, SI 2008/3229, Sch 1). See also footnote 24 above.

[40] Companies Act 2006, s 44(2), (4).

[41] Companies Act 2006, ss 44(4), 46. A document executed as a deed is a different type of document to one executed under hand in several ways as set out in this chapter. But perhaps the concept of 'delivery' is the one which most people (even lawyers who do not have a detailed knowledge of the law relating to deeds) have difficulty understanding, and the implications of which are most difficult to grasp. Unless there is something in the document executed as a deed which clearly indicates that there is a specific condition which must be fulfilled, a company which signs the deed will be bound by it as soon as they sign (ie it is delivered as soon as they sign, unless there is clear and strong evidence that it is not delivered on signature). Or if the document signed as a deed is subject to a condition then a party to the document cannot recall or cancel their intention to be bound while they wait for the condition to be fulfilled. See *Silver Queen Maritime Ltd v Persia Petroleum Services Plc* [2010] EWHC 2867 (QB) for a recent illustration of this point. If a party wishes to have control of the period between signing a deed and its delivery, then the deed will need to include wording which gives it the power to recall or cancel the document at its discretion.

[42] Companies Act 2006, s 44(5) (as amended by SI 2005/1906). A 'purchaser' means a purchaser in good faith for valuable consideration. Section 44(5) covers both deeds and other documents.

[43] See Overseas Companies (Execution of Documents and Registration of Charges) Regulations 2009, SI 2009/1917 from 1 October 2009.

- *Execution of contracts in accordance with local legal requirements.* Instead of executing a contract with a common seal, a foreign company may execute in any manner permitted by the laws of the territory in which the company is incorporated. The document should state that it is executed by the company. An individual who is authorised to act for the company may also execute the contract on behalf of a company, subject to local laws.

- *Execution of deeds.* Two authorised representatives of the foreign company may execute a deed in accordance with any local legal requirements.

1.8 Signing before the provisions of the agreement are finalised (or other situations when a signature page is signed separately from the rest of an agreement)

As noted above, it is not necessary for the parties to most types of contract to sign them[44]. Although the internet has now taken over many of the more routine contracts made between commercial parties, documents which are signed with a real signature are still of importance, even in some contracts which are of a routine nature[45]. Where a 'real' signature is required modern working practices have intruded and raise issues which were much less common.

A consequence of the reality of modern working practice is that it is now less common for parties to meet together to sign a final version of an agreement. Sometimes the parties may never meet or they do not use lawyers (whether external or in-house) to help control the process signing before they enter into an agreement. The issue here is, where the parties do wish to enter an agreement by signature, they do in fact do so by signing a final version of an agreement. Nowadays it is possible to sign an agreement in a number of ways, including:

1   the parties (or their authorised representatives) meet and sign the contract in each other's presence (the traditional way of signing);

2   the parties do not meet but each sign a final version of the agreement, and each party then sends a complete agreement (with the signature page) to the other (at least initially) electronically[46];

---

[44]   See **1.2** above.

[45]   There are many reasons why this is so. For some commercial parties it is convention that agreements need a real signature; another reason is that a signature of a real person generally requires her or him to focus on the agreement that they are signing (or have it explained to them). From a lawyer's point of view, a real signature is much easier to test, as to whether or not it is genuine, than any form of electronic signature. For more on the latter point see Mason, *Electronic Signatures in Law* (2nd Edn), Bloomsbury Professional Publishing.

[46]   'Electronically' in this section means by scanning the original paper document to a file and sending by email, uploading to a file-sharing site such as Dropbox, or by facsimile.

3   the parties do not meet but each signs a final version of the agreement, and each party then sends just the signature page to the other (at least initially) electronically, and each party puts the signature page of the other party with their final version of the agreement;

4   one or more of the parties signs a signature page in advance of the provisions of the agreement being finalised and the signature pages are then attached to the final version of the agreement and sent to the other (at least electronically).

The first option was the conventional way of signing agreements and this approach will normally cause no problems. The second option is perhaps now the most common way signing agreements. Again this will not normally cause problems, as each party will send a complete (electronic) version to the other[47]. Also it is relatively simple to protect electronic documents (either to stop the extraction of, or changes to, the text or pages or to require a password to open the document at all)[48].

The real problems arise when the signature page is attached to the final version of the agreement whether or not the signature page is signed in advance of the provisions of the agreement being finalised. It is possible for a party (or its authorised representative):

•   to sign and then for completely or substantially different provisions to be added or substituted; or

•   to sign one (complete) agreement, and then the signature page is taken from that agreement and used with another agreement.

Where either of these situations occurs there is usually no problem if the party who signs subsequently ratifies the changes made. If a party does so then the changes will normally be binding on that party[49]. Problems can occur, however, where a party subsequently alleges that what it had signed is not what was agreed.

---

[47]   The mechanics of this approach are also possible in a number of ways: one party prepares the final version of the agreement and then circulates it to the other parties for signature (perhaps with some time/date stamp or other reference). In this case it is clear that everyone is signing the same version. If each party is preparing their own final version then, deliberately or innocently, they may sign a different version. Even if the final version is supplied just for them to sign, unless the file is protected in some way, they could still make changes. These issues are examined further in Chapter 10 – Drafting, exchanging and protecting documents electronically.

[48]   There are several no-cost or low-cost programs available to create pdfs which can carry out these functions. See Chapter 10 – Drafting, exchanging and protecting documents electronically.

[49]   See *Koenigsblatt v Sweet* [1923] 2 Ch 314, [1923] All ER Rep Ext 758.

Following a case[50] where some of these problems were considered, the Law Society has produced guidance on how certain types of documents should be signed and how they should be provided to other parties. While it is *only* guidance it does provide an indicative approach which a prudent party should follow (to minimise technical disputes on how a particular document was signed).

1.8.1   Documents which are deeds or are contracts for the sale or other disposition of an interest in land

Signing. Documents which are signed as deeds or contracts for the sale or other disposition of an interest in land ('land contracts') should never be signed other than as complete documents (ie the signature page should never be signed before or separately from the rest of the agreement).

Sending electronically: If deeds or land contracts are sent electronically, they should only be sent as complete documents. As a prudent step, the parties should state in writing (at least by an exchange of emails) that they are signing documents in this way and that providing the document electronically to each other is acceptable.

1.8.2   Documents which are contracts and are not signed as deeds

Signing. It is possible either:

1 to sign an agreement as a complete document (the conventional and still the most usual way); or

2 to have the signature page signed in advance of the provisions of the agreement being finalised.

However, if option 2 is chosen then the procedure described below should be used.

---

[50]   This issue became particularly topical following the decision in *R (on the application of Mercury Tax Group and Another) v HMRC* [2008] EWHC 2721 (Admin); [2008] All ER (D) 129 (Nov). This judgment, although having nothing to do with a party alleging that what it had signed was a different agreement, contained comments on how unacceptable it was to take the signature page of one agreement and apply it to another, as well as making changes to the agreement already signed. The judge may have been partly influenced by the fact that Mercury Tax Group had created a tax-avoidance scheme (which, at the time, was perfectly legal), whereby the clients of Mercury Tax Group merely signed a series of documents. It is possible for a party to make changes to an agreement after signature, for example, if there is information which needs entering and which the parties had in contemplation before signature. An example of this would be the sale of a house, where the completion date will often be entered after the contract itself is signed.

Sending electronically If the document is sent electronically as a complete document, there will normally be no issues, but:

1 if the signature page only is sent (after a complete version of the agreement is signed); or

2 if the signature page is signed in advance of the provisions being agreed and then attached by the party signed or attached by the party who receives the document)

then the prudent approach to follow (in particular where 2 is to occur) is:

(i)   that all the parties should explicitly agree, in writing, that this is an acceptable method of signing the agreement;

(ii) that the signature page for each party is sufficiently identified so that it is obvious that it belongs to 'its' agreement (eg having a header which states the title of the agreement and the names of the parties (eg 'Sale and Purchase Agreement between Party A and Party B'));

(iii) that where 1 above applies, the person who is to sign sees the whole agreement and where 2 above applies, that the signature page is made available in good time to the person who is to sign; and

(iv) that the signed signature page is provided to a person who is authorised either to attach it to the final version of the document at the relevant time (or provide it to someone else (such as the other party or their lawyers)); and

(v)   the person who has responsibility for attaching the signature page to the final version of the agreement obtains or receives confirmation that s/he can attach the signature page to that final version of the agreement.

The documentation evidencing the agreement of the parties to attach the signature page with the final version of the agreement should be kept with the agreement.

1.9   Checklists for legally binding contracts

As has already been mentioned, this book is not a text on English contract law. However, it may be helpful to provide checklists of some of the contract law issues which the contract drafter needs to take into account when preparing or negotiating an agreement. In appropriate cases, further research or obtaining specialist advice will be necessary on these topics[51].

---

[51]   For example, in *Chitty on Contracts* (30th Edn) 2009 Sweet and Maxwell.

1.10   Checklist for formation of the contract

If a legally binding contract is to come into existence, the following elements must normally be present (in addition to the requirements that certain contracts be in writing and as to the form of deeds, already mentioned):

- *Intention to create legal relations.* This will normally be present in the case of a conventionally drafted written agreement. If there is a less formal type of document (such as a Heads of Agreement), the position may be less certain. See further the discussion of contractual and pre-contractual documents, later in this chapter at **1.11**.

  Tip: if in doubt, state specifically in the document that it is intended to be legally binding.

- *Capacity to enter into the contract.* Contracts with minors[52], those suffering from a mental incapacity and drunks may not be enforceable (with some exceptions, eg for 'necessaries'[53] such as food), because they do not have the legal capacity to enter into contracts[54]. Where a person enters into a contract with a company, that person can normally assume that the company has the capacity to enter into the contract, but in cases of doubt specialist advice should be obtained[55].

  There is a separate issue as to whether the person signing a contract on behalf of a company (or otherwise agreeing to enter into a contract) can be assumed as having the authority to do so. Legal advice should also be obtained on this issue[56]. It is difficult for a company to argue that a director or senior manager did not have authority to sign a contract on the company's behalf.

---

[52]   Persons under 18 years old: Family Law Reform Act 1969, s 1(1).

[53]   The requirement for those suffering from a mental incapacity having to pay a reasonable amount for goods delivered to them is likely to be removed following the passing of the Mental Capacity Act 2005, s 67(1) and Sch 6, para 24. This provision removes the obligation on those suffering from a mental incapacity to pay for 'necessaries'. It has not yet been brought into force.

[54]   Powers of attorney may be assigned by due legal process which allows other individuals to sign agreements on behalf of these people.

[55]   For companies formed under or regulated by the Companies Act 2006, s 43 gives capacity to a company to enter into a contract.

[56]   Many contracts are entered into without a signed agreement, perhaps via the exchange of emails. It is harder to know with emails whether the person on the other side whose name appears in the email is really that person. Another area in which technology has changed the traditional formation of contracts is online orders. For many goods and some services, for an order to be processed payment must be made in advance through a credit or debit card. For the party supplying the goods and/or services the issue of authority is minimised as they will have had payment. This technological advancement has changed who will need to deal with this issue of authority.

Tip: If in doubt, carry out (some old-fashioned) checks on the other party. For example, if a party has not had any meetings or telephone conversations with the other party, the first party might wish to telephone the person representing the other side, or carry out a search at the Registrar of Companies website on the other party, or use a credit reference agency.

- *Consideration.* As stated above, both parties need to give consideration (to a two-party agreement), or they must execute the agreement as a deed, if the agreement is to be legally binding. Normally, there will be no problem finding such consideration where goods or services are provided in return for payment of a sum of money. In some cases (eg in some confidentiality agreements), nominal consideration (eg £1) is included in the agreement to avoid doubts over whether consideration is being given. There are detailed rules on the types of consideration that are acceptable, for example, 'past consideration is no consideration'. Under the laws of some other countries there is no requirement for consideration, or the rules on consideration differ significantly from those under English law.

- *Offer and acceptance.* Although there are exceptions, a contract will not normally come into existence until one party has offered to enter into a contract on specified terms and the other party has accepted that offer, by words or conduct. A qualified acceptance (eg on slightly different terms to those offered), will generally be a counter offer, which in turn will need to be accepted before the contract comes into existence[57]. These problems are usually avoided where both parties sign a written agreement.

  Tip: If 'accepting' another party's offer, consider whether the 'acceptance' is (only) an agreement on particular points or provisions. If so further negotiations may be necessary and/or a final agreement signed by the parties may be required. Alternatively, there may be acceptance of an offer with the intention of entering into a binding contract.

- *Complete agreement and certainty of terms.* If some of the important terms have not been agreed (eg the price to be paid under a contract), the agreement may not be legally enforceable. Sometimes contracts include

---

[57] For example, Party A offers to supply six goods at £1 each within 30 days (offer). The other side purports to accept the offer but says it wants the goods within 14 days (rejection and counter-offer). The importance of carefully analysing whether a party is accepting or rejecting an offer is illustrated in the recent case of *Grant v Bragg* [2009] EWCA 1228 (where there was an exchange of emails between two parties). The decision when the case first reached the courts was that the last email was the acceptance of the first email, but on appeal, the Court of Appeal found that the emails in between the first and last email contained a rejection of the offer.

A related issue is the 'battle of the forms'. For example, Party A offers to sells goods, but subject to its terms and conditions. Party B accepts but in its written acceptance says its acceptance is subject to its terms and conditions. The traditional view is that the party that gets its terms and conditions in last is the party whose terms and conditions apply, and this view continues to be good law: see *Tekdata Internconnections v Amphenol* [2009] EWCA Civ 1209, [2010] 2 All ER (Comm) 302.

provisions stating that certain terms will be agreed at a later date by the parties. These are 'agreements to agree' and will not generally be enforceable, unless there is a mechanism for determining what those terms will be if the parties cannot agree, for example, that the terms will be settled by a third party[58]. The courts will not generally write the parties' contract for them (although a court may 'fill in' gaps in some instances). If the contract includes an agreement to agree this may invalidate either the clause in which such a provision appears, or in the worst case could make the entire agreement unenforceable.

- *Complying with specified formalities.* If the parties have negotiated and agreed that a binding agreement will only come into being when a specified formality is observed, then if it is not followed there may be no binding contract at all[59] (eg the parties state that there will be a binding contract only if they sign a written agreement, but the parties do not in fact sign any document).

In addition, the following elements must normally not be present.

- *Unconscionable bargain, undue influence or duress.* Commercial contracts are very rarely declared invalid by the courts on these grounds under English law, but these items should not be entirely overlooked. It will only be in exceptional cases that an inequality of bargaining power between parties will entitle a party to avoid his contractual obligations, particularly if the contract is between commercial enterprises[60].

- *Illegality of subject matter.* This element will not be relevant to most commercial contracts (unless common law restraint of trade is included in this category; see the comments at **1.11** on anti-competitive agreements). A few examples of the many categories of illegal agreements, which are not enforceable as a matter of public policy, include agreements to commit a criminal act; agreements to pay money in return for the procurement of a knighthood; agreements to oust the jurisdiction of the court[61]; and champerty (eg selling the right to litigate a personal claim).

---

[58]   See, for example, *Miles-Martin Pen Co v Selsdon Fountain Pen Co Ltd, Ralf Selsdon and Rebecca Selsdon (No 2)* (1950) 67 RPC 64, CA. This case concerned an agreement to settle patent litigation. The agreement included provisions on certain important issues, eg payments, duration, etc, and stated that the remaining terms would be: 'in the normal terms of a patent licence. In the event of dispute the terms shall be referred to Counsel at the Patent Bar to be agreed by the [parties].' The Court of Appeal decided that this arbitration clause was legally enforceable.

[59]   For example, in *R (on the application of Mercury Tax Group and Another) v HMRC* [2008] EWHC 2721 (Admin); [2008] All ER (D) 129 (Nov), one of the documents which needed signing contained wording that it would be signed as a deed (although there was no requirement that it had to be signed as a deed). The document was not signed as a deed (ie for a creating a deed where not complied with). The judge held that it was not a legally binding document.

[60]   *Pao On v Lau Yiu Long* [1980] AC 614, PC, per Lord Scarman: 'In a contractual situation mere commercial pressure is not enough to constitute economic duress.'

[61]   With some exceptions, for example, as permitted by the Arbitration Act 1996.

1.10.1   Examples of when a contract will be found

The following list provides a useful summary of when a contract will exist (and the points reflect some of the situations commercial parties are likely to find themselves in)[62]:

'...

(i)   Each case must be decided on its own facts and on the construction of its own agreement. Subject to that,

(ii)   where no contract exists, the use of an expression such as "to be agreed" in relation to an essential term is likely to prevent any contract coming into existence, on the ground of uncertainty. This may be summed up by the principle that "you cannot agree to agree".

(iii)   Similarly, where no contract exists, the absence of agreement on essential terms of the agreement may prevent any contract coming into existence, again on the ground of uncertainty.

(iv)   However, particularly in commercial dealings between parties who are familiar with the trade in question, and particularly where the parties have acted in the belief that they had a binding contract, the courts are willing to imply terms, where that is possible, to enable the contract to be carried out.

(v)   Where a contract has once come into existence, even the expression "to be agreed" in relation to future executory obligations is not necessarily fatal to its continued existence.

(vi)   Particularly in the case of contracts for future performance over a period, where the parties may desire or need to leave matters to be adjusted in the working out of their contract, the courts will assist the parties to do so, so as to preserve rather than destroy bargains, on the basis that what can be made certain is itself certain. *Certum est quod certum reddi potest.*

(vii)   This is particularly the case where one party has either already had the advantage of some performance which reflects the parties' agreement on a long-term relationship, or has had to make an investment premised on that agreement.

(viii) For these purposes, an express stipulation for a reasonable or fair measure or price will be a sufficient criterion for the courts to act on. But even in the absence of express language, the courts are prepared to imply an obligation in terms of what is reasonable.

(ix)   Such implications are reflected but not exhausted by the statutory provision for the implication of a reasonable price now to be found in s 8(2) of the Sale of Goods Act 1979 [if the price for goods is not fixed by the contract the buyer must pay reasonable price] (and, in the case of services, in s 15(1) of the Supply of Goods and Services Act 1982 [if the price for services is not fixed by the contract or the course of dealings between the parties, the customer has to pay a reasonable amount]).

[62]   From a discussion by Rix LJ (in *Mamidoil-Jetoil Greek Petroleum Co SA v Okta Crude Oil Refinery AD* [2001] EWCA Civ 406; [2001] 2 All ER (Comm) 193 at [69]) of the situations when such intentions can be found where commercial parties are involved.

(x)   The presence of an arbitration clause may assist the courts to hold a contract to be sufficiently certain or to be capable of being rendered so, presumably as indicating a commercial and contractual mechanism, which can be operated with the assistance of experts in the field, by which the parties, in the absence of agreement, may resolve their dispute.'

1.11   Checklist of selected matters which might make the contract or particular provisions unenforceable

Typically the following matters will not prevent the contract from coming into existence, but may make the contract, or some of its terms, legally unenforceable:

- *Anti-competitive terms.* Do the terms fit within a block exemption regulation[63]? Is the agreement unenforceable for (common law) restraint of trade? Have the parties carried out an evaluation as to whether competition law applies?

- *Penalty clauses.* Under English law a penalty clause in a contract is unenforceable but a liquidated damages clause is enforceable. If the agreement states that the consequences of a particular breach of contract are that the party in breach must pay the other party a fixed sum, is that sum a 'genuine pre-estimate' of the loss which the innocent party will suffer as a result of the breach (and is it stated to be such in the agreement)? If so, it may be upheld as a legitimate liquidated damages clause; if not, it may be struck down as a penalty clause. A penalty clause will normally exist where the stipulated sum is extravagant and unconscionable in comparison with the greatest loss that could conceivably be proved to have followed from the breach[64].

- *Tip:* at the time of drafting a liquidated damages clause, obtain (documented) evidence as to how 'genuine pre-estimate' is calculated or established, and keep this evidence on file in case of dispute.

- *Frustration.* If the parties cannot perform the agreement for reasons outside their control, it may be frustrated, in which case the agreement will come to an end. There is no automatic provision in English law allowing performance to be suspended for the duration of the frustrating events, comparable to Continental laws of *force majeure.* Consequently, English

---

[63]   Such as providing block exemption from Article 101 of the EU Treaty, eg the Technology Transfer Regulations, Regulation 772/2004/EC or the Exclusive Distribution Regulations, Regulation 1400/2002/EC.

[64]   The established principles regarding what constitutes a penalty clause were set out by Lord Dunedin in *Dunlop Pneumatic Tyre Co Ltd v New Garage and Motor Co Ltd* [1915] AC 79, HL.

law agreements commonly include a *force majeure* clause, inserted by the drafter, which allows the agreement to continue in this type of situation[65].

- *Mistake.* Occasionally, contracts are held to be void or unenforceable because of 'mistake', for example, if the parties entered into the contract on the basis of an assumption which turns out not to be true[66], or where there is a mistake as to the existence of the subject matter of the contract[67]. There are strict rules as to when this remedy is available. One of the categories of mistake is known by the Latin phrase *non est factum* (literally 'not my deed', but better understood as 'not my act'). In a very few cases it has been held that where a party is misled into signing a document essentially different from that which he intended to sign, the document is void. Most of these cases involve fraud, and are a very limited exception to the general principle that a party is bound by his signature to a document, whether he reads or understands it, or not.

- *Insolvency, bankruptcy, winding-up and death.* The winding-up or insolvency of a company, or the bankruptcy or death of an individual, may cause a contract to which that company or individual is a party to be unenforceable. Commercial contracts commonly include provisions which allow for termination of the contract on the insolvency of a corporate party[68]. Insolvency laws may override provisions in a contract, for example, allowing a liquidator of a company to terminate an agreement which imposes 'onerous' obligations on the company.

- *Breach of conditions and essential terms.* The law in this area is complex; for drafting purposes it is important to be aware that if a provision is described as a 'condition', 'condition precedent' (or 'pre-condition'), or 'condition subsequent', or as being 'of the essence', or an 'essential term' of the contract, breach or failure to comply with that provision could lead to the contract either not coming into existence at all (as in the case of some conditions precedent), or making the agreement unenforceable, or terminable by the other party.

  Tip: Use the word 'provisions' in the text of the agreement, rather than 'terms' or 'conditions' to avoid an inappropriate meaning being

---

[65]   See Clause 8.1 in Precedent 1 in Appendix for example wording.

[66]   In *Bell v Lever Bros Ltd* [1932] AC 161 the House of Lords laid down the test for when mistake can result in a contract being set aside. The mistake must, according to Lord Thankerton, 'relate to something which both [contracting parties] must necessarily have accepted in their minds as an essential element of the subject matter'.

[67]   In *Couturier v Hastie* (1856) 5 HL Cas 673, the parties contracted over a cargo of corn which both believed to be in transit from Salonica. However, the corn had deteriorated so much on the journey that the ship's master sold it before it deteriorated completely. This fact was unknown to both parties and the House of Lords set aside the contract on the ground that there was a failure of consideration.

[68]   See Clause 7.2(2) in Precedent 1 in Appendix for example wording.

inadvertently given by use of the word 'condition'; if certain provisions are intended to be 'conditions' in a formal sense, consider spelling out the consequences of breach of such provisions in the termination clause, to avoid uncertainty.

- *Misrepresentations.* The classic example of a representation is the over-enthusiastic salesperson making statements about the product s/he is selling and which are then relied upon by the purchaser. Even where the contract includes a statement by the purchaser acknowledging that the purchaser has not relied on any representations which are not set out in the contract, the seller may nevertheless be liable for certain types of misrepresentation. The purchaser may also be able to terminate the contract as a result of the misrepresentation, or the terms of the contract may be varied by a collateral contract or implied term reflecting the representation. The drafter may wish to identify what statements have been made and expressly incorporate them into the contract or cause them to be withdrawn prior to execution of the written agreement.

- *Excluding liability for death or personal injury.* A party can never exclude or limit its liability for personal injury or death resulting from its negligence[69].

- *Expiry of limitation period or laches (unreasonable delay).* Ultimately, contracts are enforceable, or not, by court action (or by arbitration/mediation). If a court action for breach of contract is brought more than six years after the cause of action accrued (in the case of contracts under hand, with some exceptions) or more than 12 years after the cause of action accrued (in the case of deeds), the action will be time-barred. A separate doctrine of laches allows the court to dismiss an action if there has been an unreasonable delay in bringing the action.

- *Law and jurisdiction.* Is the agreement made under English law and subject to the jurisdiction of the English courts? If not, or if this is not clearly stated in the agreement, and there is any international element to the agreement (eg non-English parties or a place of execution or performance outside England), foreign laws or foreign court practices may mean that the agreement is not legally enforceable, even though the agreement is valid and enforceable under English law.

1.12   Contracts and pre-contractual documents

Sometimes commercial parties wish to sign a document which is not described as a 'contract' or 'agreement'. Instead they call the document a 'Heads of Agreement', 'Letter of Intent' or other name. The terms most commonly in use are the following:

---

[69]   Unfair Contract Terms Act 1977, s 2(1).

- Heads of Agreement;

- Heads of Terms;

- Term Sheet;

- Letter of Intent;

- Letter of Agreement or Letter Agreement;

- Memorandum of Understanding;

- Comfort Letter;

Before discussing these terms, it is useful to discuss the meaning of the terms 'contract' and 'agreement'. In common legal usage these terms mean the same thing[70]. Most written contracts are described within their text as agreements (the opening line of a written contract commonly begins 'This Agreement dated …').

Occasionally different terms are used, for example, intellectual property licences sometimes begin 'This Licence dated …' or a document authorising another person to do something begins 'This Power of Attorney dated …'[71]

The expression 'Memorandum of Agreement' was sometimes used in written agreements, but is less frequently encountered nowadays, and in any case, it has an old-fashioned ring to it; the words 'Memorandum of' are unnecessary.

All of these terms, 'contract', 'agreement' and 'memorandum of agreement', are generally used to refer to a legally binding agreement. Some of the other terms listed above are used less consistently by commercial parties.

The expression 'Heads of Agreement' is generally used to describe the important commercial terms which parties negotiate, sometimes without the involvement of their lawyers. Typically, once the Heads of Agreement have been signed or initialled, the parties will negotiate a fuller, more detailed agreement incorporating the provisions of the Heads of Agreement. The expressions 'Heads of Terms' and 'Term Sheet' are often used in a similar way. Sometimes these documents are intended to be legally binding; sometimes they are not. Sometimes it is anticipated that a more detailed agreement will be negotiated after the Heads of Agreement have been signed, but it is unclear what is to happen if the parties fail to reach agreement on the more detailed terms— do the Heads take effect as a final agreement or not? A further refinement sometimes encountered is that a document entitled 'Heads of Agreements' contains some provisions which are binding and some which are not.

---

[70] A House of Lords (now the Supreme Court) judge (Lord Diplock), once famously defined a contract as a bisy-nallagmatic agreement, which caused many lawyers and judges to refer to their dictionaries. It turned out that bisy-nallagmatic meant that the parties to the agreement entered into mutual obligations.

[71] Although neither a licence nor a power of attorney need to be contractual documents.

The expression 'Letter of Intent' is typically used in negotiations where a party wishes to give reassurance on some point to the other party but the first party does not wish to be legally bound by the statement it is giving. For example, a letter of intent might state that a party intends to continue commercial negotiations with the other party. Although the distinction between letters of intent and a 'Heads of Terms' etc is in reality little more than the choice of words used by the person.

In all these cases, the only way to be certain of these matters is to state explicitly in the Heads of Agreement what their status is and what is to happen if a more detailed agreement cannot be reached. At a minimum, where it is clear that the parties do not wish to enter into legal relations based on a document labelled 'Heads of Agreement' (or some other formulation), the document should be headed 'subject to contract'[72].

The issue of the binding or non-binding nature of documents labelled 'subject to contract' is important, but fails to look at the 'bigger picture', which is the actions and intentions of the parties. The courts have repeatedly made it clear that what is important is not the labels that parties put on their documents or their actions, but rather to examine the reality of their relationship. Some of the possible variations as to what might occur if the parties to do not enter into a final, signed agreement include:

- the parties agree a non-binding Heads of Agreement, which contains outline commercial provisions, then start performing some of them, but never enter into a final signed agreement; or

- a variation to the first point, subsequent to the non-binding Heads of Agreement, the parties produce different draft agreements, none of which are finalised, but the parties perform some of the provisions; or

---

[72] An illustration of the danger of not clearly stating the (non-)legal relationship of discussions and documents exchanged between parties is found in *DMA Financial Solutions Ltd v BaaN UK Ltd* [2000] All ER (D) 411. The use of the words 'subject to contract' should normally cover the document to which this phrase is applied, *and* subsequent documents and negotiations. However, there should not be anything in the conduct of the parties (whether expressly or by implication) to make any subsequent document or communication legally binding, see *Confetti Records (a firm) v Warner Music UK Ltd (trading as East West Records)* [2003] EWHC 1274 (Ch), [2003] All ER (D) 61 (Jun). See also *ProForce Recruit Ltd v Rugby Group Ltd* [2005] EWHC 70 (QB); [2005] All ER (D) 22 (Feb). In this case the following words were in a document: 'In addition to the normal terms and conditions that exist between Rugby Cement and Proforce, it is also agreed that, subject to contract, the following conditions will apply.' It was held: 'In general, except in a very strong and exceptional case, the effect of [words such as 'subject to contract'] in an agreement is to prevent an executory contract from coming into existence because they are taken to mean that until a further contract has been executed neither party is to owe the other any contractual obligation. However, in this case, save for the alleged breach, the agreement cannot be regarded as being executory because after it was signed the parties did those things that the agreement contemplated that each should do for the benefit of the other.' Although the Court of Appeal later overturned the decision of the judge at first instance, the Court of Appeal did so on other grounds: see *Proforce Recruit Ltd v The Rugby Group Ltd* [2006] EWCA Civ 69; [2006] All ER (D) 247 (Feb).

- the parties enter into a binding Heads of Agreement which has a fixed duration but contains key terms and the parties perform some of them (beyond the fixed duration period) but never sign a final version of an agreement.

The dangers for the parties are that a court might find:

- there is no contract between parties at all (despite their subsequent conduct);

- there is a binding contract but it does not contain anything negotiated and agreed subsequent to the Heads of Terms;

- there is a binding contract but the provisions are what was negotiated and agreed subsequent to the Heads of Terms.

These are all possible outcomes (and are based on recent decisions of higher English courts)[73].

A slightly different category of document, a 'comfort letter', is where a contract is to be made by a company which is a subsidiary of another company and the parent company writes to the other contracting party to provide reassurance that it intends to continue financing the activities of the subsidiary. In the latter case, a letter of intent can be distinguished from a formal parent company guarantee. Again, it is recommended that the status of any letter of intent be stated specifically in its text, to avoid ambiguity.

Finally, the expression 'Letter Agreement' (or 'Letter of Agreement') usually means simply an agreement which is drafted in the form of a letter, and which takes effect when the recipient countersigns the letter (or, more usually, a second signed copy) and returns it to the sender. Typically, this format is used for short agreements and where a party wishes to adopt a 'friendly' format; letters are perceived as being more friendly than a contract drafted in conventional legal format. Again, it is recommended that the status of the document be stated specifically in its text[74].

---

[73]   See *RTS Flexible Systems Ltd v Molkerei Alois Müller GmbH & Co KG* [2010] UKSC 14; *Investec Bank (UK) Ltd v Zulman and Another* [2010] EWCA Civ 536; *Immingham Storage Co Ltd v Clear Plc* [2011] EWCA Civ 89. The court will need to rake through all the documentation, establish what has occurred, and what people involved in the negotiations and performance have said and written, in order to reach a decision as to what were the objective intentions of the parties, and this might be very different to what one or all the parties thought were their intentions. These recent cases provide illustrations of how hard it is determine what might be the result.

[74]   However, courts do not necessarily pay attention to the words used in a contract when the fact of the contract says something different. In *G Percy Trentham Ltd v Archital Luxfer Ltd* [1993] 1 Lloyd's Rep 25, the Court of Appeal held that a contract could be concluded by conduct, regardless of what was stated in words. Similarly, in *Immingham Storage Co Ltd v Clear Plc* [2011] EWCA Civ 89, the court ignored a clause in the draft agreement that there would not be a binding contract unless the draft agreement was signed.

1.13   Information that a party needs to include about itself in contractual and non-contractual documents

For the sake of completeness, it is useful to mention that commercial organisations that engage in selling goods and/or services must provide information about themselves (and their goods and services) to potential and actual customers/clients. But in a commercial contract there is little information that a party *must* provide about itself in order to create a binding contract (rather than that which the other party would wish to know—ie such as sufficient information to know precisely who it is contracting with).

The information a party must provide about itself (and what it provides) is a requirement under various laws. The requirement to provide this information does not have to be in the contract itself in most cases, and the failure to provide the information will not provide the other party with any directly enforceable rights. Only the government (or one its various agencies such as the Office of Fair Trading, a local authority trading standard department etc) can take action.

Chapter 2

The Structure and Format of the Contract

Key points

- *Date of agreement.* Write (or type) the date on which the agreement is signed. If signed on different dates, write the date on which the last party signed.

  Where solicitors are involved, but the signing of the agreement takes place without them being present, conventionally the agreement is not dated until after signature. The date is inserted later by agreement between the parties' solicitors.

- *Commencement date.* If the commencement date of the agreement is different to the date it is signed, the agreement should mention two dates: a commencement date (or effective date) as well as the date on which the agreement is signed. Do not confuse the two dates.

- *Names and addresses.* State the full names, legal status and addresses of the parties at the head of the agreement. Place each party's details in a separate paragraph and number the parties (eg (1) Party A, (2) Party B).

  If there are more than two parties, and the parties 'share' any obligations, make it clear whether they are jointly or severally liable, or both jointly and severally liable, for performance of those obligations.

- *Recitals.* Recitals ('whereas' clauses) can help in explaining the background to the agreement; they are not compulsory. When recitals are included, do not include any obligations on the parties under the agreement; these belong in the operative provisions part of the agreement.

- *Linking wording.* Appropriate wording should appear between the recitals and the operative provisions, for example, 'IT IS AGREED AS FOLLOWS', or 'THIS DEED WITNESSES AS FOLLOWS'.

- *Operative provisions.* There is no fixed order for operative provisions. Conventionally these start with a definitions clause, then follow the main commercial provisions, followed by secondary commercial provisions and legal 'boilerplate'. It is better to group clauses together by subject matter, rather than have a long list of obligations on Party A followed by a long list of obligations on Party B. Headings can make the document easier to read.

- *Schedules.* It is possible to place these before or after the signatures. More importantly make sure that the operative provisions of the agreement state whether the provisions of the schedules form part of the agreement.

- *Signatures.* Use the appropriate execution clauses and signature blocks, particularly where the agreement is executed as a deed. Where there is use of a traditional format, where a person places her or his signature may well need explanation (or make this clear in the wording).

- *Alternative formats.* Alternative formats for an agreement are acceptable, subject to the caveats stated in this chapter.

2.1   Introduction

This chapter considers the typical format and structure of an English law contract used by commercial parties. There is no legal requirement to draft or lay out contracts in the way described in this chapter, or any other way. Commercial contracts are sometimes put together in a completely unstructured way but the courts still hold them legally binding. Nevertheless there are advantages in adopting a conventional format, including:

- *to give a logical framework to the contract document.* In practice most well-drafted agreements follow a similar format, although alternative formats may also be logical;

- *to give a familiar framework.* When negotiating the provisions of an agreement it generally saves time and effort (and expense) to work with a draft structured in a way which is familiar to the parties and their legal advisers. If an agreement becomes the subject of litigation, it may be necessary to persuade a court of its meaning and legal effect; some courts are more conservative than others and may need to be persuaded (more than usually) of the meaning of a document which has a very unusual structure or format.

All of this begs the question, what is meant by a 'conventional format'? What is considered conventional at the beginning of the twenty-first century is very different from what was conventional at the end of the nineteenth century or earlier. What is conventional for a modern commercial contract in the UK is very different to the style of residential leases, many of which are still drafted in a very traditional way[1], let alone the style used in both many commercial and non-commercial contracts originating from the US.

This chapter recommends techniques for structuring contracts in a clear, logical way, whilst remaining within the boundaries of current conventions.

---

[1]   Over the last decade much effort has gone into drafting legal documents in clearer and simpler English. Much of the effort arose from the Unfair Contracts in Consumer Contracts Regulations 1999, SI 1999/2083 (based on an EU directive). Also there are many continuing government and non-government initiatives (such as the Plain English Campaign, and the Crystal Mark scheme and Golden Bull awards). For documents intended for use only by commercial parties, again documents are generally written in a clearer fashion, although in the authors' experience many agreements are not written in clear language.

Similar techniques are now used by many of the leading commercial law firms in England.

2.2   Main elements of a typical contract document

The main elements of a typical contract document are as follows. See Appendix 1 for an example of a contract which follows the sequence of clauses described below.

- Status of the document (ie its date and version number, whether it is legally binding: eg 'draft' or 'Subject to contract').

- Cover page (setting out the date of the agreement or draft, names of the parties and title of the agreement, and sometimes the firm of lawyers preparing the document)[2].

- Table of contents (setting out the main sections and headings and their page numbers)[3].

- Title of the agreement (eg 'patent and know-how licence' or 'asset sale and purchase agreement').

- Date of agreement.

- Names, legal status and addresses of the parties.

- Recitals (sometimes referred to as 'Whereas' clauses).

- Main provisions of the agreement (the operative provisions), including:

  o definitions;

  o conditions precedent (if any);

  o main commercial obligations, for example, supply of goods/services, price and payment, compliance with specifications, delivery;

  o secondary commercial issues, for example, risk, passing of property and retention of title, intellectual property, confidentiality, term (eg start and finish dates, length of contract) and termination (situations when termination is possible, eg for breach, insolvency etc), warranties, indemnities, liability.

- Miscellaneous 'boilerplate' clauses dealing with such matters as law and jurisdiction, notices, Contracts (Rights of Third Parties) Act 1999, entire agreement, interpretation, amendment, assignment, etc.

---

[2]   This, and a table of contents, will usually appear only in longer contracts.

[3]   Where used, it is possible to generate a table of contents automatically using a modern word processor (subject to the use of styles with the right codes contained in them to be able to do so).

- Schedules and/or appendices (these sometimes appear after the signatures in English contracts).

- Signatures.

The following paragraphs discuss in detail some legal and drafting issues relating to the above points, and give examples of some typical wording. These formal elements are distinguished from the substantive provisions of a commercial contract which are discussed in Chapter 4.

2.3   Title

The title is to indicate the type of agreement that the parties are entering into. By convention this is normally brief and will not include the names of the parties or reference number etc.

However if a party enters into many agreements of the same type, then in—or more usually underneath—the main title there could be some further wording briefly to distinguish the particular agreement from others. For example:

- an owner of a portfolio of patents who regularly enters into a standard form patent licence might include the patent number under the main title, eg:

Example

PATENT LICENCE AGREEMENT

(Patent Number [ ])

- the parties enter into a series of agreements, such as a series of confidentiality agreements (because discussions progress beyond any stated expiry date), or amending agreements all amending the same agreement.

Examples

(a)   FIRST AMENDING AGREEMENT

(b)   SECOND AMENDING AGREEMENT

(c)   FIRST CONFIDENTAILITY AGREEMENT (expiring 30 June 2011)

(d)   SECOND CONFIDENTIALITY AGREEMENT (expiry 31 December 2011)

- a party is granting a large number of leases to different property but all the leases are drafted in the same way, so each lease could be headed 'lease' and then a following line with the registered title and/or the postal address.

Example

LEASE

Registered Property Number: [ ]. Address: [ ]

Such an approach can speed going through a large number of documents to help identify a particular one. The alternative method is to record the distinctive information in a recital.

2.4   Date of agreement

Examples:

> ***Example 1***
>
> **THIS AGREEMENT** is made on _____ 201[ ] BETWEEN:
>
> ***Example 2***
>
> **THIS AGREEMENT** is made the   day of   201[ ] BETWEEN:
>
> ***Example 3***
>
> This Agreement dated _____ is between:
>
> ***Example 4***
>
> This Agreement dated as of _____ is made by, between and among:
>
> ***Example 5***
>
> **THIS AGREEMENT** is made on _____ and takes effect from _____ ('Commencement Date') BETWEEN:

Set out above are five examples of wording which typically appear in the first line of a commercial contract. If the contract is to be made as a deed, the word DEED normally replaces the word AGREEMENT. Example 1 and Example 2 are from contracts prepared by leading firms of English solicitors.

Example 3 is similar but in a simpler format. It is conventional to refer to the agreement throughout the document as 'this Agreement'.

Example 4 is from an agreement prepared by US lawyers. The main points to note in this example are the use of the phrases 'dated as of', and 'by, between and among'. 'As of' probably means 'with effect from'. It is recommended that 'as of' be avoided in English law contracts (see below). It is conventional in English agreements to use simply the word 'between' even where there are more than two parties, where grammatically the word 'among' would be more appropriate.

2.4.1   Which date should be inserted?

The date of the agreement is:

- the date on which it is signed (if signed by all of the parties on the same day);

- the date the last party signs (if the parties sign on different dates).

Conventionally, this date is not inserted until all the parties have signed the agreement and typically it is written by hand by the parties' lawyers (if lawyers are involved), who agree on the date to be inserted. There is nothing wrong with typing in the date before the parties sign, but if this approach is used there is an increased risk that the date might turn out to be wrong if the agreement is signed by one or more of the parties on another date.

If the agreement is signed in counterparts (see discussion of counterparts, below), it is dated when the counterparts are exchanged. If the anticipated date of signing is typed in prior to signature, there is a risk that the parties may sign on a different date. It is bad drafting practice to misstate the date of execution, and it may amount to a forgery[4].

These points assume that signing the agreement takes place in the traditional way, with a real signature. If the agreement is signed electronically (such as typing the name of the person who is signing on behalf of a party in the signature), the same points as to dating the agreement after (electronic) signature still apply.

2.4.2   Reasons for dating an agreement

There are several reasons why contracts are dated:

One practical reason is to be able to refer to the agreement at a later date (as in 'the agreement between X and Y dated Z').

Another practical and evidential reason is that the date can be the date when the parties reached agreement to enter into a legally binding contract.

Often an agreement will include provisions which take effect by reference to the date of the agreement (eg where royalties are to be paid on each anniversary of the date of the agreement or the date of termination of the agreement is calculated by reference to the date of the agreement).

Where there are several contracts concerned with the same subject matter (eg if an agreement is amended on several occasions it may be essential to know the order in which the amendments were made). Particularly, where the agreement is signed in counterparts and the parties' solicitors agree to date the versions in their possession, dating also acts as a formal acknowledgement that the agreement has come into existence.

2.4.3   What format to use for the date

When the date is inserted (whether in writing or typed), best practice is to do so in full; this will mean that the month part of the date is written as a word

---

[4]   See the Forgery and Counterfeiting Act 1981, s 9 which specifically mentions the misdating of contracts.

not as a numeral. The use of numerals can cause confusion or uncertainly given that some countries place the month first in dates written numerically (such as in the US and countries which follow US practice). For example, a date written numerically as 12.1.2012 will mean, in England and Wales, 12 January 2012, while in the United States it will mean December 1, 2012.

2.4.4   Date of agreement and effective (or commencement date) date

Do not confuse the date of the agreement (the date the agreement is signed) with the date on which the agreement is stated to take effect (often called a commencement date). If they are different, then they need distinguishing.

The usual way of distinguishing between the two is to include a definition of the commencement date and/or wording in the operative provisions of the agreement to state when the agreement comes into effect (ie when the parties start performing some or all of their obligations under the agreement).

It is best not to state the commencement date at the head of the agreement, to avoid confusion with the date of the agreement; if, however, the parties insist, wording as in the last of the above examples could be used. The alternative method is to include a specific definition for when performance of the contract will start and refer to that definition in the rest of the agreement as needed (see Appendix 1—Precedent 1—definition of 'Commencement Date' and Clause 3.1) for an example.

2.5   Names and addresses of the parties

Examples:

Example 1

(1)   **ABC LIMITED**, a company incorporated in England and Wales [under company registration number 123456789, and] whose registered office [and principal place of business] is at ABC House, ABC Street, ABC City, AB12 C99 (the 'Company'); and

(2)   **ABC PLC**, a company incorporated in England and Wales [under company number registration 987654321, and] whose registered office [and principal place of business is at ABC House], ABC Street, ABC City, AB12 C99 (the 'Guarantor');

(the Company and the Guarantor being referred to collectively below as the 'Group'); and

(3)   **DEF, INC.**, a Delaware corporation, whose principal place of business is at 99th floor, Business Towers, 15th 2nd Avenue, New York, NY12345, United States of America (the 'Consultant').

Example 2

This Agreement dated [ ] is made by and between **DEF, Inc**. ('DEF' which expression shall include its successors and assigns) a US corporation incorporated in the State of Delaware and having a place of business at 1234 San Antonio Boulevard, La Jolla, California, and **GHI Services Limited** a company incorporated in England and Wales whose registered office is at Twenty-First Century Business Park, Greentown, Loamshire G1 2AG, United Kingdom, a wholly owned subsidiary of **GHI Plc** having the same registered office as GHI Services Limited ('GHI' which expression shall include its successors and assigns).

Example 1 is drafted in a conventional English style, whereas Example 2 includes some undesirable wording and formatting (although the layout is fairly conventional in US agreements), which will be discussed further below. In particular, note the following:

- *Numbering.* Numbering is useful to distinguish the parties from one another. In the second example, it is not entirely clear whether GHI Plc:

    (a)   is an entirely separate contracting party from GHI Services Limited; or

    (b)   is to be treated as the same party as GHI Limited (perhaps it is intended that they should be jointly and severally liable for the obligations of 'GHI'); or

    (c)   is not to be a party at all, and is named simply as part of a description of who GHI Limited is.

    Use of numbering and paragraphing makes these points clear. If it is intended that GHI Plc and GHI Services Limited should be treated as one, this could be made clear in the drafting of this section of the agreement by including them both under (2) in Example 1 above and adding words such as 'GHI Plc and GHI Services Limited being collectively referred to in this Agreement as GHI'. The question of their joint and/or several liability should be addressed elsewhere in the agreement (see discussion of this topic below).

    Before numbering became conventional, phrases such as 'on the one part' and 'on the other part' or 'of the first part', 'of the second part', etc were placed after the parties' names, to distinguish them; it is recommended that this antiquated practice be avoided.

- *Names.* The full names of the parties should be used, including any part of the name which describes its status, such as 'Limited', 'Plc', 'llp', etc. Sometimes, to avoid any uncertainty, the number with which a company or limited liability partnership is registered is also stated; whilst the name of the company or limited liability partnership may change (and even be swapped with that of another company), the number remains constant and therefore identifies with certainty the contracting party.

If it is not clear from the name of the party or the use of the words such as 'Limited' etc, it is sometimes also helpful to indicate the status of the parties, for example, to state that a party is a company limited by guarantee[5] or is incorporated by Royal Charter.

In international contracts, the country or state of incorporation should also be stated. The purpose of including all this information is to be clear as to the identity (and status) of the entity which is entering into the contract.

- *Addresses.*

  Companies. In the case of a UK company limited by shares (ie 'limited' or 'Plc') or a limited liability partnership ('llp'), the registered office is normally stated. For other bodies corporate (ie not formed or regulated by the Companies Act 2006, such as those formed by Royal Charter), a principal or main address can be used.

  Overseas companies. With overseas companies, the principal place of business is more often stated.

  Individuals. Where an individual is a party, the person's home address is normally stated.

  Unincorporated partnership. For a partnership the home address of each of the partners is normally used.

  One of the reasons for stating the parties' addresses is that it is clear where to send notices under the agreement.

  Although the addresses are stated in the Parties Clause, there will normally also be a notices clause included in the agreement (see Chapter 4) and this may cross-refer to the addresses set out at the head of the agreement. Technically, it is not necessary to state the parties' addresses at the head of the agreement, and in the contracts of some other countries the addresses are sometimes stated in the notices clause (such as in most US agreements).

- *Successors and assigns.* It is not conventional in modern, English contracts to include a reference to successors and assigns in the names and addresses section of the contract, although this practice is occasionally encountered (see Example 2 above, which includes such wording).

  Relatively few published English precedents for commercial contracts include such wording (although there may an 'interpretation' clause in the main body of the agreement that has a similar effect). This practice is more commonly encountered in contracts drafted by overseas lawyers. Assignment of contracts is discussed in more detail in Chapter 6.

---

[5]   In some cases charitable organisations are established as companies limited by guarantee. They can apply not to use the word 'limited' in their name.

- *Requirement to include name and address of a party.* In most commercial contracts in England and Wales there is no legal requirement to include any details about a party with one important exception. For companies formed or regulated by the Companies Act 2006, the registered name of the company must appear in all 'documentation' that the company produces[6], which would cover contracts. The registered office, the part of the UK in which it is registered and its registered number need to appear in a more restricted range of documents (its business letters, order forms and websites)[7]. These are not necessarily or indeed often the same as a contractual document.

When deciding who are to be the parties to a contract, a number of legal questions need consideration; some of the more common questions are:

- *Is it necessary to be a party in order to benefit from the contract?* The general rule is that a person who is intended to benefit under a contract needs to be named as a party; in order for the person bring an action to enforce it. There is now one important exception, which allows a person who is not a party, but it is intended by the parties to it to benefit from the contract (following the implementation of the Contracts (Rights of Third Parties) Act 1999)[8]. Although the 1999 Act provides an important exception to the principle of the privity of contract, the position under English law contrasts with the position under the laws of some other countries, where the rules on privity of contract are not so strict.

- *Defining the parties as including their group companies.* Where a company is part of a group of companies (whether as a parent or subsidiary), there is often a statement that references to that company include members of its group in agreements to which the company is a party. Depending on the wording used there can be uncertainty as to whether group companies are intended to be parties to the agreement. In view of the privity of contract rules referred to above, group companies can only be parties to the contract if either:

    ○   they are named as parties and sign the contract; or

---

[6]   Companies (Trading Disclosures) Regulations 2008, reg 7. Companies must disclose their registered name in a range of documentation, which in addition to specific types of document (orders, letters), includes 'all other forms of its business correspondence and documentation'. This latter phrase appears to be a catch all and therefore would appear to include a contractual document. The failure to disclose this is a criminal offence (ie not something which a party to a contract can do anything about).

[7]   Companies (Trading Disclosures) Regulations 2008, reg 7. This information must be disclosed in both printed and electronic documentation (ibid, reg 1(d)).

[8]   See Chapter 4 for a discussion of the Contracts (Rights of Third Parties) Act 1999.

○   one of the group companies acts (and is empowered and stated in the contract to act) as their agent to sign the contract on behalf of each of them[9].

The Contracts (Rights of Third Parties) Act 1999 does not in itself alter this position, but would allow group companies to enforce a contract term where the contract was entered into with the intention that they might enforce a term and states that they may do so, or a contract term purports to confer a benefit on them. The advantage of being a party would normally be that as a party the group companies would have greater and more encompassing rights than those specific benefits provided by the 1999 Act.

•   *Joint and several liability.* In a multi-party agreement, two or more parties may have obligations to another party. An example is an agreement between a customer and a supplier, to which the supplier's parent company is made a party in order to guarantee performance of the supplier's obligations. Another example is where a client wishes to have various design and print services provided and the supplier is divided into a number of companies (each of which provides a discrete part of the services, such as one company providing print design, a second buying advertising space, a third designing and implementing websites, and so on). A joint and several liability clause would ensure that all of the supplying companies would be liable for the failure to perform any of the services (or would avoid one of the supplying companies going into liquidation and the client having paid large sums to it and the other supplying companies being able to avoid liability).

In such agreements it is important to be clear:

(a)   which of the parties has rights or obligations under a particular clause of the contract and, if more than one party has such obligations;

(b)   whether the obligations give rise to joint, several, or joint and several liabilities on the parties concerned. Simply naming someone as a party to the agreement, without specifying any obligations on that party, does not make that person liable. In the first example given above, clauses creating obligations on both the Company and Guarantor might refer to the Group having such obligations, whilst clauses imposing obligations on only one of them would refer to the Company or to the Guarantor, as appropriate.

Where the obligations are expressed to be on the Group, the question then arises whether such obligations are intended to give rise to joint and/

---

[9]   A discussion of other potential mechanisms, eg making one group company trustee for the others, is beyond the scope of this book. See further Chapter 18 *Chitty on Contracts* (30th Edn, 2008) Sweet and Maxwell.

or several liability on the part of the Company and Guarantor. To avoid doubt, this should be stated; commonly the other party to the agreement (ie the Consultant, in the above example) would prefer the liability to be joint and several for all the obligations. The following examples illustrate the differences between joint and several liability.

- *Several liability.* A and B undertake that they will each pay C £10. There are two separate undertakings, and C can sue each of them for £10.

- *Joint liability.* A and B undertake to pay C £10. There is a single undertaking binding on both A and B. Therefore, C should normally sue them together. If A pays the £10, C cannot sue B.

- *Joint and several liability.* A and B undertake to pay C £10. There are three undertakings (ie by A, by B and by A and B together).

The full implications of joint and several liabilities are discussed in the standard contract law books[10]. The best option is joint and several liability, which gives maximum flexibility to the party to whom the liability is owed when bringing actions for breach of undertakings. An example of a clause stating that certain parties are jointly and severally liable follows, and in turn is followed by an example of a clause under which the parties who have accepted such liability apportion it between them (perhaps in a separate agreement between those parties). In detailed agreements, the latter provision might be part of a more detailed clause describing the respective obligations of the parties.

> References in this Agreement to an undertaking being given by the Group shall mean that each of the Company and the Guarantor jointly and severally accept liability for performance of the undertaking.
>
> As between themselves, any liability which any one or more of the parties may bear under or pursuant to any Guarantee (including any legal costs incurred by or which any party is required to pay pursuant to or in connection with such liability) shall irrespective of whether they or any of them are liable as co-sureties or whether they are liable jointly and/or severally be borne by the parties in their respective Relevant Proportions (as defined below).

Where an undertaking is given (by one party) to two or more parties (beneficiaries?) separate issues arise. It seems that if the undertaking is given to the beneficiaries jointly, and only one of the beneficiaries has given consideration for the undertaking, the undertaking is enforceable, but if the undertaking is given to the beneficiaries severally, and some of the beneficiaries have not given consideration for the undertaking (and the undertaking is not given in a deed), the undertaking is not legally enforceable by those beneficiaries.

---

[10]   For a detailed explanation of the law, see Chapter 17 on Joint Obligations, *Chitty on Contracts* (30th Edn) 2008 Sweet and Maxwell. For a summary of the law see Anderson and Warner, *A-Z Guide to Boilerplate and Commercial Clauses* (2nd Edn) 2006 Bloomsbury Professional, pp 334–335.

2.6   Recitals

Example

WHEREAS:

(a)   X owns all right, title and interest in the Patents.

(b)   Y wishes to acquire an exclusive, worldwide licence under the Patents and X is willing to grant such a licence to Y in accordance with the provisions of this Agreement.

2.6.1   Purpose of recitals

Recitals are normally used to explain the background to the agreement. For example, recitals are used:

- to describe the negotiating history;

- to describe what the parties have done to prepare to enter into the agreement;

- to set out the relationship between the parties (and, if relevant, other persons who are not parties but are involved with the parties, such as through other agreements);

- to describe the status of the agreement;

- to provide information on its relationship to other (linked) agreements, its nature and effect, and so on.

Recitals are not the place to include obligations and it is bad drafting practice to include any in the recitals, not least because a court may hold an obligation as not legally binding (although sometimes obligations set out in recitals are held to be legally binding). There is long-established case authority on the legal status of wording which appears in recitals[11].

2.6.2   Are recitals needed at all?

The use of recitals is not obligatory and they should be included only if they will help to explain the background to the agreement. In some shorter agreements it may be appropriate to omit recitals altogether.

---

[11]   The courts are prepared to consider recitals when interpreting the provisions of the main body of the contract, but if these provisions are clear they will not be qualified by any wording in the recitals. A party may be prevented ('estopped' in legal jargon) from denying a statement made in the recitals if that statement is clear and is made by him rather than the other party. See, eg, *Re Moon, ex p Dawes* (1886) 17 QBD 275 at 286, CA. In *Square Mile Partnership Ltd v Fitzmaurice McCall Ltd* [2006] EWCA Civ 1690 the court observed that where a recital is included which explains what the parties did to prepare to enter into the agreement, then such recitals are useful in interpreting the provisions of the agreement.

2.6.3   Wording to use and not use in a recital

Sometimes recitals use wording such as 'X *has agreed* to grant Y a licence under the Patents'. This is not recommended, unless what is meant is that the present agreement is made pursuant to another agreement. If this is what it meant then the recital should specifically state that, with details of the earlier agreement, including its date, name of the agreement, etc.

Example

A.   Party A and Party B entered into a Research and Development Agreement dated 1 January 2000 (the 'Research Agreement'). Under the Research Agreement the Parties agreed to enter into a licence agreement when the Results occurred (as defined in the Research Agreement) in a form substantially the same as this Licence Agreement.

B.   By a written notice from Party A to Party B dated 1 March 2011 Party A indicated that the Results had occurred.

C.   Party B is now willing to grant a licence under the Research IP (as defined in the Research Agreement) to Party A, and Party A is willing to take the licence, all in accordance with the provisions of this Licence Agreement.

If all that is meant is that X and Y *are willing* to sign the present agreement it is confusing to suggest that they have already reached an agreement; and this may lead to one party arguing that other terms, not stated in the present agreement, govern the contract between them.

2.6.4   Layout and number of recitals

Some published precedents do not clearly distinguish between recitals and operative provisions. Instead they use a format where recitals are clause 1, definitions clause 2, and so on. This practice is not recommended. There should be clear labelling that there are recitals, followed by some wording which makes clear that they have come to an end and that operative provisions are about to begin. The conventional way of labelling the results is to begin them with an introductory word such as 'WHEREAS' or 'RECITALS' or even 'BACKGROUND'.

Where there is more than one recital in an agreement, the modern English drafting style is to list each recital in a separate paragraph, numbered A, B, C, etc. There is nothing to stop the use of different numbing (eg 1, 2, 3, etc), but it is advisable to avoid using the same numbering system as in the operative provisions, either on stylistic grounds or to avoid confusion in cross-references as to whether one is referring to a recital or an operative provision. The English style of numbering recitals contrasts with the practice in some jurisdictions of starting each new recital with the word 'WHEREAS' or not using numbering at all (such as in some US contracts).

2.6.5   Recitals and overseas practice

Agreements made under the laws of other European countries often have more detailed recitals than are encountered in English law agreements. In some jurisdictions, certain types of relationship (eg between a distributor and his principal) are defined in the *Code Civil* or other laws, and a purpose of the recitals may be to identify which type of standard relationship the parties intend. Once this is established the operative provisions of the contract are sometimes less detailed than in an English law agreement, because certain provisions are determined by the *Code Civil*.

Moreover, the distinction between recitals and operative provisions may be less clear cut under the laws of some other European countries. This is reflected in European Community legislation—for example, the various block exemption regulations which give automatic exemption from Article 101(1) of the EU Treaty. These include very detailed recitals which have been held to be as legally binding as operative provisions.

2.7   Operative provisions—introductory wording

The main part of the agreement consists of the operative provisions (ie the obligations on the parties and related provisions). The detailed content of those provisions, and how they might be drafted, are subjects which are discussed in Chapters 3 to 6. The operative provisions are conventionally introduced with wording such as the following. Where the agreement includes recitals, one of the following phrases might be used:

> NOW, THEREFORE, IT IS HEREBY AGREED as follows:

> IT IS AGREED AS FOLLOWS:

The authors are not aware of any reported decision where the words 'now', 'therefore' or 'hereby' have been considered critical in this introductory wording. Generally, the word 'hereby' is unnecessary, and not used on stylistic grounds (see further Chapter 3). However, there may be advantages in using the word 'hereby' in certain limited situations[12]. Where recitals are not included, the following phrase is sometimes used:

> WHEREBY IT IS AGREED as follows:

The differences between these versions are stylistic. Use of the word 'whereby' assumes that all of the introductory wording up to start of clause 1 consists of a single sentence.

---

[12]   See **6.5.9.**

Agreements drafted in a traditional style by US lawyers often include more lengthy wording at this point, which seeks to address the issue of consideration (see Chapter 1). This type of wording is not normally encountered in English law agreements[13]:

> NOW, THEREFORE, in consideration of the foregoing and the mutual covenants and obligations hereinafter set forth and other good and valuable consideration, the receipt and adequacy of which the parties hereby acknowledge, and intending to be legally bound, and otherwise to be bound by proper and reasonable conduct, the parties agree as follows:

Where the agreement is to be executed as a deed, the conventional (English) wording is:

> THIS DEED WITNESSES AS FOLLOWS:

Where the deed does not include any recitals, the words THIS DEED are sometimes omitted at this point, on the basis that these words have already been used in the first line of the deed and do not need to be stated again. This is a matter of personal preference and style. Until a generation or two ago, the word 'witnesseth' was used, but even lawyers have now stopped using this archaic form.

2.8   Definitions

As a general principle, the drafter should use words consistently throughout an agreement. Definitions of words are useful for a number of reasons, including:

(a) to avoid repeating a long list of words, such as in the example definitions shown below; and

(b) to avoid ambiguity as to what is, or is not, meant when a particular word is used.

This is particularly important where the sense in which a word is used is other than its natural dictionary meaning, or where there are several dictionary meanings[14]. Also definitions clauses should not include any obligations on the parties.

- *Location of definitions.* It is conventional to place the definitions at the beginning of the operative provisions, usually as clause 1. The courts will

---

[13]   Such wording may not, in any case, be effective in the US in some cases, see Kenneth Adams, *A Manual of Style for Contract Drafting*, 2009 American Bar Association, sections 2.63–2.71.

[14]   For example, stating that a fact is true 'to my knowledge' can mean (a) it is within my knowledge that this fact is true, or (b) as far as I am aware this fact is true, but my knowledge may be incomplete, so this fact may not be true. This problem, which is sometimes encountered in warranty clauses, can be avoided by use of different, less ambiguous words.

read agreements 'as a whole'; therefore, strictly speaking, the definitions do not need to appear first.

A written agreement is not like a computer program written in machine code where it is necessary to define a term before it is possible to use it in the computer program (and without the defined term the computer program will not work).

Some agreements are drafted in a more 'commercial' way than others. Some clients hate wading through pages of definitions before they reach what they consider the 'meat' of the agreement. Also, they criticise their lawyers for drafting documents which are not 'user friendly'.

In such situations there is a temptation to place the definitions at the end of the agreement or in a schedule. Although this is occasionally encountered (mostly with North American agreements), it is not yet conventional in most English agreements. It is, however, becoming increasingly common to place interpretation clauses at the end of the agreement with other 'boilerplate' provisions, rather than in their traditional place, immediately after the definitions.

Sometimes definitions appear in individual clauses of the agreement. The English drafting convention is that this is acceptable if the defined term only appears in the clause in which it is defined. Otherwise, the definition should appear in a separate definitions clause, so that there is one place where all the definitions can be found. If it is convenient to define a word within the main body of the contract, the wording in the definitions clause could use wording such as: '"Patents" has the meaning given in clause 3 below.'

- *Introductory wording.* Definitions clauses commonly begin with words such as the following:

    (i)   In this Agreement the following words shall have the following meanings:

    (ii) In this Agreement the following words and phrases shall have the meanings set out below, unless the context requires otherwise:

The phrase 'unless the context requires otherwise' is reflected in the definitions sections of some UK statutes[15]. It is a kind of safety valve in case words are used in a different sense at some point in the agreement. Occasionally, introductory phrases such as those set out above are omitted altogether. Even if such words are not used, the court may be prepared

---

[15]   For example, the Insolvency Act 1986, s 436 begins: 'In this Act, except in so far as the context otherwise requires …', whilst the Interpretation Act 1976, s 36 begins: ' In computing time for the purposes of any enactment, unless the contrary intention appears …'

to imply them into the contract, but stating them explicitly should give greater certainty[16].

- *Layout.* The layout of definitions clauses is a matter of personal preference. An important objective is to make it easy to find and understand a definition. Examples of two alternative approaches follow, the first using columns:

(i)	Patents	any and all patent applications and patents, and substitutions, extensions, reissues, renewals, divisions, continuations, continuations-in-part and foreign counterparts and including supplementary protection certificates, patent term restorations and similar instruments.
(ii)	'Patent Rights'	shall mean all rights arising under any patents, patent applications, inventor's certificates and applications therefore, throughout the world, now or hereafter made or issued, and any substitutions, continuations, continuations-in-part, divisions, reissues, re-examinations, renewals, or extensions of the terms thereof.

- *Use of capital letters.* It is conventional to capitalise the first letter of a defined word, both in the definitions clause and whenever the word appears in the agreement. This signals the fact that it is a defined term. A common US drafting practice is to place all defined terms in block capital letters, but this is not conventional in English agreements. It is becoming increasingly common to put defined terms in bold text throughout the agreement.

- *Order of definitions.* The modern drafting practice is to place the definitions in alphabetical order, particularly now that most modern processors allow for a collection of definitions to be kept together in a table. The use of a table allows for the entry of definitions in any order; it is possible then to sort them alphabetically. Use of an alphabetical order makes it easier to find the definition. An alternative approach, which is still favoured by some drafters, is to place the definitions in the order in which the defined words appear in the agreement. This alternative approach is fine if there are only a small number of definitions (say three to five) and they all fit on one page, but any greater number may cause problems with trying to locate a particular definition.

---

[16]   See *Meux v Jacobs* (1875) LR 7 (HL) 481 at 493 per Lord Selbourne. See *Oxonica Energy Ltd v Neuftec Ltd* [2009] EWCA Civ 668 for a recent illustration where the court was able to find that a definition had another meaning, although the words 'unless the context requires otherwise' were absent.

2.9   Conditions precedent and subsequent

Conditions precedent (or pre-conditions) and conditions subsequent have both technical aspects (in that they affect the coming into existence of the agreement or its provisions, or their continuation in force) and commercial aspects[17]. The following paragraphs describe technical aspects of the different types of conditions precedent and subsequent and consider where such conditions should appear in the agreement.

Examples of conditions precedent and conditions subsequent follow. In the first example the effect of the condition is that the entire agreement does not come into effect, in the second example only certain provisions of the agreement do not come into effect. The third example is a condition subsequent, which in effect is a termination clause:

(i)   This Agreement shall not come into effect until X shall have obtained Planning Consent for the Property. If X fails to obtain Planning Consent for the Property on or before 30 June 1990, this Agreement shall not come into effect and neither party shall have any obligations to the other hereunder.

(ii)   The obligations on X under clause 4 of this Agreement shall not come into effect until the day after the date on which X receives formal notification from the Patent Office that the Patent has been granted.

(iii)   If Planning Consent is refused, or if X fails to obtain Planning Consent for the Property by 30 June 1990:
        (a)   this Agreement shall terminate;
        (b)   any rights or obligations under this Agreement which have accrued prior to such date of termination shall remain effective; and
        (c)   clauses 1, 3 and 6 of this Agreement shall survive termination.

As has already been mentioned, conditions precedent could logically appear at the beginning of the agreement or as part of a clause dealing with all aspects of commencement and termination of the contract. Conditions subsequent are more likely to appear in, or near, a termination clause. The main problems in the drafting of such clauses are:

*   the clause fails to state clearly whether it is the entire agreement or only certain clauses which do not come into effect (or, in the case of conditions subsequent, cease to have effect) if the condition is not met;

*   no time limit is put on the condition being met, which can lead to uncertainty;

---

[17]   The use of the phrases 'conditions precedent' and 'conditions subsequent' are merely convenient labels for a particular type of contractual provision. It is not necessary to use the label 'condition precedent' for a court to construe a clause as a condition precedent: *Eagle Star Insurance Co Ltd v J N Cresswell* [2004] EWCA Civ 602, [2004] 2 All ER (Comm) 244.

- the condition is so vague that it is void for uncertainty[18];

- it is unclear whether either party has any obligation to try to ensure that the condition is met, and if so how extensive that obligation is[19].

2.10   Sequence of clauses

It is recommended that the main commercial issues appear early in the agreement. For example, in a contract to supply services, a description of work to be done could be set out in clause 2 (assuming clause 1 sets out the definitions) with clause 3 setting out the payment provisions. After these clauses other commercial provisions would appear such as warranties, confidentiality, liability and termination clauses. Commencement provisions (including any conditions precedent) might, typically, appear either at the beginning of the agreement (after the definitions), or in the same clause as the termination provisions. Miscellaneous provisions, sometimes known as 'boilerplate', are normally placed at the end of the agreement. Examples of boilerplate include law and jurisdiction, notices, *force majeure* and entire agreement clauses.

Modern drafting practice is for each clause to address a new topic, with the more important commercial topics at the beginning and the 'legal' provisions towards the end. This contrasts with the older convention which is still encountered in some older property leases of listing most, or all, of one party's obligations in one clause, and the other party's obligations in another clause.

2.11   Schedules

Sometimes, parts of the contract are set out in one or more schedules. For example:

- detailed description of the consultancy tasks that a consultant is to perform in a consultancy agreement is set out in a schedule; or

- a list of the materials a party will use in a work and materials contract is listed in a schedule; or

- a standard set of terms and conditions which do not change from agreement to agreement are put in a schedule; or

---

[18]   *Lee-Parker v Izett (No 2)* [1972] 2 All ER 800.

[19]   Although such an obligation may be implied (*Kyprianou v Cyprus Textiles Ltd* [1958] 2 Lloyd's Rep 60), the extent of any implied term will be limited: see *C Czarninkow Ltd v Centrala Handlu Zagranicznego Rolimpex* [1979] AC 351.

- particularly sensitive information (such as financial, commercial or personal data) is set out in a schedule in order that the main agreement is available for disclosure to third parties[20].

Traditional English drafting practice is to place the schedules before the signatures.

By contrast, US drafting practice places the schedules after the signatures. Either the traditional or US format is acceptable nowadays. Sometimes schedules are drafted by technical or commercial staff and 'tacked on' to the main agreement, prepared by the legal adviser. In this situation, it can be convenient to place the schedules after the signatures.

Schedules are typically numbered, for example, 'Schedule 1', 'Schedule 2', etc. The older practice of describing them as 'Schedule the First', 'Schedule the Second' is no longer common. Sometimes the Schedules are called Annexes, Annexures, Appendices, Attachments or other names. Some drafters make a distinction between Schedules (which set out provisions affecting the parties' rights and obligations under the present agreement) and Attachments (which are not part of the present agreement but have been included for some good reason, eg to show the format of a licence which the parties will sign if certain conditions are met). This is a matter of personal preference; the important point being to identify clearly the status of any documents attached to the main agreement (ie whether the provisions in such documents are to form part of the agreement).

---

[20] Some organisations must disclose particular information to various governmental and regulatory authorities. Putting sensitive information in a schedule can allow the disclosing organisation to fulfil its obligations easily while clearly demonstrating it has separated out truly sensitive information from the non-sensitive kind. Also, some organisations are subject to the Freedom of Information Act 2000. Public bodies are required (subject to available exceptions), when requested, to provide information that they hold which can include agreements entered into with commercial organisations. Separating out information which is truly sensitive or commercial into a schedule may afford the public body (and the commercial organisation, when relevant) a better opportunity to argue that such information should have the benefit of one of the permitted exceptions to the 2000 Act. The importance of separating out confidential information from the body of the contract is particularly important in light of the Information Tribunal's decision in EA/2006/00014, where it was decided that confidential information contained in a concluded agreement would not normally benefit from the confidential information exemption under the Freedom of Information Act 2000, as it would not be obtained by the public body (one of the criteria under the Act relating to whether such confidential information is exempt from disclosure). The Information Tribunal held that such confidential information was to be regarded as no more than recording the mutual obligations of the parties to the agreement. However, confidential information which was not only recording the mutual obligations of the parties and which could be said to be obtained by the public authority might still be exempt under this confidential information exemption, and might also benefit from the commercial interests exemption.

2.12   Execution clauses[21]

Examples for contracts under hand:

(i)   *Modern wording.* **AGREED** by the parties through their authorised signatories

(ii)   *Traditional wording.* **AS WITNESS** the hands of the duly authorised representatives of the parties to this Agreement on the day and year first before written

Examples for deeds:

(i)   *Modern wording.* **EXECUTED** as a deed by the parties on the date first above written

(ii)   *Traditional wording.* **IN WITNESS WHEREOF** the parties have executed this Deed on the day and year first above written

An execution clause is not needed[22] but often included.

It may be important to use this formal language in some situations, particularly for some types of documents (such as deeds and powers of attorney) and in some types of transaction (such as those relating to real property (sale or purchases of land and buildings, leases, trusts etc). There are other formal requirements for such documents, and this may lead the court to take a stricter view on the need to comply with drafting formalities. For contracts made under hand, where the form of the document is less important, it is suggested that the use of words such as 'as witness' are not necessary and are avoided, on account of their archaic language.

In the first of the above examples, the words 'through their authorised signatories' are used. These words are designed to focus the minds of the individuals signing the contract on whether they do, in fact, have authority to sign the contract (eg on behalf of a corporate party)[23]. If a person signing the contract does not in fact have actual authority to sign it, he may nevertheless have apparent authority, on which the other party to the contract can rely, such that the contract will be binding[24]. The words 'through their authorised signatories' will not affect the legal position.

---

[21]   Traditionally known as testimonium clauses.

[22]   Reason for its inclusion: 'is not necessary to the validity of the instrument but is added merely to preserve the evidence of its due execution. For this reason it may be of importance and, except in instruments relating to registered land, it should never in practice be omitted' *Encyclopaedia of Forms and Precedents*, vol 12(2), para 18, 1530.

[23]   In some US agreements, next to the place where a person signs (eg on behalf of a company), the word 'by' is inserted to indicate clearly that the person is not signing in a personal capacity.

[24]   See *Freeman and Lockyer (a firm) v Buckhurst Park Properties (Mangal Ltd)* [1964] 2 QB 480, CA.

2.13   Signature blocks[25]

2.13.1   *Examples in deeds*

Examples:

Example 1

SIGNED [and **DELIVERED**] as a **DEED** by the
above-named [*name of individual*] in the presence
of: (signature of executing party)

[Signature, name, address and description of attesting witness]

Example 2

EXECUTED [and **DELIVERED**] as a Deed by
[*name of company*] acting through [a director][26]
[two of its directors] [a directory and the company
secretary]   (signatures of director(s)) (or)
                                                    (signatures of director and
                                                    company secretary)

Example 3

SIGNED [and **DELIVERED** upon signature] as
a **DEED** by [*name of individual*]   Witnessed by:
_____   _____
signature   signature

                                                    _____
                                                    description

                                                    _____
                                                    address

Example 4

SIGNED [and **DELIVERED**[27]] as a Deed by [*name of company*] acting through
[a director][28] [two of its directors] [a director and the company secretary]

_____   _____
director's signature   [director] [company secretary]'s signature

---

[25]   Traditionally known as attestation clauses.

[26]   Where the default provisions of the Companies Act 2006 s 44 apply, if one director is signing
then s/he needs to sign in the presence of a witness.

[27]   This wording refers to the deed being 'delivered' to avoid uncertainty as to whether delivery
is intended on signature or at some later date; clearly if delivery is to take place at a later date,
different words should be used, eg a reference to the circumstances or date on which delivery
will take place (eg on notification by the signatory's solicitor, following receipt of funds). See
Chapter 1 for a discussion of the requirement for delivery of deeds.

[28]   Where the default provisions of the Companies Act 2006 s 44 apply, if one director is signing
then s/he needs to sign in the presence of a witness.

2.13.2   Examples in contracts under hand

Examples:

Example 5

SIGNED by [*name of person signing on behalf of company*] [as director] [duly authorised] for and on behalf of [*name of company*]   (*signature of person signing*)

Example 6

For, and on behalf of [name of company/individual]

_____
signature

_____
print name

_____
job title

_____
date

After the execution clauses appear the signature blocks. The above examples show a range of different styles for signatures by individuals and companies in contracts under hand and deeds. The traditional English style is to leave a space for signatures on the right-hand side of the page, as in Examples 1, 2 and 5. This seems easy enough once one is familiar with the convention. However, the commercial parties who actually sign the agreement will not always be aware of the convention, and may not know where to sign. This may not matter if their solicitors are present at a signing ceremony. However, it is common for many types of commercial contract to be signed by one party without its solicitor present, and then posted to the other party for signature. In such cases detailed instructions may be required to ensure that the agreement is properly executed.

A common mistake occurs with signature blocks prepared as in Example 1 above. The drafter's intention is that the name of the signatory be printed immediately after the typed words 'SIGNED by:' and that the agreement be signed to the right of the brackets. What sometimes happens is that the signatory signs next to 'SIGNED by:' and does not print its name. Perhaps this does not matter, but it seems pointless having an elaborate layout for signatures if it is misunderstood by the person who has to use it. This problem is avoided in Examples 3, 4 and 6 above, which do not use the traditional layout.

Example 6 includes a space for the date of signature to be inserted. Some English solicitors would regard this practice as inappropriate, since the date should be inserted in the first line of the agreement, and other dates are irrelevant or misleading. This is fine as long as the parties' solicitors are in control of the signing process and ensure that a date is inserted. However, with some types of commercial contracts and parties, (a) the parties do not involve their solicitors once final versions of the agreement have been prepared, and (b) the parties may omit to date the agreement (despite their solicitor's detailed instructions), and it may be difficult to establish later exactly when it was executed, particularly if there was no signing ceremony, and instead one party signed the agreement then posted it to the other party for signature. As a 'belt and braces' measure, therefore, the authors sometimes include a date line in the signature blocks. This practice is common in some other countries.

2.14   Clause numbering

The numbering of clauses is a matter of personal preference and modern word-processing programs include automatic numbering facilities which allow the drafter to choose different standard styles of numbering for clauses and sub-clauses, or create their own numbering style.

The traditional English drafting style often followed the practice of UK statutes. The hierarchy of clauses and sub-clauses used in statutes is demonstrated in the following excerpt from s 1 of the Freedom of Information Act 2000:

> '3   **Public authorities**
> (1)   In this Act "public authority" means—
>   (a) subject to section 4(4), any body which, any other person who, or the holder of any office which—
>   (i)   is listed in Schedule 1, or
>   (ii) is designated by order under section 5, or
>   (b) a publicly owned company as defined by section 6.
> (2)   For the purposes of this Act, information is held by a public authority if—
>   (a) it is held by the authority, otherwise than on behalf of another person, or
>   (b) it is held by another person on behalf of the authority.'

Thus, the hierarchy of clauses is 1(1)(a)(i). For further subdivisions, another distinctive letter can be used, for example: (A). Under this system, 1 is a clause, (1) is a sub-clause, and lower level subdivisions are referred to as paragraphs.

In contrast under the numerical style of numbering commonly used in the US, the same clause (in a contract) would use numbers throughout.

A disadvantage of the traditional English style becomes apparent when a clause runs over a page or several pages of the agreement. It may be necessary to turn back through several pages to find whether a sub-clause forms part of (for example) clause 4 or 5. The user of the agreement may find this frustrating. The numerical style avoids this problem, because the numbering of a sub-clause includes all the numbers in the hierarchy, and it is immediately obvious which is the main clause of which the sub-clause under discussion forms part. For example, renumbering s 1 of the Freedom of Information Act 2000 using the US system of number would result in:

> '3   **Public authorities**
> 3.1   In this Act "public authority" means—
> > 3.1.1   subject to section 4(4), any body which, any other person who, or the holder of any office which—
> > > 3.1.1.1   is listed in Schedule 1, or
> > > 3.1.1.2   is designated by order under section 5, or
> > 3.1.2   a publicly owned company as defined by section 6.
> 3.2   For the purposes of this Act, information is held by a public authority if—
> > 3.2.1   it is held by the authority, otherwise than on behalf of another person, or
> > 3.2.2   it is held by another person on behalf of the authority.'

It will be always clear which clause the wording which carries over a page belongs to.

A disadvantage of the numerical style is that the numbering can look inelegant, particularly if the drafter needs to go down to the fourth or fifth level in the hierarchy of clauses, for example, 4.3.1.2.1. Also some users find a string of numbers hard to interpret.

The authors' personal preference is a mixture of these two styles, which distinguishes between clauses (stand-alone provisions, which it is possible to read without referring back to an earlier clause) and paragraphs (which it is possible to understand when read in conjunction with an earlier main clause). In the following example, the words referring to VAT in paragraph (b) would be classed as a paragraph because it can only be understood if put together with the introductory wording 'All sums due under this Agreement'. This approach results in the following numbering in the above example:

4.   Payments

…

4.3 All sums due under this Agreement:

…

(b)   are exclusive of Value Added Tax which where applicable will be paid by Consultant to Company in addition; …

Finally, on the subject of clause numbering, it is conventional to refer to clauses in a contract, but sections or paragraphs in a schedule to the contract. This is done to avoid confusion over which provision is being referred to. In some countries, contracts are drafted with Articles and Sections (eg in the above example, Article 4, section 4.3), which is a style to be found in some international treaties.

2.15   Headings

To make the contract easier to read and understand, headings are now commonly used.

It is conventional to include a clause stating that the headings are to be disregarded when construing the meaning of provisions which appear beneath a heading. The format of headings is a matter of personal preference. Headings can either be integrated into the numbering of clauses or appear above clauses. Although the former is more common (as in the examples given in the discussion of clause numbering, above), headings which are independent of clauses can be useful at times. The formatting of individual clauses for ease of reading, including the use of headings, is discussed further in Chapters 4 and 5.

2.16   Engrossments (final version ready for signature) and counterparts

The old-fashioned term for the final versions of an agreement which is ready for signature, was often referred to by English lawyers as 'engrossments'[29]. In modern usage, it is the originals, and not the copies, which are the engrossments.

The authors' experience is that majority of commercial clients and most UK commercial and foreign lawyers are not familiar with this term. It can therefore fairly be described as English lawyers' jargon. In the absence of an alternative ('final copies' is misleading, and 'final versions for signature' is clumsy although accurate) it is, however, useful jargon.

The common practice with most commercial contracts is for one party (or their lawyer) to prepare one copy of the final version of the agreement (engrossment) for each party signing the contract if using the traditional practice of having them sign a document physically provided by that party. Where this is the practice then all the parties sign all the engrossments, thereby enabling each party to retain an original version of the contract.

These originals are sometimes inaccurately described as counterparts. Where a (two-party) agreement is signed in counterparts, each party signs one original and the parties then exchange those originals. Thus each party retains an original signed by the other party only. This practice is common in conveyancing transactions, such as leases.

---

[29]   This term has its origins in the medieval legal practice of preparing fair copies of important documents en gross (usually deeds).

However more common nowadays is the practice that documents are circulated electronically, again with one party usually being responsible for preparing the final version. In such cases, each party receives the document electronically, and in order to sign it has to print the document to paper, sign the signature block, and then either send the original document by post or scan at least the signature page and return the whole document or just the signature page to the other party electronically. There are dangers in returning the signature page by itself and this is something that in most cases a party should not do. They should normally return the whole agreement (so that there is no doubt as to what they have signed). The worst danger of just returning a signature page is that the other party may claim that the signature page belongs to a different version of the agreement)[30].

2.17   Alternative formats—letter agreements; terms in schedules

Sometimes parties prefer to draft their contracts in the form of a letter from one party to the other. The other party accepts by countersigning and returning a copy of the letter. A letter format can appear less formal and intimidating to the non-lawyer than a conventional agreement format. Even though the content of the agreement is the same as if it was set out in a conventional agreement format; all that has changed is that the agreement has been 'topped and tailed' to make it into a letter. As was stated at the beginning of this chapter, whether the agreement is in conventional format, or in the form of a letter, or in any other format, is not legally significant; what matters is the content of the document and whether parties have agreed to enter into a legally binding agreement.

Another practice which is sometimes encountered is to move all the 'boilerplate', definitions and standard provisions of the contract to one or more schedules, leaving the main part of the contract as a short document, perhaps no more than a page long, which sets out the names and addresses of the parties, describes the main provisions of the contract, incorporates the schedules into the contract by reference, and provides a space for each party to sign at the bottom of the page. This format can be particularly useful where a form (on one page) is used to capture all the key facts for a contract.

2.18   Obsolete drafting conventions

For a fuller understanding of how modern contracts are drafted, it is useful to consider how they differ from what was the convention for previous

---

[30]   This practice, consequences and suggested solution(s) are dealt with at 1.8.

generations. Some of the former conventions (most of which are no longer used) included the following:

- *Avoiding use of punctuation.* Traditionally, there were no full stops and commas in contracts. Typically, they were drafted as a single sentence running to several pages. Before the invention of typewriters, documents were often written by hand. If the document included punctuation, there was a danger that the insertion of a comma or full stop after the contract was signed could change its meaning.

  This practice of avoiding punctuation has now died out.

- *Beginning each new paragraph with a word in block capitals.* This *was* designed to make clear where a new subject began, and in modern drafting is replaced by the use of headings and different weights of fount (such as bold, italic) and spacing. This practice survives in the use of block capitals in certain words in the preliminary sections of the agreement, as in 'THIS AGREEMENT dated …', 'WHEREAS …', and 'IT IS AGREED as follows'. The use of block capitals in these places is entirely optional and is a matter of personal drafting style.

- *Using special engrossment paper.* Another practice which is no longer prevalent (at least in England) is to prepare final versions of agreements on special 'engrossment' paper, which includes lines down the left and right hand margins, typically printed in red ink and is longer than A4 size paper[31]. The idea was that the document should be written in such a way that the words went right up to the margins, so that there was no space for extra words or letters to be inserted after the signature which might change the meaning of the document.

  In contracts drafted by US lawyers, another practice has developed, which is to state 'REMAINDER OF THIS PAGE LEFT INTENTIONALLY BLANK' at the end of pages which are not completely filled with text. This sometimes happens because lengthy clauses are kept on a single page. However, this practice is not common in English law agreements.

---

[31] This practice is prevalent in some Commonwealth countries, particularly for traditional, non-commercial legal areas such as conveyances of land.

Chapter 3

Contract Drafting Techniques

Key points

The drafting techniques described in this chapter can be summarised as follows:

- use simple, direct language (preferably in the active and not the passive tense);

- use consistent language and defined terms (where needed);

- use a correct word order;

- make clear who has the obligation and to whom it is owed;

- use short sentences;

- use a logical sequence of clauses;

- use headings, numbering, punctuation and other techniques to make the contract easier to understand; and

- use a sensible size of typeface and plenty of white space around text.

3.1   Introduction

This chapter considers some techniques for the drafting of contracts. These are not formal rules which must always be followed; rather they are suggestions to help the drafter to achieve their objectives. The main objectives when drafting a contract are likely to be the following.

3.1.1   Legal interpretation

One of the most important aims for the drafter is to try to ensure that the court will interpret the contract in the way the drafter intended. Over the years, legal drafters have developed standard ways of expressing particular concepts, which will be readily understood by the court. For example, a contract might state that an event 'is deemed' to take place; this is understood by the courts and by most lawyers but sometimes causes clients problems. Some words have taken on a particular legal meaning; for example, an obligation to use one's 'best endeavours', or a document which is labelled 'subject to contract' or the nature and effect of a no 'assignment' clause which the courts have interpreted in several court cases[1].

The courts have also developed rules and general techniques for 'construing'[2] contracts. The drafter should therefore be aware of how words are used and understood by other legal drafters and by the courts. The interpretation of contracts by the courts is the subject of Chapter 5 of this book, whilst Chapter 6 considers words which have a particular legal meaning.

3.1.2   Intelligibility

Traditional contract language includes jargon and old-fashioned language which is not part of everyday speech, for example, 'hereinafter', 'determine' (meaning *terminate*), and 'in the event that' (meaning *if*). It may be necessary to use some technical language in the contract, but for the most part it is possible to write contracts in plain, modern English.

Litigation over contracts is relatively rare, and it may be just as important to the commercial client that the contract can be understood and used as a commercial document. It may be necessary to strike a balance between using technical language which will ensure that the contract is interpreted in a particular way by the court, and avoiding legal jargon which the commercial client does not understand.

The use of plain English is desirable in any contract; it may be essential when one of the parties to the contract is a consumer. Recent consumer legislation[3] requires the use of 'plain, intelligible English' in contracts with consumers, failing which particular terms in the contract or the whole contract may not be enforceable against the consumer.

This chapter will recommend some techniques for drafting contracts in plain English, using technical language where necessary to achieve a particular legal result, but avoiding unnecessary legalese, old-fashioned language and jargon. Some of these techniques are recommended for most types of business or

---

[1]   Over time, the courts have made different interpretations as to what the nature and effect of these words mean.

[2]   The word 'construe' is a classic example of an old-fashioned word used by lawyers. It is technically different from 'interpret', but in modern English the latter word would suffice, see the *Oxford English Dictionary* (2th Edn) which gives in a legal context one of definitions of 'construe' as 'To explain or interpret for legal purposes'. This definition is identified by the dictionary as an application of another definition of the word: 'To give the sense or meaning of; to expound, explain, interpret (language)'. Its use in a legal sense is explained in the judgment of Lindley LJ in *Chatenay v Brazilian Submarine Telegraph Co* [1891] 1 QB 79, CA: 'The expression "construction" as applied to a document, at all events as used by English lawyers, includes two things: first the meaning of the words; and secondly their legal effect, or the effect to be given to them.'

[3]   Unfair Terms in Consumer Regulations 1999, SI 1999/2083. See Chapter 7 for more on this subject.

official communication: to write directly and to the point, in a logical order, avoiding jargon where possible, and in such a way that the meaning is clear.

Other techniques for drafting contracts differ from those used in many types of communication: for example, the need for consistent use of words to express the same idea in different parts of the contract, avoiding ambiguity, sacrificing (if need be) elegance for the sake of certainty.

Most of us speak and write in a more colourful or complex way than is appropriate for the wording of a contract. A business letter, conversation or office memo may include some 'talking around' the main subject, softening of hard statements, commentary on the main subject, or references to opinions or feelings. This more informal way of communicating is even more likely to occur now that most people communicate via email, twitter feeds or text messages. These newer methods of communication, and the devices which allow them to be sent from anywhere, emphasise shortness (and the use of short-cut expressions).

For example, a common technique for softening statements which might offend or irritate is to make them indirect or passive, to write 'it is requested that X do (whatever)', or even more obliquely, 'it would be a good idea to do (whatever)'. A drafter should avoid such modes of expression when drafting a contract. Some people are uncomfortable with the directness of good contract drafting: such as 'I require that you perform (whatever) by (whenever)', or 'you *shall* do the following things, or else the following consequences *will* result'. For some, such a direct mode of expression can appear rude or untrusting. As one of the main purposes of contract wording is to set out clearly that what the parties are legally obliged to do is as they have promised, directness and precision are essential.

3.2   Topics to be covered in this chapter

This chapter deals with the following main areas: *use of language*, including use of plain, modern, direct English, consistent use of words, sentence structure and length, and *clause structure*, including the sequence of clauses and the use of headings, numbering and paragraphing. The following topics will be discussed:

- stating obligations clearly—who, what, when;
- active and passive, indicative and subjunctive;
- avoiding jargon and archaic language:
  - simplest form;
  - plain, intelligible style for consumer contracts;
- definitions and consistent use of words;

- avoiding unnecessary words;
- sentence structure and length;
- word order and use of punctuation;
- conciseness and comprehensiveness;
- length of individual clauses;
- formatting, use of paragraphs and tabulation;
- type size and white space;
- use of headings;
- logical sequence of clauses;
- grouping of clauses;
- use of schedules.

3.3   Stating obligations clearly—who, what, when

Examples:

Example 1

X shall be paid the sum of £500 as consideration for its obligations under this Agreement.

Example 2

Y may only use the Confidential Information for the purposes of this Agreement.

Example 3

Y shall pay X the sum of £500 within 30 days of the date of this Agreement.

Example 4

Y shall not use the Confidential Information other than as shall be necessary for it to achieve the Permitted Purpose.

Example 5 (from a modern US software licence, using US spelling)

You may not copy, modify, sublicense, or distribute the Program except as expressly provided under this License. Any attempt otherwise to copy, modify, sublicense or distribute the Program is void, and will automatically terminate your rights under this License. However, parties who have received copies, or rights, from you under this License will not have their licenses terminated so long as such parties remain in full compliance.

Good contract wording is direct and unambiguous. Ideally, it should state each party's rights and obligations in such a way that there can be only one

57

interpretation of the words used. The wording in Example 1 above has several deficiencies. It is not stated who is to pay X the sum of £500, nor is it stated when this sum is to be paid. To address these points, consider Example 3.

The wording in Example 3 states:

- *who* has the obligation ('Y shall pay');

- *to whom* it is owed ('shall pay X');

- *what* the obligation is ('shall pay ... the sum of £500'); and

- *when* that obligation must be performed ('within 30 days of the date of this Agreement').

It is conventional to state the obligation with the emphatic word *shall*. This does not mean that the obligation arises in the future. Unless otherwise stated, the obligation arises on signing the agreement. In plain English, you could say 'Y must pay X the sum of ...' and this would avoid any suggestion that the obligation arises in the future; but this is not the conventional way to draft contracts. Under traditional rules of English grammar, the word 'shall' can be used in either a future sense or an emphatic sense. The traditional rule is to say 'I shall', 'you will', 'he/she/it will', etc for the future sense, and to reverse this sequence when using the empathetic sense, that is 'I will', 'you shall', 'he/she/it shall'. Hence the use of the word 'shall' in contracts (ie 'Party A shall ...'). It may or may not be appropriate to refer to the sum being consideration for X's obligations under the Agreement. In some cases this will be obvious and not worth stating; in other cases, words such as 'In consideration for X's obligations under this Agreement' might be added at the beginning of the clause.

In Example 2 the phrase 'for the purposes of this Agreement' may well be unclear. Unless those purposes have been clearly stated, the extent of Y's rights to use the Confidential Information will be uncertain. It is possible to avoid this problem by including a definition of, say, the 'Permitted Purpose' and using this defined term in the clause.

In Example 2 a further problem is that the phrase 'may only' is weak, and the clause could state more explicitly that Y is prohibited from using the Confidential Information for any other purpose (which, presumably, is the other party's intention). Although it might be argued that this is implicit, it is better (from the other party's point of view) to make the obligation clear. An alternative form of words to address these points would be that of Example 4.

Another example of the use of the word 'may' in this sense is found in Example 5, taken from the GNU General Public License[4]. The clause clearly forbids the

---

[4]   GNU General Public License, version 2, available from http://www.gnu.org/licenses/gpl-2.0.html.

copying etc of the licensed software except as the rest of the licence permits, which the second sentence of the quoted clause appears to indicate. The rest of the licence mainly consists of what it is possible (but not obligatory) to do under the licence and where the word 'may' is more appropriate. The clause in Example 5 is a clause of prohibition and the use of the word 'shall' as suggested above, is the more appropriate verb to use: 'You *shall* not copy, modify, sublicense, or distribute the Program except as expressly provided…' [emphasis added]. The other explanation for the choice of wording used in Example 5 is differing drafting styles as the GNU General Public License (largely) originates in the US, where there is some difference is the use of the emphatic verb.

In some contexts the use of the word 'may' can have another purpose, particularly where a party is given the discretion to exercise a right, ie it can do so but does not have to do so. For example, giving a party the right to terminate an agreement if another party is in breach or the right to terminate after a particular date, but not requiring it to do so, eg: 'Any of the parties may at any time after (date) terminate this agreement immediately by notice in writing to the other parties'. In such circumstances, the use of the word 'may' is an appropriate choice.

In summary, contractual obligations should state clearly who has the obligation, to whom it is owed, exactly what the obligation is, and when that obligation arises—*who, what and when.* In some cases it should also be made clear *where* the obligation is to be performed (eg if there is an obligation to supply goods, are they to be supplied 'ex works'—made available at the supplier's factory— or delivered to the customer's address, or to some other location)? In some cases it will be important to state *how* the obligation is to be performed (eg is payment to be made by cheque, in cash, by letter of credit, or other method).

3.4   Active and passive

Examples:

Example 1
X shall be paid the sum of £500 by Y within 30 days of the date of this Agreement.

Example 2
Y shall pay X the sum of £500 within 30 days of the date of this Agreement.

Both of these examples say the same thing, in effect. The only difference between them is that the first uses the passive form, and the second the active form, of the verb 'to pay'. The second version is more direct. Although both versions are clear and easy to understand, use of the passive can make the meaning unclear, particularly in long or complex sentences. There is also a danger, when using the passive form, of omitting to state who has the obligation. In Example 1, this mistake has not been made, as the phrase 'by Y' has been included. In general, the drafter should use the active rather than the passive form.

There are a limited number of situations which require the use of passive; such as:

- if it is not known who carries out or is the subject of an action;
- if there is no requirement to identify who is to do something.

For example, a payment clause might provide that 'X shall pay the Royalties to Y within 60 days of the end of each quarter …'. Related payment clauses can use the passive, as it will be obvious from the context who is required to do them, for example, 'All sums due under this Agreement shall be made by the due date … and shall be paid in pounds sterling …'.

3.5   Indicative and subjunctive

Examples:

Example 1
Y should pay X the sum of £500 within 30 days of the date of this Agreement.

Example 2
Y shall pay X the sum of £500 within 30 days of the date of this Agreement.

Example 3
If A were to become insolvent, B would be entitled to terminate this Agreement.

Example 4
If A becomes insolvent, B will be entitled to [or, B may] terminate this Agreement.

A statement, such as Example 2, that Y shall pay a sum, uses the indicative sense of the verb 'to pay'. A statement, such as in Example 1, that Y should pay a sum, uses the subjunctive sense. The latter is ungrammatical, and should be avoided. If the words 'Y should pay' are used, an English court might interpret them simply as a polite way of stating the contractual obligation, or as a poor use of English, which in either case would not change the contractual meaning. However, they might be interpreted in a quite different way, as meaning that Y ought to pay the sum, but he does not have a contractual obligation to do so[5]. Similarly, the wording used in Example 4 is preferable to

---

[5]   One of the authors was involved in negotiations with a well-known international computer company some years ago, in which in-house lawyers from the computer company, based in the US, indicated that this was their intention when using the term 'should' in a contract clause.

that used in Example 3. Although it could be argued that the wording of the third example is perfectly grammatical (and even preferable to the fourth in its use of English), nevertheless the wording of the fourth example is to be preferred as contractual wording, as it is more direct.

3.6   Avoiding jargon and archaic language

Examples:

Example 1

In the event that there shall be a determination of this Agreement by the vendor, the purchaser shall be entitled to a reimbursement of all financial consideration given by him pursuant to clause 4 hereof.

Example 2

If the seller terminates this Agreement, the seller shall repay to the buyer all payments made by the buyer under clause 4 of this Agreement.

Example 2 means (almost) the same as the first but uses simpler and more modern language, for example:

- 'In the event that' is replaced by 'if';

- 'determination' is replaced by the less ambiguous 'termination';

- 'financial consideration' becomes 'payments';

- 'hereof' is replaced by the longer but less old-fashioned phrase 'of this Agreement', and might be dispensed with altogether[6];

- 'reimbursement' becomes 'repay' (or 'return' or 'reimburse' depending on the precise circumstances of the underlying agreement);

- 'Pursuant to' is replaced by 'under';

- 'vendor' is replaced by 'seller';

- 'purchaser' is replaced by 'buyer'; and

- the more complex construction 'there shall be a determination of this Agreement by the vendor' is replaced by the simpler and more direct 'the seller terminates this Agreement'.

The result is a shorter sentence (23 words rather than 34) which is easier to understand.

---

[6]   Particularly if another clause is included stating that references in the Agreement to 'clauses' mean 'clauses of the Agreement'.

3.6.1 Old fashioned words and jargon

A few examples of old-fashioned words or jargon which can, in most cases, be avoided, are listed below; together with suggested alternatives. There are many other words, which are not listed here, which a drafter should also avoid. There may be situations in which the drafter decides that the old-fashioned word or phrase more accurately reflects the drafter's intended meaning (or reflects some specific legal meaning based on a court ruling) in which case it should be used. The use of such words should not be simply out of habit. The important point is to look critically at what you have drafted, to check that it is written in clear English and means what you intend.

By reason that	Because
Forthwith	Immediately
Furnish	Give, provide
Hereinafter	Below (*or omit altogether*)
Heretofore	Above (*or omit altogether*)
In as much as/In so far as	Since
In excess of	More than
In the event that	If
In view of	Because
Determine	Terminate *or* decide
On the part of	By
Prior to	Before
Pursuant to	Under
Qua	As such
Said (eg the said Party)	*Omit altogether*
Until such time as	Until
Vendor	Seller
Whence	From where

3.6.2 'Acceptable' legal jargon

In commercial agreements, there is certain legal jargon which has a special meaning for lawyers but generally, there is no easy way to substitute shorthand alternatives. Where none of the parties to a contract is a consumer, there is normally no issue with their use. The main ones are listed here for convenience:

- assignment/assign

- covenant

- condition precedent/subsequent

- force majeure

- indemnity

- material/substantial breach

- novation

- of the essence

- representations

- time is of the essence

- warrant/warranty.

3.6.3   Using pairs of words when one will do

Pairs of words are sometimes used by lawyers. This is another type of unnecessary jargon unless the words mean something different from one another. An example with which most non-lawyers are familiar is the phrase 'last will and testament'. Other examples include 'sell and convey', 'goods and chattels', 'fit and proper', 'free and clear', 'save and except' and 'settle and compromise'. The reasons for these particular paired phrases are historical, dating back to the years following the Norman Conquest. The Anglo-Saxon and Norman legal customs were to some extent merged into a single legal system. To avoid legal uncertainty, Anglo-Saxon and Norman legal terminology were used together—for example, *will* is Anglo-Saxon whilst *testament* comes from the Norman French. It is sufficient to use the word *will* on its own nowadays. This practice became irrelevant for legal purposes a long time ago, but still persists in some legal terminology[7].

3.6.4   Use of Latin

Another type of legal jargon is to be found in Latin words and phrases. Sometimes, these are not even proper Latin but a kind of 'dog Latin' developed over centuries by lawyers. Fortunately the use of Latin phrases has mostly died out, particularly in the wording of contracts. Much of the recent drive to stamp out the use of Latin comes from the reforms to the civil litigation system in 1999 which replaced all Latin words with modern English.

---

[7]   The use of both Anglo-Saxon and Norman French names can be seen in other areas, eg the names for animals and food. The English names for meat—pork, beef, venison, mutton, veal—are French in origin and similar to the modern French names for both the meat and the animal, whilst the corresponding English names for the animals—pig, cow, deer, etc—are Anglo-Saxon in origin.

In some situations there is a good reason for the inclusion of a phrase, for example, where saying the same thing in English would be clumsy or take many more words to say. Nevertheless, it is recommended that most of these phrases should be avoided[8].

3.6.5   Other jargon

There are many other types of jargon, which should also be avoided in contracts unless the meaning is clear. Some of the terms used in the computer industry, for example, are meaningless to the uninitiated, and may be understood in different ways by computer specialists.

If the meaning of a technical term is disputed in court, the litigating parties may need to call expert witnesses as to the meaning of the term used. It is best to avoid the use of any word which is not part of ordinary speech unless (a) its meaning is clear from the context, or (b) it is defined in the agreement (or a reference is provided as to where a definition may be found). A discussion of how the courts approach the task of interpreting words used in a contract appears in Chapter 4.

3.7   Simplest forms

In recent years much effort has gone into simplifying the language of 'official' legal documents, including making such language far more direct and understandable by non-lawyers. A good illustration of this approach is the Civil Procedure Rules[9] (CPR) on which the following examples are based:

Example 1

IT IS ORDERED THAT ... the Defendant do forthwith disclose to the Plaintiff's Solicitors the full value of his assets within and without the jurisdiction of this Court identifying with full particularity the nature of all such assets and their whereabouts and whether the same be held in his own name or by nominees or otherwise on his behalf and the sums standing in such accounts such disclosure to be verified by affidavit to be made by the Defendant and to be served on the Plaintiff's Solicitors within 7 days of the service of this Order or notice thereof being given.

Example 2

9 (1) Unless paragraph (2) applies, the Respondent must [immediately] [within hours of service of this order] and to the best of his ability inform the Applicant's solicitors of all his assets [in England and Wales] [worldwide] [exceeding £ in value] whether in his own name or not and whether solely or jointly owned, giving the value, location and details of all such assets.

---

[8]   A Latin phrase which the authors find difficult to avoid is '*inter alia*'. This phrase is also used by non-lawyers, so perhaps is not truly legal jargon.

[9]   SI 1998/3132,

(2) If the provision of any of this information is likely to incriminate the Respondent, he may be entitled to refuse to provide it, but is recommended to take legal advice before refusing to provide the information. Wrongful refusal to provide the information is contempt of court and may render the Respondent liable to be imprisoned, fined or have his assets seized.

10 Within [ ] working days after being served with this order, the Respondent must swear and serve on the Applicant's solicitors an affidavit setting out the above information.

Example 1 is taken from an old court order (known as a Mareva injunction and now known as a freezing order under the CPR). It was typical of the court order style before the introduction of the CPR—heavy and impressive, but difficult to understand, covering several issues in a single, very long sentence, and using some very old-fashioned language (eg 'without' used as the opposite of 'within', and 'with full particularity'—perhaps the closest in modern English would be 'giving full details'). Before the introduction of the CPR, the likely argument as to why such a way of expressing a document in this way was used was that as long as the defendant had a lawyer, the lawyer could translate the order into simple English. But why should this be necessary? Why not write the order in simple English in the first place[10]?

Example 2 attempts to cover the same ground as Example 1, using more modern English, a more direct style, and breaking up the text into numbered paragraphs. Some parts of the second version could be criticised; for example, using the term 'serve' in place of the word 'deliver' as the word 'serve' is unlikely to mean much to a non-lawyer. However, the CPR comes with a glossary so that words like 'affidavit' and 'serve' are given definitions, much like a modern commercial agreement. For example, 'service' means 'Steps required by rules of court to bring documents used in court proceedings to a person's attention'.

3.8   Plain, intelligible style (particularly for consumer contracts)

Examples:

Example 1

This is a copy of your proposed credit agreement. It has been given to you now so that you may have at least a week to consider its terms before the actual agreement is sent to you for signature. You should read it carefully. If

---

[10]   It might, perhaps, be argued that the heavy old-fashioned style is an important aspect of the legal process—like the wearing of wigs and gowns, it is designed to intimidate the public into respecting the law. If such a view is held, it is, in the authors' view, misguided. In the twenty-first century, people do not respect attempts to overawe them with fustiness and legal impedimenta.

you do not understand it, you may need to seek professional advice. If you do not wish to go ahead with it, you need not do so.

Example 2

Contract creation and electronic contracting

The technical steps required to create the contract between you and us are as follows:

* You place the order for your products on the Website by pressing the confirm order button at the end of the checkout process. You will be guided through the process of placing an order by a series of simple instructions on the Website.

* We will send to you an order acknowledgement email detailing the products you have ordered. This is not an order confirmation or order acceptance from John Lewis Direct.

* As your product is shipped from our warehouse we will send you a despatch confirmation email.

* Order acceptance and the completion of the contract between you and us will take place on the despatch to you of the Products ordered unless we have notified you that we do not accept your order, or you have cancelled it in accordance with the instructions in Change or cancel an order[11].

This section of the chapter is headed *plain, intelligible style* but many of the techniques described in other sections are designed to help the drafter write in a plain, intelligible style. The techniques described in this section go one stage further than the techniques described elsewhere and are particularly relevant to the requirement, under the Unfair Terms in Consumer Contracts Regulations 1999, that contracts with consumers be drafted in a plain, intelligible style[12].

Example 1 is of wording which must be included in certain types of consumer credit agreement under the Consumer Credit Act 1974 and subsidiary legislation; it is written in very plain, intelligible language. Example 2 sets out modern contract drafting aimed at consumers. This wording sets out, in clear language using short sentences, the sequence of events to order goods from the supplier. But readers will no doubt spot that the wording is not entirely clear as to when a contract actually comes into being (see the last paragraph in Example 2).

Contractual language, particularly between commercial parties, tends to be formal in tone, even where the worst excesses of jargon and complex sentence construction have been removed. It is possible to lighten the tone, and make the words more intelligible, using some or all of the following techniques.

---

[11] Taken from online terms and conditions for the purchase of goods from John Lewis Direct.

[12] See discussion of the Regulations at Chapter 7 – Drafting Consumer Contracts.

It may not always be appropriate to use these techniques. For example, use of the words 'you' and 'we', rather than names such as 'the Company' and 'the Purchaser', may be helpful in a consumer contract or where one of the contracting parties is an individual, but would often be out of place in a detailed agreement between commercial parties.

- *You and we/us.* Nowadays, many of the standard terms and conditions of supply provided by major consumer suppliers (eg utilities companies) refer to the customer as 'you'. This technique is not compulsory, but conditions of supply do become slightly easier to understand, and less intimidating, using this technique rather than terms such as 'Customer' and 'Supplier'. This technique is recommended for other types of contract with individuals, for example, employment or consultancy contracts. Also consider (although it can sound abrupt) using 'must' rather than 'shall', as in 'We must tell you …' rather than 'The Company shall notify the Customer …'.

- *Avoiding technical language.* It is a difficult decision to take, whether to avoid all technical and legal language in an agreement. The Office for Fair Trading (OFT) has expressed a strong preference that legal jargon or wording is not used in contracts with consumers. The OFT's starting point on this issue is that a consumer should be able to understand and deal with a contract without the benefit of legal advice[13]. Language such as 'consequential loss', 'time being of the essence', '*force majeure*', 'all conditions and warranties are excluded', 'vicarious liability', 'mitigation' and 'this is without prejudice to your statutory rights' are best avoided[14]. Where 'legal' wording is used then explain its meaning. Some phrases, for example, 'service of notices' are probably best replaced with modern English (eg 'notify us in writing'), even if the technical meaning of a word like 'serve' is lost in the process[15].

- *Keeping it simple.* Much of this chapter is concerned with using simple, straightforward language in contracts. This is particularly important in consumer contracts, where the consumer will generally not take legal advice on the terms of the contract, nor be expected to understand complex contractual language. In consumer contracts, not only the style, but also the content should be kept as simple as possible, if only to avoid

---

[13]   See OFT Bulletin 3, para 19 (available from http://www.oft.gov.uk).

[14]   See Chapter 5 for more on this drafting issue.

[15]   See the example above taken from the CPR where the word 'serve' is specifically defined in the glossary to the CPR.

having the terms declared unenforceable by a court[16]. This is not to imply that the content of contracts between commercial enterprises should be intentionally complex, but in practice commercial parties often require their contracts to be detailed and comprehensive. In some commercial contracts, and in many consumer contracts, it may be desirable to draft wording which is not comprehensive in the interests of making the contract understandable.

- *Provide explanations.* A distinctive feature of some consumer contracts is that more explanation is provided as to the meaning of certain terms and, for certain parts of the contract, more descriptive language of what is to happen is used. In the former instance, a contract between commercial parties might state that goods are of satisfactory quality; but a contract with a consumer might spell out the meaning of satisfactory quality or if the goods have an easily scratched surface, this fact could be added. For the latter, more descriptive wording for a consumer contract might be used for example when describing, when delivery will and will not take place, and what a delivery person will and will not do (ie not take goods other than to the ground floor) as opposed to a commercial contracts where a statement simply stating that delivery will take place at the customer's premises would be used.

3.9   Definitions and consistent use of words

The same words should be used to express the same ideas at different places in the agreement. If different words are used, the court is likely to assume that a different meaning is intended. Thus if the contract refers to 'the company and its subsidiaries' in one clause, and to 'the company, its subsidiaries and affiliates' in a later clause, the court may assume (perhaps incorrectly) that the drafter or parties meant to exclude affiliates in the earlier clause[17]. In reality, the drafter may simply have 'cut and pasted' these clauses from different sources and failed to notice the inconsistency. Partly to avoid such risks, and partly to avoid repetitive use of long phrases, it is preferable to use a word such as the 'Group' throughout, and to define the Group carefully at the outset.

---

[16]   In addition, drafters who draft contracts where a consumer is a party, should regularly consult the bulletins and guidance issued by the OFT. The bulletins provide specific examples of unacceptable wording. The guidance provides the OFT's views on unacceptable wording in particular industries or service sectors (such as tenancy agreements, care home contracts, fitness club contracts, etc).

[17]   The same principle applies where the parties use a defined word (eg 'Sample' has a specific meaning (identified by the use of a capital letter) in parts of the agreement but in other places, the same word is used but not as a defined word.

The drafter should also avoid the use of 'elegant variations'. In non-legal writing it may be acceptable, and even desirable, to avoid repeating a word in a document, even where the same meaning is meant on each occasion. For example, a newspaper article, essay or even business emails between parties who know each other well and adopt a less formal style of communication, might refer in one sentence to a 'contract', in the next to an 'agreement' and in the third sentence to a 'bargain struck by the parties'. This type of literary technique should be avoided when drafting contracts.

While the use of definitions can undoubtedly aid the process of making the wording in an agreement more consistent, their extensive use can interfere with readers' understanding of the meaning of individual clauses. For example:

> The Client grants to the Contractor the right to Use the Client Software on the Equipment that is used in the Delivery of the Services for the performance of the Work in the Territory during the Term of this Agreement[18].

Without consulting the definitions section, the reader of this clause will not be able to determine its full meaning (in this example, they will need to look up eight definitions). There is a danger with the extensive use of definitions in a single sentence that the reader will not fully focus on the implications or consequences of the clause. Practically, the reader will have to turn back and forth from the clause they are reading to determine the meaning of each defined word, which can be irritating and cause loss of concentration. In some cases, where a definition is repeated only a few times, it may be appropriate not to use one at all, but rather to type out the full text that would have appeared in the definition, in each relevant clause.

There are several common types of definition, including the following.

3.9.1   Means

Examples:

Example 1

ABC LIMITED, a company incorporated in England and Wales whose registered office is at Twenty-first Century Business Park, Greentown, Loamshire G1 2AB (the 'Company')

Example 2

'Know-how' means all unpatented technical information developed in the laboratory relating to the Patents or the Materials.

---

[18] And some of these definitions are merely listings of further definitions which need to be consulted.

This is the most common type of definition. The meaning of the defined term is set out in a phrase or sentence, and the boundaries of the definition are clear. These examples are slight variations on this type of definition. In Example 1 the full name of a party to the contract is abbreviated by use of the defined term 'Company'. In Example 2, the definition explains what is meant by 'Know-how', and enables the drafter to set out the meaning only once in the agreement, rather than have to explain the meaning each time the term is used. These types of definition may be contrasted with definitions which state that the meaning of a defined term includes or excludes items, as described below.

3.9.2 Includes

Examples:

Example 3

'Person' includes a partnership or corporation.

Example 4

'Know-how' includes without limitation any results, data, methods, techniques, drawings, DNA sequences and formulae and any commercial and marketing information relating to Products.

This type of definition is particularly useful in a situation where there might be some doubt as to whether such items are included. In the first of the above examples, 'person' might not be understood by non-lawyers as including 'legal persons' such as a company. The definition clarifies that partnerships and corporations are to be understood as persons for the purposes of the agreement. In the second example, it is made clear that the meaning of 'Know-how' should be understood as including several types of technical information and also (surprisingly) commercial and marketing information. Such definitions do not, by themselves, set limits on how the defined term is to be understood, and are therefore less 'complete' than the type of definition discussed in the previous paragraph.

Example 3 uses 'includes' while Example 4 uses 'includes without limitation'. The view of the English courts is that the word 'including' (or include) will enlarge or extend the meaning of the word or phrase that precedes it[19]. The phrase 'including without limitation' is intended to set beyond doubt that 'includes' is intended not to be restrictive, although strictly unnecessary. In effect 'includes' and 'including without limitation' have the same meaning.

---

[19] *Stroud's Judicial Dictionary of Words and Phrases* (7th Edn), Sweet & Maxwell, definitions of 'includes' and 'including'.

3.9.3   Excludes

Examples:

> **Example 5**
>
> 'Know-how' excludes any information developed by the licensee under this Agreement.

> **Example 6**
>
> 'Know-how' means all unpatented technical information and know-how developed in the Laboratory relating to the Patents or the Materials, including without limitation any results, data, methods, techniques, drawings, DNA sequences and formulae, but shall exclude any information developed by the Licensee under this Agreement.

Example 5 is self-explanatory. It may be important to exclude information developed by the Licensee, for example, if the Licensee has confidentiality obligations to the Licensor in relation to know-how (but should not have such obligations in respect of information which the Licensee himself developed). Sometimes a definition will include all three types of definition, as in Example 6.

3.10   Avoiding unnecessary words

There are several types of unnecessary wording:

- *Verbose phrasing*. For example, writing 'In the event that there is a reduction in the number of explosions' rather than 'If fewer explosions occur'.

- '*Belt and braces*' *words*. For example, writing 'the said company' (or, even worse, 'the aforesaid company') or 'such company' rather than 'the company', when it is perfectly clear from the context which company is being referred to. Occasionally, it is useful to write 'the said …' but in most cases it is unnecessary. Another example is 'termination or expiry', which is sometimes found in several places in a contract. This could be avoided either by referring to 'termination by expiry' in the clause dealing with expiry, so that it is clear that expiry is a type of termination, or better by defining termination as including termination by expiry.

- *Clearly redundant words*. For example, consider the following sentence:

  Claims shall mean all claims and demands brought against the Policyholder by third parties (including without limitation any person injured by the Equipment, any personal representative of any such injured person, and any other person whomsoever).

It is clearly not necessary to use the phrase 'and any other person whomsoever' at the end of a phrase beginning 'including without limitation', since the point of the latter phrase is to make clear that what follow are merely examples.

The general point seems rather obvious—to avoid 'flabby' or unnecessary wording which does not add anything to the intended meaning. In practice, this is not always easy, particularly where the drafter is uncertain whether his choice of words covers all that he intends it to cover.

3.11   The use of pronouns (in non-consumer contracts)

Many contracts with consumers are drafted so that parties are identified by the use of pronouns ('you', 'we', 'us'), instead of using the names of the parties or a defined term.

In itself this is not a problem; but for commercial contracts, it can cause difficulties particularly with a pronoun such as 'we'. For example

- 'we' can refer only to one party, eg, the party who is providing the goods or services under a contract, but could just as easily refer to both parties to a contract;

- even if the intention is to refer to only one side of the contract (eg the side that provides the goods and services), it is unlikely to be suitable if there is more than one party on that side (such as a supplier of goods and a second supplier who is providing some services, or several members of a group of companies). The use of 'we' could refer to one or both suppliers or just one, but then the second would need identifying by another word or pronoun; but there may not be a suitable pronoun available to distinguish it from the other supplier.

Partly this issue can be overcome by definitions at the beginning of the agreement, such as

'In this Agreement 'we', 'us' and 'supplier' shall mean [*name of the party*]'.

However it is dependent on a user of the agreement being aware of how the word 'we' is being used. The user may not start by reading the definitions section; or may go straight to a clause that is relevant or of interest to them or after reading many paragraphs simply not remember the specific meaning of 'we' and 'us'. The safest course to minimise confusion is to use either:

- the names of the parties (or a suitable contraction of the name); or

- the name which clearly reflects the role the party plays in the contract.

3.12   Numbers

Some agreements contain provisions where any figure is expressed in both words and figures such as:

The Company shall pay the Consultant one thousand, three hundred and ninety five pounds sterling (£1,395.00) within 30 days of the date of this Agreement.

or

The Company shall pay the Consultant £1,132,395.00 (one million, one hundred and thirty two thousand, three hundred and ninety five pounds sterling) within 30 days of the date of this Agreement.

There is no legal requirement that such an approach is required or necessary in English contracts. The idea of expressing an amount twice is to provide an extra level of certainty that the amount is correctly stated (ie on the basis that one amount is checked against another, or perhaps that typing figures is more likely to lead to error whereas it is much more laborious and requires more thought to write out numbers in words). As far as the law is concerned, there is a presumption that where an amount is written in both formats, then it is the words that are assumed to be correct (on the assumption that it is easier to mis-type or write an amount as a figure[20], but it is no more than a presumption).

However, having to type, let alone read, amounts and figures twice is time consuming and, in the case of higher amounts expressed in words, the number of words might be off putting and lead the reader to skip over the written version of the number and rely on just the figure.

3.13   Formulas and the like

Formulas appear in most contracts where any form of payment or calculated amount is stated. Formulas indicate how an amount is calculated and it is possible to express the method of calculation either in words or figures (using arithmetic or algebra). Whichever method is used, the order of the words or the order of the operators and parentheses can all make the difference in the calculated figure.

---

[20]   See eg *Re Hammond* [1938] 3 All ER 308.

3.13.1   *Formulas expressed mathematically*

For calculations expressed mathematically it is important to understand some basic notation of mathematical convention:

1   Where figures are added and multiplied in the same calculation, the multiplication is calculated first, for example:

$12 + 3 \times 12 = 48$

But a person who does not understand mathematical conventions might make the calculation starting from the left and end up with $12 + 3 = 15 \times 12 = 180$

2   Where figures are added and subtracted, then the calculation is done from left to right, for example:

$12 + 3 - 15 + 12 = 12$

3   Anything in parentheses is calculated first, for example:

$(12 + 3) \times 12 = 12 + 3$ is first calculated and then result of this is multiplied by 12.

The problem is that many users of an agreement may not understand the mathematical conventions used in the order of calculations.

3.13.2   *Formulas expressed in words*

Similarly where words are used to express the calculation and the order in which items are subtracted, added or multiplied can make a difference to the amounts payable. In some cases the order in which the user of the agreement is to make the calculation may not be clear.

Take the following example:

the Consultant shall pay to the Company a royalty of 50% of the Price of all Products sold by the Company, less the Expenses during the period of 10 years from the Commencement Date.[21]

The word order can lead to a number of interpretations:

(for the purposes of this example Price = £20, Expenses = £8)

1   First deduct Expenses from Price (£20 – £8 = £12) and then take 50% of £12 = £6; or

---

[21]   Similar wording to this ambiguous type of contract drafting as used in the example came under consideration in the *Chartbrook Ltd v Persimmon Homes Ltd and Another* [2009] UKHL 38.

2   First calculate the royalty from the Price (50% of £20 = £10) and then deduct the Expenses (£8) = £2.

In this simple example, the Consultant might have to pay three times the amount to the Company depending on when the Expenses are deducted.

There are other possible interpretations but either of these two views is permissible. The first will mean the consultant pays a much lower royalty than the second[22]. Other problems include the use of the definitions, all of which will need referencing before the meaning of the formula might be understood.

3.13.3   Formulas—suggestions

Other than the simplest calculation, particularly where more than two operators are in use, to avoid ambiguity and ensure precision, the following is suggested:

1   mathematical notation is used and not words; and

2   the mathematical notation has an explanatory key; and

3   one or more examples are provided.

Where mathematical notation is *not* used, then the wording should have examples accompanying it.

The use of examples can serve two purposes: first, they can serve as a check to the drafter whether they have expressed what the parties intend and secondly, over the life of the agreement (or in the event of a dispute), the intentions of the parties at the time of the agreement will be easily understood.

3.14   Sentence structure and length

Short sentences are easier to understand than long sentences[23]. There is a long-established principle in official writing: 'only put one idea in each sentence'. This principle was almost certainly not devised by a lawyer. Contractual obligations are often complex, with many ifs and buts, and it

---

[22]   Clause 4.2 in Precedent 1 in Appendix 1 provides an example of the type of clause under consideration; but not drafted in the poor way of this example and also with different definitions. In the precedent the definition of Net Sales Value (the equivalent of Price in the example used here) indicates clearly that it is net of various costs of sales, etc (the equivalent of Expenses) *before* the royalty percentage is applied.

[23]   There are also government-backed codes concerning the length of sentences in some foreign countries, such as in the United States and certain Commonwealth countries.

may be necessary to cover several aspects of an obligation in one sentence. Consider the following:

> The Licensee undertakes at all times during the subsistence of this Agreement and thereafter to keep confidential (and to ensure that its officers and employees shall keep confidential) the terms of this Agreement and any and all confidential information which it may acquire in relation to the business or affairs of the Proprietor, save for any information which is publicly available or becomes publicly available through no act of the Licensee; provided that the Licensee shall be at liberty to disclose such terms and confidential information under a duty of confidence to its professional advisers and to others if and when required to do so by force of law.

The above clause is found in a published precedent. The word order is good—the main obligation appears first and is then qualified and embellished by further phrases. The language is fairly clear and covers, in a very concise way, most of the issues which are commonly addressed in a confidentiality clause. The main problem with the clause is that several ideas are crammed into a single, very long sentence which runs to 109 words. These ideas include the following:

(i)   The obligations set out in the clause continue during the life of the agreement and after it comes to an end.

(ii) The Licensee is required both to comply with the obligation and to take steps to ensure that its officers and employees do so.

(iii) The Licensee is required to keep confidential both the terms of the agreement and any confidential information relating to the Proprietor's business.

(iv) These confidentiality obligations do not apply to publicly available information unless the Licensee caused the information to become publicly available.

(v) The Licensee may disclose information to his professional advisers if they are bound by a duty of confidence to keep the information confidential.

(vi) The Licensee may disclose information if required to do so 'by force of law'[24].

---

[24]   Whatever this means—would an instruction given by a constable be a requirement 'by force of law'? More typical wording for this type of exception would be 'by order of a court of competent jurisdiction'.

Thus, the clause deals with at least six ideas in a long sentence of unbroken text. An alternative way of setting out the above clause, without any substantive redrafting of the words used[25], would be as follows:

1.   Confidentiality

1.1   The licensee shall keep confidential the terms of this Agreement and any and all confidential information which it may acquire in relation to the business or affairs of the Proprietor ('Confidential Information').

1.2   The obligations set out in clause 1.1 shall not apply to any information which is publicly available or becomes publicly available through no act of the licensee.

1.3   The licensee shall be at liberty to disclose Confidential Information:

(a)   under a duty of confidence to its professional advisers; and

(b)   to others if and when required to do so by force of law.

1.4   The obligations set out in this clause 1 shall apply at all times during the subsistence of this Agreement and thereafter.

1.5   The licensee shall ensure that its officers and employees comply with the licensee's obligations under this clause 1.

This version uses a few more words than the earlier version, but is considerably easier to understand. Each of the six main ideas appears in a separate sentence or (in the case of clause 1.3) separate paragraphs. The clauses are numbered for additional ease of reading. Even if the numbering had been omitted, and the text had been put together as a single paragraph of five or six sentences, it would still be easier to understand than the original version.

3.15   Word order and use of punctuation

Examples:

Example 1

If the Borrower fails to make any monthly payment on the due date or if any information about the Borrower which the Borrower furnished to the Lender hereunder proves incomplete or inaccurate or if the loan is used for the repair or improvement of any building which is subsequently sold or destroyed or if the Borrower ceases to live in such building or if the Security is or becomes at

---

[25]   This is not the appropriate place to comment on the substance of the obligations and whether further obligations or exceptions should be included. See Mark Anderson and Simon Keevey-Kothari, *Drafting Confidentiality Agreements* (2nd Edn) 2004 Law Society Publishing for a detailed discussion of the terms of confidentiality agreements.

any time unenforceable against the Borrower or the Borrower fails to observe or perform any of the terms of the Security or of any prior charge then the Lender shall be entitled after the expiry of proper notice to demand immediate repayment of the unpaid balance of the loan together with all other sums then owing but unpaid.

Example 2

We may demand immediate repayment of the [entire] unpaid balance of the loan, and all other sums then owing to us, if [after expiry of proper notice][26]:

(a)   you fail to make any monthly payment on the due date; or

(b)   you have provided us with incomplete or inaccurate information about yourself; or

(c)   the loan is used to pay for repairs or improvements to any building and the building is sold or destroyed, or you cease to live in the building; or

(d)   the Security is or becomes unenforceable against you; or

(e)   you do not comply with the terms of the Security, or the terms of any other Mortgage on the Property.

This section considers two related issues. First, clauses should be drafted in such a way that, if a comma is inserted in a sentence, the meaning of the sentence will not be changed. However, this is not always realistic. Commas, other punctuation (eg semi-colons) and brackets (parentheses) can be very useful to break up a sentence which covers several points, and reduce it to phrases of manageable length. Indentation, paragraphing and numbering can also help, and these topics are discussed in a later section.

Secondly, as a matter of general writing style, it is desirable to 'get to the point' early in a sentence, rather than leave the main part to the end of the sentence. In the first of the above examples, the point of the clause—that a demand for payment may be made—is left to the end of the sentence. It is therefore necessary to read to the end of the sentence before discovering what the clause is about. The second of the above examples uses a different word order and also introduces some punctuation, formatting and other drafting techniques to make the clause easier to understand.

Incorrect word order can sometimes change the meaning of a sentence; clearly this should be avoided. For example:

Example 1

Being ignorant of the law, the barrister argued that his client should receive a light sentence.

---

[26]   This phrase was used by the drafter to take account of the requirements of the Consumer Credit Act 1974. Ideally, it should be made clear what the 'proper notice' period is, or the clause should cross-refer to the termination provisions, eg by adding words such as 'subject to clause X'.

Example 2

The barrister argued that his client, being ignorant of the law, should receive a light sentence.

Example 3

The barrister, being ignorant of the law, argued that his client should receive a light sentence.

Example 1 is ambiguous. Try asking a group of people what the first sentence means, and in particular who is being referred to in the phrase 'being ignorant of the law'. You may find that some people think it refers to the barrister, others think it means the client (lawyers tend to assume it is the client). To avoid any ambiguity, the position of this phrase should be moved, as in Example 2 and Example 3, depending on the drafter's intention.

It is not difficult to find the correct word order in this example. In more complex contract clauses it can be very difficult. A 'rule of thumb' is to move the ambiguous phrase as close as possible to the subject to which it relates. Thus, in the above example, the phrase 'being ignorant of the law' is moved next to the word 'client' or 'barrister', depending on which is being described as ignorant.

These examples demonstrate what Sir Ernest Gowers calls 'that mathematical arrangement of words which lawyers adopt to make their meaning unambiguous'[27].

3.16   Conciseness and comprehensiveness

No drafter wants to forget provisions which might turn out to be important at a later date. There is therefore a tendency to make contracts longer rather than shorter. This tendency is fuelled by the use of standard contract precedents in many law firms; these documents often cover a wide range of unlikely eventualities. It is a brave lawyer who decides to cut out provisions from an office precedent which might prove to be important later, however peripheral these provisions might seem at the time of drafting the contract.

Competing with this pressure to be comprehensive is the desire to be concise, to avoid irrelevant wording. Sometimes, in trying to be comprehensive, it is possible to have the opposite effect. Consider the following examples.

Example 1

Neither party shall have any liability to the other party for any delay or failure in performance of this Agreement resulting from circumstances beyond the

---

[27]   *The Complete Plain Words* (3rd Edn) 1987 Penguin.

reasonable control of that party, including without limitation labour disputes involving that party.

Example 2

Neither party shall have any liability to the other party for any delay or failure in performance of this Agreement resulting from war, acts of warfare, hostilities (whether war be declared or not), invasion, incursion by armed force, act of hostile army, nation or enemy, riot, uprising against constituted authority, civil commotion, disorder, rebellion, organised armed resistance to the government, insurrection, revolt, military or usurped power, civil war, acts which hinder the course of or stop, thwart, prevent, interrupt or breach the supply and/or provision of any material and/or power which is instrumental to the continuance of this Agreement, any hazardous, dangerous, perilous, unsafe chemical, substance, material or property, which renders liable or endangers the health and safety of either party or the general public, flood, fire, arson, storm, lightning, tempest, accident or other Acts of God, epidemic, explosion, earthquake, hijacking, sabotage, crime, cracking or fracturing of equipment, plant or property, landslip, nuclear radiation and/or accident, death, injury or illness of key personnel.

In Example 2, most of which is taken from a published precedent, the drafter has attempted to think of all *force majeure* events which might possibly arise. In most situations, a long list of events will be unnecessary, if these are merely examples of events beyond the reasonable control of a party. The long list may be counter-productive if an event occurs which is not mentioned in the list—the court may take the view that by listing the events so extensively, the parties did not intend any event not listed to be within the scope of the clause. However, with some types of contract there may be good reasons for having a list of events—for example, if work is to be performed in a country that is close to, or embroiled in, a civil war.

Example 1 takes a different (and much more concise) approach, referring to events beyond the reasonable control of the parties. Labour disputes are specifically mentioned, mainly to avoid any doubts as to whether they are beyond the control of the party affected by them.

3.17   Length of individual clauses

The traditional English drafting convention was that each clause should be limited to a single sentence. However, as agreements have become more sophisticated and detailed, this convention is followed less often as it tends to increase the overall length of the document. Nowadays a clause can often continue for several lines of text (rarely more than, say, ten lines unless the clause is broken up into numbered paragraphs) and perhaps for two or three sentences. It is not yet conventional to have very long clauses which extend for more than a page of unbroken text, as is sometimes seen in North American agreements.

An example of a lengthy clause, which deals with at least six different issues in a single sentence, is given in the discussion of sentence structure and length at **3.14**.

3.18   Formatting, use of paragraphs and tabulation

Examples:

Example 1

Owner hereby grants Licensee, subject to the terms of this Agreement, an exclusive, worldwide licence under the Patents and to use the Materials, with the rights to sub-license, and a non-exclusive, worldwide licence to use the Know-how, to develop, manufacture, have manufactured, market, use and sell Licensed Products and use the Licensed Property in any processes.

Example 2

Owner hereby grants Licensee, subject to the terms of this Agreement, the following worldwide licences:

(a)   an exclusive licence under the Patents, with the right to sub-license; and

(b)   an exclusive licence to use the Materials, with the right to sub-license; and

(c)   a non-exclusive licence to use the Know-how, without any right to sub-license;

to develop, manufacture, have manufactured, market, use and sell Licensed Products and use the Licensed Property in any processes.

The layout of a clause may greatly affect how easily it is understood, particularly if the ideas being expressed are complex. The section on word order, at **3.14**, included an example of a clause which could be made easier to understand by splitting a long sentence into numbered paragraphs. Set out above are some more examples.

3.19   Size of typeface and use of white space

Going hand in hand with formatting is the size of the type used, whether the type is justified and the line length chosen. These factors can all dramatically affect how *readable* the agreement is. Although this chapter concentrates on drafting techniques, the next step after drafting is to read and check what is drafted[28]. An agreement that is printed on paper with a small typeface will

---

[28]   Specific techniques for checking agreements are dealt with in Chapter 9.

be difficult to check, even though it uses the drafting techniques suggested in this chapter. The same is true if the type is printed close together, without sufficient space between clauses and the other elements in the agreement (such as headings).

Much of the appearance of a document can be controlled through the use of styles and other formatting features[29]. Nowadays most drafters will be typing directly into a word-processing program, and most reading and checking is done directly on the computer screen[30]. This is not always convenient or practical, particularly where definitions or other sections of the agreement need checking. This will involve going back and forth through the document and will often not be practical (even with the use of bookmarks or hyperlinks)[31]. Also many users of document are not comfortable with reading documents on screen for extended periods. This will mean that documents need printing to paper.

3.20   Use of headings

Headings are very useful as an aid to finding clauses on a particular topic and for understanding the general subject area of the clause[32]. Where headings are used in an agreement, it is conventional to include a clause along the following lines:

> Headings used in this Agreement are for convenience only and shall not affect the interpretation of this Agreement.

Headings can be used for both clauses and sub-clauses if required. An example of an agreement which uses headings at several levels of a clause is to be found in Appendix 1.

---

[29]   Including the use of automation features such as macros and programming tools built into modern word processors.

[30]   The type size displayed is normally controlled by the zoom functionality. Other ways of improving the readability of text on screen is to change styles (which can control the spacing between paragraphs) or specific features of word processing programs such as Microsoft Word with its Full Screen Mode. One less well-known way is to use a feature built into the operating system—displaying text (and everything else) on the screen vertically (assuming that it is possible to swivel the monitor into a vertical rather than its normal horizontal).

[31]   Even users who have two (or more screens) attached to their computer can find it difficult to go through a long document on screen. One screen may contain one copy, and another screen shows another copy of the agreement.

[32]   And if the default heading styles of many word processing programs is used, such as with Microsoft Word or LibreOffice/OpenOffice, it is possible automatically to generate a table of contents (with hyperlinking).

3.21   Logical sequence of clauses

As has already been mentioned, a logical sequence of clauses is:

- to start with the definitions;

- perhaps followed by any provisions dealing with commencement of the agreement;

- then followed by the main commercial provisions; and

- less important provisions (including 'boilerplate') might appear towards the end of the agreement.

The more traditional practice of having a long list of obligations upon one party, followed by a long list of obligations on the other party, each introduced by words such as 'The Company shall:' at the beginning of the list, should, in general, be avoided.

3.22   Grouping of clauses

We recommend the grouping of provisions dealing with the same general topic. For example, the clauses which state the amount of any payments to be made should appear near to general payment provisions, for example, stating how quickly invoices must be paid, whether VAT is included, and whether interest is payable if payment is made after the due date.

3.23   Use of schedules

Another method for the logical organisation of contract wording is the use of one or more schedules. If the contract involves performance of work, a schedule can contain the detailed description of that work, as can any standards or acceptance criteria which the work must meet, a detailed timetable for completion of the work and a detailed payment schedule.

If documents are to be executed after signature of the main agreement, the agreed form of these documents is commonly set out in a schedule. Schedules are also useful for setting out information, for example, lists of the patents which are the subject of a licence agreement, or a list of assets, equipment, property, software licences etc subject to a business sale.

If the schedule sets out any obligations on the parties, it is important to state in the main agreement whether the provisions of the schedule form part of the agreement, or else they may not be legally binding on the parties. Wording along the following lines is commonly included in the main agreement:

The provisions of Schedule 1 to this Agreement shall form part of this Agreement as if set out here.

3.24   The question of gender

A few words about the question of gender[33]. When addressing a document the traditional practice has been to refer to men only, for example:

- addressing a letter to an organisation with 'Dear Sirs'[34]; or

- referring to a person in an agreement by using 'his' or 'he' (eg 'The Consultant shall carry out the Work and he shall be responsible for performing to work to a satisfactory standard').

It is a fact that more than half the entrants to the legal profession in England are women (the same is of course, true outside the legal profession), and there are strong arguments that modern legal practice should also move with the times so that communications are expressed in a gender-neutral way. For some, the question of gender is a non-issue but some people do find it at least old-fashioned to receive correspondence or documents which refer to men only. This chapter is about contract drafting techniques and part of that technique is to not offend the receiver, particularly in situations where it is easy to avoid gender-specific wording. For example:

- in an agreement where an organisation is providing the services of a consultant the agreement can use a defined word for the particular consultant: 'If the Consultant is or becomes unavailable to work on the Project the Consultant shall inform the Client as soon as possible' rather than '... he shall inform the Client as soon as possible'.

- in an agreement with a consumer, use the word 'you' or 'the consumer' as per the wording from the online terms and conditions for the purchase of goods from John Lewis Direct reproduced above[35].

---

[33] For more information about this topic and some practical ways of avoiding the use of gender-specific wording, consult, eg, Michèle M Asprey, *Plain Language for Lawyers* (3rd Edn) 2003 The Federation Press, pp 152–161.

[34] Still particularly true in inter-law firm correspondence. There are, perhaps apocryphal, stories about letters sent to all-women law firms being addressed 'Dear Sirs'.

[35] See **3.8** above on plain, intelligible style for consumer contracts.

Chapter 4

Advanced Drafting Techniques

4.1 Introduction

This chapter is purposively located between Chapter 3 (Contract Drafting Techniques) and Chapter 5 (Basic Commercial/Legal Issues Affecting Contract Drafting). It contains some pointers for looking at the 'bigger picture' in the drafting of a commercial contract. The other two chapters focus primarily on detailed aspects of an agreement: the first on writing a clear, consistently expressed and legally binding agreement; and the latter on individual legal elements in an agreement. This chapter deals with some 'bigger picture' matters in contract drafting outside of the specific words used and their legal effect. Given their nature, they do not provide 'answers', but indicate the questions which often need consideration.

4.2 The role of the contract drafter

The contract drafter should have (or play) a larger role than simply preparing the wording; ideally they should also help their party achieve the best deal it can. The first role will usually encompass the following:

- creating a legally effective and binding agreement which clearly expresses the stated commercial intentions of the parties;

- adding wording which is necessary to fulfil those intentions (including filling in gaps in draft agreements provided to the contract drafter);

- making certain (as far as it is possible to do so) that the wording used (or the commercial goals behind them) will accord with the way the courts have interpreted such wording in previous decisions;

- checking that the obligations that the parties are entering into are legally effective (eg avoiding wording which does not comply with the law, such as excluding liability for personal injury or death, or wording that is against competition law).

The second part of a contract drafter's role focuses more on commercial points including:

- providing information on the implications of the parties entering into an agreement on its proposed terms;

- suggesting different ways of entering into the proposed deal (whether by using different wording, or using different terms which better express the intentions of the parties, or suggesting a different type of agreement);

- guiding the parties away from deal structures which are not thought through, or which are too complex[1].

The second part of the role might often be useful or sometimes essential to 'save' the parties from themselves. However, this role may need to be performed at an early stage; once a particular type of agreement is selected as the basis for a deal and the parties have carried out negotiations, it may be difficult if not impossible to get them to move away from it. If the intervention comes too late, the 'better solution' may not be acceptable, and the deal however constructed is what will be used, and the contract drafter will have to make it work.

Whether a contract drafter is able to play the second role is subject to their position within an organisation. If they work in a fairly junior position, whatever their level of experience or skill, they may simply have no say in such matters. More senior staff (commercial negotiators, marketing or accounting personnel) may be in charge and they may see the role of the contract drafter as being to do no more than to create the agreement translating (to the limited extent necessary) the marketing/accounting language provided to them.

Often where a party uses lawyers (whether in-house or external) they can help with the second role, and this is where they can add the most value to a deal. The lawyer's past experiences of similar situations can enable them to help prevent a party having to 're-invent the wheel'.

4.3   Negotiating and drafting policies

For those regularly involved in negotiating agreements which cover the same subject area they will understand what is acceptable commercially and the type of wording that is acceptable, or not.

---

[1]   This can cover situations where the parties have simply selected the wrong type of agreement (less likely to happen with experienced commercial parties), or in order to help the parties to clarify which agreements they need to enter into. Take the following example: the parties wish to exchange technical information, to allow one party to perform consultancy services, and then to allow for that party to manufacture a product using the intellectual property of the other. The parties may wish may to enter into one agreement, but it might make better sense to separate out the different elements of the deal and have a separate agreement for each block of work, a confidentiality agreement for the technical discussions, a consultancy agreement for the services, a manufacturing agreement for the product manufacture and an intellectual property licence agreement for the licence. Such an approach may also help the parties to focus on the commercial priorities and objectives of each element, instead of mixing everything up together.

Typically this will arise where a party is regularly entering into the same type of deal covering the same subject matter. Often there will be negotiations or differences on the same points over and over again.

Where this occurs a party may wish to develop (written) policies on how a contract negotiator and/or drafter should deal with particular commercial issues. Such a policy may cover the following:

- areas in an agreement which are particularly problematic;

- the default commercial position of the party and acceptable and unacceptable variations;

- suggested wording to deal with each variation of the commercial position;

- suggested wording which will always or usually be unacceptable; and

- who at a party is to approve any variation or alternative wording.

The policy can include commercial positions and wording proposed or accepted in the past from other parties.

For example, if a party is in the business of providing statistical consultancy services to clients they may always provide a report at the end of the consultancy. The consultant's default position (as reflected in its terms and conditions) is:

- the consultant owns the intellectual property in the reports it provides; and

- the client only gets a licence to use the reports for their own internal positions; and

- the consultant offers no warranties as to whether the report or its contents will achieve any result etc.

The policy could then go on to deal with variations. Regarding the ownership of intellectual property, these could include the following reasonably foreseeable different variations:

- a client wishing to have the right to reproduce the report (such as having the right to incorporate the report in a publication of its own, or the right to reproduce it);

- a client wishing to own the intellectual property rights to the report (without the consultant having a licence to use it);

- a client wishing to own the intellectual property rights to the report (with the consultant having the right to use it, whether to produce further reports or more generally);

- a client having ownership of the intellectual property rights to those parts of the report other than specific 'core' elements (eg statistical techniques etc);

- a client owning certain intellectual property rights in the report but not all of it (and whether with or without the right of the consultant to able to use the report)[2];

- a client owning the intellectual property to the report but not to any rights belonging to a third party[3];

Where a party enters into a number of similar types of agreement, having an agreed position on commercial points which frequently arise can help to focus minds on what is (commercially) important to it, as well as speeding up the negotiating and agreeing of a contract. For example, the policy could state who in a party's hierarchy needs to consider particular variations from the default position. A minor variation from the default position may require approval or involvement of less senior management, while a major variation may need the involvement of senior management to approve or consider the draft contract.

Cynically, having an agreed policy may be of use as a negotiating tactic. A contract negotiator/drafter could justify its position as being necessary because they have to follow the policy.

4.4   Agreements with a large number of parties

With agreements where there are a large number of parties, particularly if the parties are located in different countries, there are dangers:

- in managing the process of drafting a clause which each party will agree with;

- that each change by one party will lead to every other party commenting on the specific change but not focusing on the contract as a whole;

- that the clause in question becomes verbose, complex and with a large number of exceptions or additions to incorporate the wishes of all the parties.

In the authors' experience, a party who regularly enters into agreements where there are several parties will usually find that they will end up with an agreement that is more lengthy and less coherent.

---

[2]   A report may contain more than one type of intellectual property, for example there might be several copyright rights, such as in the written expression, database rights, in any arrangements etc, as well as the use of any trade marks.

[3]   For example, if the reports contain statistical information or analysis, then the party may need to licence from a third party statistical information or statistical tools which it needs in order to carry out the consultancy services and/or to produce the report. The party may not be able to (sub)-licence such information or tools on particular terms.

The authors' view is that where there are several parties involved, one party to the negotiations will need to exercise strong direction in managing the process of negotiating, commenting and drafting. This lead role should go beyond the mere responsibility for drafting but also extend to:

- where there are inconsistencies, suggesting solutions to remove the inconsistencies;

- requesting the parties make decisions within a stated timescale[4].

Faced with multi-party agreements, where there are proposals from several of the parties as to changes and for which negotiations and internal approvals can take months, a party may need to set clear objectives as to changes or wording:

- which it can live with; and/or

- which it must make strong efforts to change (but can live with if not changed substantially or at all); and/or

- which it cannot live with (the 'deal breakers').

In the authors' experience, the length of multi-party negotiations can extend beyond any length of the contract, and a party is sometimes faced with a very difficult choice as to whether to start work without a signed agreement and without agreement on key commercial provisions (or no meaningful agreement at all)[5].

4.5 International negotiations

Where the parties involved come from different countries, there will often be problems concerning some or all of the following issues:

- differing drafting styles (ie a party in one country will express the performance of the obligation one way, whilst a party in another will do so differently)[6];

---

[4] With some parties, a contract negotiator/drafter may need to consult internally after a change (however minor)—a process that can take months in the worst case.

[5] It is never a good idea to start work without a signed, final agreement. For some of the reasons see Chapter 1, **1.12**.

[6] For example, a party based in an European country such as France, Germany etc may wish to express contractual obligations in a more general way, relying on the Civil Code to 'fill in the gaps', while an English party may wish express obligations with more precision.

- the legal requirements and laws of each country may be different (eg as to the regulations on how a party operates[7]);

- although English is often the default language of business, and many international contracts are now drafted in English, legal and commercial issues may still need resolving including those which are unique to international agreements, such as:

  o under which country's law the contract is made and which country's courts will decide on disputes;

  o which language will determine the meaning of the provisions expressed in the contract (ie in some countries, although it can sign an agreement in English, in order to 'use' the agreement in their country they may need to have it translated into their own country's language);

  o whether the agreement might be disclosed in a public register (and therefore that the parties agree a redacted version for such registration)[8];

  o the meaning of certain terms may not translate into the legal system of another country or may not have a direct equivalent or could be known under a different name[9].

Consider the following grant of a licence of intellectual property[10]:

1 Licences

Subject to the provisions of this Agreement, ABC hereby grants to the Licensee:

(a) an exclusive licence under the Patents, in the Field and in the Territory, [with the right to sub-license, subject to Clause [ ]], to [research,] develop, manufacture, have manufactured, market, use and sell Licensed Products; and

---

[7] For example, if the parties are negotiating an agency agreement, and for the party who is to become the agent, in its country it may require registration with a regulatory authority or other compliance procedures which the other party may not be aware of. In addition, such a requirement may also require that certain obligations that the party granting the agency wishes the potential agent to comply with are simply ineffective.

[8] For example, in the United States a party may have to file certain types of agreement with the Securities and Exchange Commission, which are then publicly available. Only a limited amount of redaction is permitted.

[9] For example, many agreements drafted in England contain a provision that prices stated are exclusive of VAT. In another country, there may be no such tax, but there may be a similar tax with another name (eg sales tax).

[10] This clause is from Anderson (ed) *Drafting Agreements in the Biotechnology and Pharmaceutical Industries* (OUP), Precedent 8e.

(b)   [a non-exclusive][an exclusive] licence to use the Know-how, in the Field and in the Territory, [with the right to sub-license, subject to Clause [   ],] to [research,] develop, manufacture, have manufactured, market, use and sell Licensed Products.

To consider some potential issues:

- If the licensor is based in the European Union and wishes to reserve the right to manufacture then the licence agreement may fall outside the protection afforded by the Technology Transfer Regulation[11].

- If the party granting an exclusive licence is based in Germany, then they may not consider it necessary to include any wording as to right to granting of sub-licences (if it wishes to do so) as, under German law, this is automatically permitted. Such an assumption would not normally be made in England.

- If an exclusive licence is granted, the position in England is generally that the licensor is also precluded from working with the licensed intellectual property, however if Dutch law applies or a party is based in Holland then whether this is permitted or not may need stating.

In addition to the points made above relating to the use of English, other more practical issues may arise such as:

- if the draft agreement begins as one drafted based on English law, then concepts or legal words (such as 'indemnity', 'term', 'warranty' etc) may not 'translate' exactly into the legal system in which the agreement is to operate[12]; local legal advice may be needed in the country whose law is to govern the contract; or

- more fundamentally, the level of understanding of English of a party in another country may mean that they fail to grasp the meaning of particular 'legal' words; or

- if a party in another country is preparing the first draft of the agreement, it may use the wrong template as a starting point, and therefore it may not contain the 'right' provisions[13].

---

[11] Commission Regulation (EC) No 772/2004 of 27 April 2004 on the application of Article 81(3) of the Treaty to categories of technology transfer agreements, OJ 27.4.200 L 123/11.

[12] In appropriate cases, a translation may be required so that the correct legally effective meaning in the target language is chosen, preferably with a qualified translator skilled in translating legal documents.

[13] For example, an Italian subsidiary of a US company that wishes to grant a distribution agreement to an English company but the available templates provided by the US parent do not include a distribution agreement, and therefore the Italian subsidiary chooses an intellectual licence agreement as the starting point; but the agreement will not have any provisions that entitle the English company to distribute products.

Chapter 5

Basic Commercial/Legal Issues Affecting Contract Drafting

5.1　Introduction

This chapter considers some of the issues which often need to be addressed in a commercial contract, almost irrespective of the specific subject matter of the particular contract. For example, which legal entities are to be the parties to the contract, how and when a party is to perform the subject of the contract, when and how a party is to pay, when does the contract come into effect and when does it come to an end, and (in international contracts) which country's law is to govern the contract?

Many of these topics are regarded as legal issues by the commercial representatives of the parties and as commercial issues by their lawyers. The truth is, both perspectives are correct; they are fundamental commercial and legal issues and, either way, may need to be addressed by the contract drafter. Ideally, a party should consider all of the topics in this chapter; but the reality is that most parties will find many of the topics of little interest. To take the first (who the parties should be), this normally causes no problem but if a party is dealing with a group of companies, they may find that they are entering into a contract with a member of the group who has no resources.

5.2　Who should the parties be?

Anyone who has rights or obligations under the contract should be a party. Sometimes parties are added to the contract who have no rights or obligations under it. This is generally a mistake; either the contract should state what their rights or obligations are, or they should not be parties to the contract.

There is also a danger that a person mentioned in the contract might benefit from the provisions of the Contracts (Rights of Third Parties) Act 1999[1].

---

[1]　Unless the rights of third parties are explicitly excluded with wording—see Contracts (Rights of Third Parties) Act 1999 at **5.12.5** (which is usually the case in most contracts). For a third party to be able to enforce the provisions of a contract , the parties to the contract must clearly intend that the third party can benefit, see *Dolphin Martime & Aviation Services Ltd v Sveriges Angartygs Assurans Forening* [2009] EWHC 716 (Comm), [2009] All ER (D) 119 (Apr).

The importance of stating the parties' names accurately has already been mentioned[2].

Where a company is part of a group of companies, it is not always clear which member of that group should perform the contractual obligations. Sometimes the parent company will be made a contracting party, either:

(a) instead of the subsidiary (with performance of the contractual obligations being delegated or sub-contracted by the parent to the subsidiary); or

(b) in addition to the subsidiary, and the parent will undertake to guarantee performance of the contract by the subsidiary[3].

5.3   Commencement, duration, extension of term

Sometimes contracts are signed after performance of the contractual obligations has begun. Where this occurs, it may be necessary to have a different commencement date to the date of signature of the contract. As has already been mentioned, the parties should not misstate the date of execution of the agreement[4].

Contracts are sometimes stated to be for a fixed term (eg three years), with a right for each party to terminate on notice to the other party (eg 90 days). Where this is the case, the drafter should clearly state whether a party may give such notice:

• at any time during the fixed term; or

• at any time after two years and nine months (so that the earliest termination is after three years); or

• only after the fixed term has expired (so that the minimum term is, in effect, three years and three months).

If the contract also allows for termination on breach or insolvency, the clause providing for the fixed term should state that it is subject to the clause(s) providing for earlier termination.

---

[2] See Chapter 2 at **2.5**.

[3] Or a parent company can obtain the benefit of an obligation of another party by being named as a party.

[4] Eg if the parties start performing the contract on 1 January 2011 but do not sign the contract until 1 February 2011, they should not date the agreement as 1 January 2011, but use 1 February 2011 as the date, and have a definition of 'commencement date' of 1 January 2011. See Chapter 2 at **2.4.1**.

It is also possible for a contract not to be for any fixed period of time, or that it continues from one period of time to another automatically. In such cases, provisions for when it is possible to give notice to terminate and the length of any notice need stating.

Sometimes contracts are stated to be terminable only at fixed times, for example, at a year end, and provided a minimum period of notice has been given. Again, careful drafting is required.

If the contract does not include any provisions for termination at all, then at common law it may be terminable on reasonable notice or (less commonly) it may not be terminable at all[5]. In view of these uncertainties, it is highly desirable to include in the contract a provision stating its duration or allowing a party to terminate the contract at any time.

5.4   Main commercial obligations

These will be at the heart of the contract and will often receive the most attention from the commercial parties. As already mentioned, the contract should make clear what the obligations are and when they are to be performed (and sometimes it may be necessary to state how and where they are to be performed and the standards to be met). There may also be provisions concerning the reports to be provided, meetings to be held to review progress, packaging and delivery requirements, etc.

Conditions precedent are often placed at the beginning of the main commercial obligations. If there are conditions precedent, the consequences of what is to happen if one or more of them are not met needs consideration. For example, whether there is a contract at all, whether the contract comes automatically to an end and whether any of the other obligations in the contract remain in force (such as confidentiality obligations).

---

[5]   For cases where termination on reasonable notice was allowed, see *Martin-Baker Aircraft Co Ltd v Canadian Flight Equipment Ltd* [1955] 2 QB 556 and *Crediton Gas Co v Crediton UDC* [1928] Ch 174. However, termination on reasonable notice might not be implied: see *Berker Sportcraft Ltd's Agreements, Re Hartnell v Berker Sportcraft Ltd* (1947) 91 Sol Jo 409, (1947) 177 LT 420. For a recent illustration of where an agreement was not terminable on reasonable notice see *Harbinger UK Ltd v GEI Information Services Ltd* [2000] 1 All ER (Comm) 166. In this case a clause in an agreement stated that the support and maintenance of certain computer networks and software was to be provided in perpetuity. It was held by the Court of Appeal that the words 'in perpetuity' meant that obligation was to continue without limit of time and would extend beyond termination of the agreement. In this case, the obligation would eventually come to an end only when the technology was superseded and the software outdated. The contract was not terminable on reasonable notice.

5.5   'Best endeavours', 'all reasonable endeavours', 'reasonable endeavours (and absolute obligations)

5.5.1   Measuring the effort needed

An agreement will usually contain an obligation on a party to do something (eg sell some goods and deliver them by a certain date, provide services, etc). Often the party will have to fulfil the obligation in a particular way. It is possible to express the way the party will have to fulfil the obligation in:

- absolute terms (eg 'the Consultant shall perform the Services in accordance with the Specification'); or

- evaluative terms (eg 'the Consultant shall use reasonable endeavours to perform the Services in accordance with the Specification').

Fundamentally, the commercial issue is to what standard is the party to perform its obligations under an agreement? The related commercial issue raised is, if a party fails to meet that standard, does the party have the right to terminate the agreement or does it have to give the party who has failed an opportunity to remedy its failure?

Many agreements seek to make a party perform its obligations according to some notional amount of effort but without specifying exactly what the party must do. Often terms such as 'best endeavours', 'all reasonable endeavours and 'reasonable endeavours' are used. These terms have received a considerable amount of attention from the courts.

Typically, the court will be asked to interpret a contractual obligation where a party has agreed to 'use its best endeavours' to do something (X). Inevitably, the extent of such an obligation can be uncertain and the subject of dispute if X is not achieved. One party may claim that X was not achieved *because* best endeavours were not used, whilst the other party may claim that X was not achieved *despite* using its best endeavours.

5.5.2 Use of the 'best endeavours' obligation

A client who is considering giving an undertaking to use its best endeavours should be warned that this is understood in English law to be an onerous level of commitment.

Sometimes, if a party is asked to accept an obligation to use best endeavours, their lawyer will try to negotiate an obligation to use 'all reasonable endeavours', or 'reasonable endeavours' on the understanding that this is a less onerous obligation. There is some limited case law which supports this view[6], although the authors' personal view is that most of the cases on best endeavours do not address this issue. In some contracts it will undoubtedly be preferable, and lead to greater contractual certainty, to avoid using any of these terms and to state specifically what the party in question is expected to do. A brief summary of some of the cases on the meaning of 'best endeavours' follows.

The case[7] which is traditionally cited on the meaning of 'best endeavours' concerned two licence agreements relating to inventions and designs. The agreements contained clauses requiring the licensees to use 'all diligence' to promote sales of the inventions and designs and to use their 'best endeavours' to exploit these. It was held that the licensees' obligation was at least that of taking reasonable steps to exploit the inventions and designs, having regard to both the interests of and their contractual obligations to their shareholders. The licensees' financial and commercial position and capabilities, and the chance that the inventions would prove commercially successful, were relevant in assessing the amount of damages.

In a case concerning the sale of land, a contract of sale included an obligation on the purchaser to use its 'best endeavours' to obtain planning permission. In the Court of Appeal, it was held that an undertaking to use one's best endeavours involved taking 'steps which a prudent and determined man acting in his own interests and desiring to achieve that result' would take[8]. In that case, by failing to appeal against a refusal of planning permission, the purchaser was held not to have used his best endeavours (where the appeal offered a reasonable chance of success).

There is also some case law on the extent of a 'best endeavours' obligation accepted by directors of a company, for example, to obtain shareholders' approval for a sale of shares. It was held (in the particular circumstances of these cases) that such an obligation does not override a director's duty to act in the best interests of the company[9].

---

[6]   In *UBH (Mechanical Services) Ltd v Standard Life Assurance Co* (1986) *The Times*, 13 November 1986, Rougier J held that an obligation to use 'reasonable endeavours' was less onerous than 'best endeavours'. Where a lessee undertook to his landlord to use reasonable endeavours, the lessee could take into account other commercial considerations as well as his obligation to the landlord.

[7]   *Terrell v Mabie Todd & Co Ltd* (1952) 69 RPC 234; also briefly reported in the Court of Appeal where the appeal was dismissed by consent: (1953) 70 RPC 97. In an earlier case the obligation was stated to be 'to leave no stone unturned', but this probably overstates the position. See *Sheffield District Rly v Great Central Rly* (1911) 14 Ry & Can Tr Cas 299, cited by Melville, para 9.11. See also *B Davis Ltd v Tooth & Co Ltd* [1937] 4 All ER 118, PC; and *Western Geophysical Co v Bolt Associates* 200 USPQ 1 (2d Cir 1978).

[8]   *IBM United Kingdom Ltd v Rockware Glass Ltd* [1980] FSR 335, CA. For a case where an obligation to use best endeavours was considered in a preliminary motion before the court, see *Imasa Ltd v Technic Inc* [1981] FSR 554.

[9]   See *Rackham v Peek Foods Ltd* [1990] BCLC 895; *John Crowther Group Plc v Carpets International Plc* [1990] BCLC 460; and *Dawson International Plc v Coates Patons Plc* [1990] BCLC 560.

Right to promote competing products? It has been held that an implied term in a contract that a company would use its best endeavours to promote another's product was to be construed in the context of the circumstances of the contract. Such a term was not inconsistent with the company being at liberty to promote similar products made by competitors of the other, but required the company to treat the others at least as well as it treated the competitors[10].

The promotion of sales? A requirement in a distributorship agreement that a claimant was to 'promote sales to the best of its ability in the UK and all countries in the schedule' was found to be a best endeavours clause as was an obligation that 'the claimant will endeavour to increase sales year on year'[11]. These best endeavours obligations were placed in the context of making a business investment:

> 'Increased sales, provided they earned or commercially could reasonably be expected in the future to earn a reasonable return, were in the interest of [the claimant and the defendant]. I agree with [counsel for the defendants] that where appropriate the obligation could require the claimant to invest and to take the risk or failure but only where there was a reasonable prospect of commercial success.'

In an Australian case[12] (not binding on an English court) a licence agreement contained an obligation on the licensee 'at all times to use his best endeavours in and towards the design fabrication installation and selling of the [licensed product] throughout the licensed territory and to energetically promote and develop the greatest possible market for the [licensed product]'. The five judges hearing the case on appeal in the High Court reached different conclusions on whether this obligation, by implication, prohibited the sale of competing products by the licensee.

Using best endeavours to negotiate and agree a contract: A provision in a heads of terms[13] document stated that the parties to the document would use their best endeavours to negotiate and agree a final settlement concerning the repayment of a loan (the loan being the subject matter of an earlier agreement). It was held that, based on the facts of the case, the parties had to use best endeavours to negotiate and agree an agreement, but the parties were not obliged to enter into any form of agreement[14].

---

[10]   *Ault & Wiborg Paints Ltd v Sure Service Ltd* (1983) *The Times*, 2 July 1983.

[11]   *Days Medical Aids Ltd v Pihsiang Machinery Manufacturing Co Ltd* [2004] EWHC 44 (Comm); [2004] 1 All ER (Comm) 991. The views expressed by the judge were *obiter*, as this case was concerned with the issues of restraint of trade and whether the distributorship agreement was in breach of community law.

[12]   *Transfield Pty Ltd v Arlo International Ltd* [1981] RPC 141.

[13]   See Chapter 1 at **1.12** for the meaning of this type of document.

[14]   *Beta Investments SA v Transmedia Europe Inc* [2003] EWHC 3066 (Ch); [2003] All ER (D) 133 (May).

5.5.3 How to deal with best and reasonable endeavours provisions

There are a number of ways to overcome the inherent weakness of best and reasonable endeavours, including:

- *Avoid such expressions altogether.* Define specifically the standards to be met; or

- *Use a comparator or benchmark.* This enables the best or reasonable obligation to be set to the activities that a notional third party would undertake within the relevant industry or sector. For example, a sales agent might be subject to an obligation to use 'reasonable endeavours' to obtain sales of a particular product, with 'reasonable endeavours' defined as follows:

  > 'Exerting such efforts and employing such resources as would normally be exerted or employed by a reasonable third-party sales agent for a product of similar market potential at a similar stage of its product life, when utilising sound and reasonable business, sales and market-specific practice, judgment and knowledge in order to develop a market for, and generate sales of, the Product in a timely manner and maximise the economic return to the Parties from such sales.'

However the problem will always remain that the exact meaning of such phrases will depend, in the event of a dispute going before the courts, on the view of a judge and the facts of the case[15].

In some US contracts the expression 'best efforts' is used. It appears that a 'best efforts' obligation under US laws may be less onerous than an obligation to use 'best endeavours' under English law[16].

5.6   Payment provisions

If the price is a fixed amount, the payment clause will be relatively easy to draft. If it is calculated by reference to a rate (eg a rate per task, for time spent or as a percentage of sales revenue—as with intellectual property royalties,

---

[15] In perhaps the most recent case to reach the courts, *Jet2.com Ltd v Blackpool Airport Ltd* [2011] EWHC 1529 (Comm), the court held that the meaning of an endeavours clause will depend on the facts of the particular case before the courts and not on the meaning(s) of endeavours clauses in other cases.

[16] For a US view on the meaning of 'best efforts' see Kenneth A Adams, *A Manual of Style for Contract Drafting,* 2004 American Bar Association and 'Understanding "Best Efforts" and its Variants (Including Drafting Recommendations)', *The Practical Lawyer,* August 2004. In the article, an analysis of case law appears to suggest that the standard to be used for measuring a best efforts obligation is higher than using good faith, and that reasonable methods and/or reasonable diligence need to be used. Another point indicated by the article is that the standard to be met by a 'best efforts' obligations is the same as for 'reasonable best efforts', 'reasonable efforts' and so on.

or payments of commission such as in agency and distribution agreements), then this will generally require more careful drafting. Particular attention is required where the calculation of the payment amount is expressed in a formula (especially where the formula is expressed in words), so that the right amounts are deducted, added and multiplied in the correct order[17].

A number of secondary payment issues may also need to be addressed, including the following.

- Does the price stated include VAT?

- When are payments to be made? (If periodically, how frequently?)

- How are the payments to be made (by cheque, online, letter of credit, etc)?

- Is interest payable on late payments[18]?

- Is time of payment 'of the essence'? (Is termination of the contract allowed for late payment? Is any one late payment, regardless of how late, sufficient to entitle party to terminate)?

- In what currency are payments are to be made (in contracts with an international element)? What currency conversion method is to be used, and who bears the risk of any change in the exchange rates?

- Are deductions or set-offs allowed, including withholding of taxes and avoiding double taxation (eg for royalty payments)?

- Are any payments refundable or to be treated as an advance against future payments?

- Who bears any ancillary costs (eg packing, carriage, insurance)?

- Are any statements, receipts or other documents required to be provided in support of payment claims?

---

[17]   See Chapter 3 at **3.13** (Formulas and the like). The case referred to, *Chartbrook Ltd* v *Persimmon Homes Ltd and Another* [2009] UKHL 38, illustrates the dangers.

[18]   If a right to charge interest is not stated in the contract, a party can rely on the provisions of the Late Payment of Commercial Debts (Interest) Act 1998. This provides for interest to be payable on qualifying debts in contracts for the supply of goods or services where the purchaser and the supplier are each acting in the course of a businesses (Late Payment of Commercial Debts (Interest) Act 1998, s 2(1)). A qualifying debt is a debt created by virtue of an obligation to pay the whole or any part of the contract price. A term is implied into contracts that the debtor will pay interest as specified in the 1998 Act (s 1). The statutory rate of interest under the 1998 Act is 8% over the official dealing rate per annum (Late Payment of Commercial Debts (Rate of Interest) (No 3) Order 2002, SI 2002/1675, art 4). A creditor is also entitled to a fixed sum in addition to interest, the amount of which starts currently at £40 for debts of less than £1,000 up to £100 for debts of £10,000 and above (s 5A). If the creditor is not entitled to charge interest, then the creditor is to have some other substantial contractual remedy for late payment of a contractual debt (s 8(1)).

5.7   Warranties

Commercial contracts often include warranties given by one or more parties. The content of the warranties will vary from contract to contract. Many warranties come within a number of well-defined categories, for example that the parties have the necessary authority and capacity to enter into the transaction or are in compliance with the laws and regulations or that the goods and/or services being provided meet a particular standard and what is to happen if they do not.

Amongst the commercial issues to be considered are the following:

- Is a party willing to give the warranty at all, or does it deal with something for which that party should not be responsible, or which the other party should check for itself?

- If the party is willing to give the warranty, should it be limited to matters within the party's knowledge?

There are two main types of knowledge warranty, as demonstrated by the following examples:

Example 1

X warrants that to the best of its knowledge, information and belief it is not a party to any current legal proceedings.

Example 2

X warrants that as far as it is aware, but without having conducted any searches or investigations, it is not a party to any current legal proceedings.

With Example 1 the court may consider that it is implicit in the warranty that X has taken reasonable steps to establish the truth of the warranted statement. In Example 2 it is made explicit that this is not a part of the warranty being given. It is generally considered unwise merely to use the phrase 'as far as [a party] is aware' without an express disclaimer of investigations (or whatever kind of disclaimer is appropriate to the warranty in question), as this might be interpreted as a 'best of knowledge' type of warranty.

It is common specifically to exclude from the warranties matters formally disclosed to the other party. Such disclosures are often included in a separate document (often called a 'disclosure letter') which is sent by the party giving the warranties to the other party at the time of signing the agreement. (The agreement will make specific reference to this letter.)

Sometimes:

- time limits (eg that a breach of warranty is brought to the attention of the party within a certain time period); or

- financial limits (lower or upper limit) are agreed in relation to the bringing of claims under the warranty.

5.8   Liability and indemnities

The legal effectiveness of exemption clauses, and techniques for drafting such clauses, are discussed in Chapter 5. Liability and indemnity clauses can be viewed as attempts to apportion commercial risk between the contracting parties. The parties will often wish to consider whether, commercially, those risks are acceptable, whether it is possible to insure against them at a reasonable price, and whether the price to be paid under the contract takes proper account of the risks being borne by each party.

Ultimately these are commercial rather than legal issues, but they are often rather remote issues, which the parties' lawyers may have spent more time considering than their commercial colleagues or clients. Moreover, the contractual language needed to deal with such issues may of necessity be legalistic (and nowadays where most legal jargon is encountered).

Accordingly, this is an area where lawyers are often asked to take the lead in contractual negotiations.

5.9   Confidentiality; announcements

Parties sometimes wish to keep some or all aspects of their agreement out of the public domain. Sometimes this is not possible, for example, where one (or more) of the parties:

- notifies the London Stock Exchange about the agreement; or

- places the agreement on a public register[19]; or

- discloses its existence under the Freedom of Information Act 2000 (if one party to the agreement is a 'public body').

Sometimes the parties wish to agree the text of any public statement that is to be made about the agreement, and may attach an agreed form of press release to the contract.

As a separate issue, parties may wish to provide that information disclosed between them, (eg technical or marketing information), must be kept confidential and used only for the purposes of the agreement. Amongst the issues commonly covered in confidentiality undertakings are the following:

---

[19]   For example, if notified to the Securities and Exchange Commission in the United States (subject to 'redaction'—blacking out—of confidential details).

- restrictions on disclosure and use[20] of information;

- security precautions to be taken by the recipient of the information;

- the extent to which disclosure to employees and consultants (and third parties) is allowed, and restrictions or conditions on such disclosure;

- exceptions to the confidentiality obligations;

- rights to disclose if ordered to do so by a court, etc;

- the duration of the obligations and whether they survive termination of the agreement;

- rights to have information and copies returned on request;

- (sometimes) provisions dealing with information developed under the agreement—who it belongs to, who can use it, etc;

- (sometimes) non-competition covenants going beyond the ordinary confidentiality obligations.

5.10   Termination and consequences of termination

It is common to include provisions allowing a party to terminate the contract if the other party is in breach[21] or becomes insolvent. Where one of the parties is not a UK company or individual, it should be borne in mind that standard English 'boilerplate' language for termination on insolvency or bankruptcy

---

[20] Sometimes the drafter of a confidentiality undertaking fails to mention *use* of the information.

[21] A clause concerning breach and whether the agreement terminated at the expiry of the notice (and worded in similar fashion to that found in Appendix 1 at clause 7.2(b), 7.2(b)(1)) has been considered in a case decided by the Court of Appeal (*Artpower Ltd v Bespoke Couture Ltd* [2006] EWCA Civ 1696, [2006] All ER (D) 35 (Nov)). The clause stated: '9.3— This Agreement may be terminated:—(a) by either Licensor or Artpower with immediate effect if the other commits a material breach of any term of this Agreement which in the case of a breach capable of remedy shall not have been remedied within thirty (30) working days of the receipt by the other of a written notice identifying the breach and requiring its remedy. Upon remedy, the party in breach shall provide proof of remedy within this same thirty (30) working days …' Despite this wording the CA held that, even if the breach was not remedied at the end of the 30 days' notice, the contract still remained in existence. The CA held that a further step was needed to bring it to an end: 'In my judgment clause 9.3 confers a right on the party, if he wishes to do so, to terminate the agreement in the circumstances described in that clause. But he is not bound to take that step … In my judgment, the party who was not in breach had to take some positive step to bring the agreement to an end' (at [13] and [14] of the judgment). The decision may have been influenced by letters written by the party not in breach which indicated that the party would decide at the end of the 30 days' notice whether to terminate the agreement. Perhaps, the practical outcome from this case is (i) to add wording to this type of clause, which indicates that the agreement will terminate automatically without the party not in breach having to do anything further; (ii) that party not writing anything following the giving of the notice which causes any doubt as to whether the agreement will terminate automatically; and (iii) the initial notice should state explicitly that if the breach is not remedied then the agreement will terminate automatically.

may not be appropriate, as this will generally describe situations arising under UK insolvency or bankruptcy laws.

Sometimes omitted from contracts is a description of what is to happen on termination. It can be very important to state that certain terms survive termination, for example, confidentiality obligations. There may be a need for a 'wind-down' phase, particularly in long-term contracts. In some contracts, for example, some complex joint venture agreements, agency/distributorship agreements, or where sub-contracts are entered into or those involving the licensing of intellectual property, the clauses dealing with termination issues and post-termination issues may run to many pages.

5.11   Law and jurisdiction

A common mistake in the drafting of commercial contracts is to state which country's (or state's) laws are to apply, but then fail to state which courts are to have jurisdiction. This is more relevant in contracts which have an international element, for example:

- where one or more parties are based outside England and Wales; or

- where offer or acceptance took place outside England and Wales; or

- where work is to be done under the contract or goods are to be delivered outside England and Wales.

If the contract concerns only English parties and obligations arising only in England, a law and jurisdiction clause will in most cases be unnecessary.

In the case of contracts with an international element, the drafter will need to take account of the Contracts (Applicable Law) Act 1990 (which implements the Rome Convention) and the EU Brussels Regulation[22]. The Brussels Regulation includes a set of rules for determining where a dispute between parties based in different jurisdictions (in countries which are parties to the Regulation) should be heard. In certain circumstances this may be the place where the defendant is based, or the place where the contractual obligations are to be performed. Of particular importance is Article 23 under which, if the parties agree to litigate their contractual dispute in a particular place, the courts of that place will have jurisdiction to settle the dispute.

The jurisdiction clause should also make clear whether the courts which are to have jurisdiction are to do so on an 'exclusive' or 'non-exclusive' basis. If this is not stated and the clause merely refers to 'submitting to the jurisdiction'

---

[22]   Council Regulation (EC) No 44/2001 of 22 December 2001 on Jurisdiction and the Recognition and Enforcement of Judgments in Civil and Commercial Matters, implemented in the UK by the Civil Jurisdiction and Judgments Order 2001, SI 2001/3929. The Brussels Convention (which the Brussels Regulation was intended to replace) still applies to Denmark.

of a particular court, and if the Brussels Regulation applies, this will probably mean that the court in question has exclusive jurisdiction and therefore all claims must be brought in that court. If on the other hand the jurisdiction clause provides for non-exclusive jurisdiction, it is likely that this will mean that a party may commence proceeding in that court, but may alternatively bring proceedings in any other court which is entitled to hear the claim.

A question sometimes considered by the courts is whether the parties have 'submitted' to the jurisdiction of those courts; if they have submitted, the court is more likely to accept the case. It is therefore considered desirable in the jurisdiction clause of the contract to use this slightly arcane terminology. A typical law and exclusive jurisdiction clause might read as follows:

> The validity, construction and performance of this Agreement shall be governed by English law. Any dispute arising under or in connection with this Agreement shall be subject to the exclusive jurisdiction of the English courts to which the parties to this Agreement hereby submit.

5.12   Boilerplate clauses

The following paragraphs will very briefly mention some of the more common boilerplate clauses[23].

5.12.1   Notices

Notices clauses are regarded by some lawyers as amongst the most important of the boilerplate clauses. Even in contracts which contain very few boilerplate clauses there will normally be a notices clause and (particularly in contracts with an international element) a law and jurisdiction clause. The notices clause generally states the procedure for how one party informs another and will include whether the notice must be in writing and how delivery will take place (by hand or sent by post; sometimes recorded delivery or first-class post is specified).

Often the clause will refer to sending notices by fax, e-mail, etc, although sometimes such forms of communication must then be confirmed by post. The addresses to which notices must be sent are generally specified. (In English law contracts these addresses are generally stated at the head of the agreement, although they could be stated in the notices clause, as is the practice in US agreements.) The notices clause will often state a time period after which notices will be deemed to be received. A typical notices clause might read as follows.

---

[23] 'Interpretation' clauses are discussed briefly in Chapter 6.

1.   Notices

1.1   Any notice to be given under this Agreement shall be in writing and shall be sent by first class mail or air mail, or by fax (confirmed by first class mail or air mail), to the address of the relevant Party set out at the head of this Agreement, or to the relevant fax number set out below, or such other address or fax number as that Party may from time to time notify to the other Party in accordance with this clause 1. The fax numbers of the Parties are as follows: Party A: 01234 567 890; Party B: 01234 123 456.

1.2   Notices sent as above shall be deemed to have been received three working days after the day of posting (in the case of inland first class mail), or seven working days after the date of posting (in the case of air mail), or on the next working day after transmission (in the case of fax messages, but only if a transmission report is generated by the sender's fax machine recording a message from the recipient's fax machine, confirming that the fax was sent to the number indicated above and confirming that all pages were successfully transmitted).

A further issue sometimes addressed in a notices clause is whether the notice is to be marked for the attention of a particular job title or a named person. For example, a notice seeking to terminate an agreement, sent in compliance with the above example wording, might not be specifically addressed to a person sufficiently senior and may not come to his or her attention quickly. Sometimes wording is added to state that notices need to be sent to a particular person[24].

5.12.2   Force majeure

Force majeure is a legal concept which exists in the laws of some European countries but not in English law. It allows a party to be excused from performance of its contractual obligations if it is prevented from performing them by circumstances beyond its control, such as terrorism, civil wars, floods, earthquakes etc. Under English law there is no automatic 'safety valve' of this kind—if the contract cannot be performed, it may be *frustrated* and come to an end. To avoid this happening, a clause is sometimes included in English law agreements stating that a party is not liable for delays in performance resulting from circumstances beyond its reasonable control. Sometimes those circumstances are defined. A simple form of clause might read as follows.

Neither Party shall have any liability or be deemed to be in breach of this Agreement for any delays or failures in performance of this Agreement which

---

[24]   See *Bottin (International) Investments Ltd v Venson Group Plc* [2004] EWCA Civ 1368; [2004] All ER (D) 322 (Oct) where a notice clause in a commercial agreement that stated 'Any notice … shall be in writing and delivered personally or sent by pre-paid recorded delivery post to the addresses set out in this agreement' was interpreted by the court in such a way that a notice left at the reception desk of one the parties was held as being sufficiently served.

result from circumstances beyond the reasonable control of that Party, including without limitation labour disputes involving that Party. The Party affected by such circumstances shall promptly notify the other Party in writing when such circumstances cause a delay or failure in performance and when they cease to do so.

5.12.3   Entire agreement

As is discussed elsewhere in this book[25], the drafter may wish to consider including an entire agreement clause in the contract.

5.12.4   Assignment

In general, a party may assign its rights under a contract unless the contract is one with a 'personal' element. A party may not transfer his obligations under the contract without the consent of the other contracting party. If such consent is given and rights and obligations are transferred, there will typically be a *novation* of the contract. It is incorrect to refer to 'assigning this Agreement'[26]. In general, a party may delegate or subcontract performance of his obligations under the contract, unless there is an express or implied term to the contrary in the contract.

The parties will often wish to address the question of whether they are to be permitted to transfer or subcontract their obligations under the contract. A corporate party may wish to be permitted to transfer his rights or obligations to another member of the same group of companies or to a purchaser of its business.

5.12.5   Contracts (Rights of Third Parties) Act 1999

This Act made a modification to the common law doctrine of privity of contract. It allows persons who are not parties to a contract (a 'third party') to enforce certain provisions directly. A third party can have this right if the contract explicitly stipulates to this effect, or a term of the contract purports to confer a benefit on the third party[27]. The practical effect of this Act is that most properly drafted commercial agreements now seek to exclude the application of this Act with wording such as:

---

[25]   See Chapter 1 at **1.10** and Chapter 6 at **6.5.5** and **6.5.22.10**.

[26]   See *Linden Gardens Trust Ltd v Lenesta Sludge Disposals Ltd* [1994] 1 AC 85 at 103, per Lord Browne-Wilkinson.

[27]   Contracts (Rights of Third Parties) Act 1999, s 1(1).

For the purposes of the Contracts (Rights of Third Parties) Act 1999 [and notwithstanding any other provisions of this Agreement] this Agreement is not intended to, and does not, give any person who is not a party to it, any right to enforce any of its provisions.

Agreements often mention third parties (such as members of staff carrying out one party's obligations, subcontractors, or affiliates of a party), but fail specifically to identify them with sufficient precision and/or fail to state that the particular wording is used for their benefit and to enable them to enforce their rights under the relevant agreement[28].

5.12.6   *Who signs the contract—are they authorised to do so?*

Where a contract is signed on behalf of a company by a senior employee, and the contract concerns matters which might be expected to be within that employee's area of responsibility (eg where the head of research signs a research and development agreement), it is generally difficult for the company to disown the contract on the basis that the person who signed it was not authorised to do so[29]. It will be virtually impossible to disown the contract if the person signing is a director of the company[30]. Unless the company has made clear to the other contracting party in advance of the signing of the contract that the person signing does *not* have authority to do so, the company is likely to be bound. These principles will apply even where there are internal rules within the company, limiting the powers of its employees to enter into commitments, although if those rules were brought to the attention of the other contracting party, the position might be different.

The authority of agents is a large subject and complete books have been written on agency law[31]. The main drafting issues are as follows:

- If a person does not have actual or apparent authority to sign a contract on behalf of his employer, nothing said in the contract can affect the position. Thus words such as 'The undersigned is authorised to sign this contract on behalf of XYZ Limited' will not protect the other party. Such words may prompt the individual to check whether he is, in fact,

---

[28] See *Nisshin Shipping Co Ltd v Cleaves & Cleaves & Co Ltd* [2003] EWHC 2602 (Comm); [2004] 1 All ER (Comm) 481 and *Laemthong International Lines Co Ltd v Artis* [2005] EWCA Civ 519; [2005] 23 All ER (Comm) 167 as illustrations of the dangers of not specifying whether a third party could enforce the terms of a contract.

[29] See, eg, Chapter 3 of *Bowstead and Reynolds on Agency* (19th Edn) 2010 Sweet and Maxwell, regarding apparent (ostensible) authority of an employee to act as the agent of his employer.

[30] See s 40(1) of the Companies Act 2006 (as amended). Section 40(1) provides: 'In favour of a person, dealing with a company in good faith, the power of the board of directors to bind the company, or authorise others to do so, shall be deemed to be free of any limitations under the company's constitution.'

[31] For example, *Bowstead and Reynolds on Agency* (19th Edn) 2010 Sweet and Maxwell.

authorised, and might give the other contracting party a right to sue that individual if he or she does not have such authority, and for these reasons such a statement may be useful.

- The methods by which a company can execute a contract are discussed in Chapter 1. Examples of execution clauses and signature blocks are discussed in Chapter 2.

- If the contract is of great importance, the other contracting party might insist on being provided with a certified copy of a Board resolution of the company approving the execution of the contract and giving the individual signing it delegated authority to do so. This would avoid any doubt over whether the agreement has been validly executed by the company. However, with many contracts this will not be appropriate—a small supplier entering into an agreement with a major multinational company can hardly expect the latter to call a Board meeting to approve each run-of-the-mill commercial agreement.

Chapter 6

Interpretation of Contracts by the Courts— Implications for the Drafter/Negotiator

6.1 Introduction

This chapter considers the methods the English courts use for interpreting contracts. It focuses particularly on how the drafter of a contract should take account of such methods. The courts have developed these methods over decades, in some cases over centuries, to the point where some are regarded as hard rules or principles of contractual interpretation. The principles have become known as the 'canons of construction', a name which implies great authority, commanding respect from all who go near[1]. The reported cases indicate that the courts take these principles very seriously, and seek to apply them when interpreting contracts. Yet it is not always easy to predict how a court will apply the principles or what the practical result will be; sometimes it seems that the courts pay lip service to the principles, whilst deciding cases on the 'merits' of the situation before them. On some issues there are so many principles that it seems the court can choose which principle to apply[2].

Some of the principles will be considered in more detail later in this chapter. To give a flavour of what this chapter will cover it may be helpful at this point to list some of the more important topics to be discussed.

6.2 Establishing the terms of the contract and their meaning

- *General approach of the courts:* how to determine the intentions of the contracting parties; relevance of past decisions.

- *Which terms comprise the contract:* express terms; terms of other documents; parol evidence rule; representations and collateral contracts.

---

[1] And from time to time, these principles are said to be overturned, as some have argued following the speech of Lord Hoffmann in *Investors' Compensation Scheme Ltd v West Bromwich Building Society* [1998] 1 All ER 98.

[2] For example, when considering whether to admit evidence of terms not set out in the main contract document, the courts may apply the parol evidence rule (and exceptions to that rule), or treat the terms as part of a collateral contract or prior representation. This is discussed later in this chapter.

- *The meaning of words used in contracts:* the 'golden rule'; ordinary words; technical terms; legal terms (in outline)[3]; special meanings given by the parties.

6.3   Interpreting a given set of contract terms

- *General approach:* (1) interpret the document as a whole; (2) give effect to all parts of the document; (3) special conditions override standard (usually printed) conditions.

- *Express terms:* (1) if some items are mentioned, and similar items are not mentioned, it may be assumed that the omission was deliberate; (2) if the contract includes express terms on a topic, it is unlikely that the court will imply terms on that topic; (3) the *ejusdem generis* ('of the same kind') rule—where the contract includes a list of items followed by words such as 'or other [items]', the 'others' will be interpreted as being limited to items which are similar to those specifically listed.

- *Who has the benefit of the doubt:* (1) unclear contract wording will be interpreted against the interests of the party seeking to rely on it, or the party which drafted the wording; (2) the court is unlikely to interpret contract wording so as to allow a party to take advantage of his own wrongdoing (and only the clearest and most explicit words will allow a party to can take such an advantage, where it is possible to do so); (3) if there are two possible interpretations, one of which is lawful and the other unlawful, the court will apply the lawful one; (4) if by one interpretation the contract is valid, and by the other the contract is invalid, the valid interpretation will be applied; (5) an interpretation which leads to a reasonable result may be preferred over one which leads to an unreasonable result; (6) an interpretation which requires a party to do something which is possible will be preferred over a requirement to do something which is impossible.

- *Implied terms:* terms implied by statute or common law or implied into the particular contract, for example, under the business efficacy rule.

- *Special rules for exemption clauses:* how the courts interpret such clauses, and restrictions on exemption clauses under the Unfair Contract Terms Act 1977, the Misrepresentation Act 1967 and the Unfair Terms in Consumer Contracts Regulations 1999[4].

Some of these principles are concerned simply with interpreting obscure or ambiguous wording and the message for the drafter is simple—draft the

---

[3]   Legal terms, words whose meaning have been decided by the courts or by statute, and lawyers' jargon, are considered together in Chapter 8.

[4]   SI 1999/2083.

contract as clearly as possible. General techniques for clear drafting are discussed in Chapter 3. In other cases there may be very little the drafter can do: the court may apply general principles of interpretation which override even the most careful drafting. In other cases there are specific techniques which can be used to try to ensure that the court interprets the contract in the way the drafter intended. This chapter will focus mainly on this last category— principles of interpretation which can be addressed by particular contract drafting—whilst giving an overview of all the main principles of interpretation which are followed by the courts[5].

Some of these principles may contradict one another, when applied to a particular contract or contract term. This gives the courts some scope for selecting which principles they wish to apply to a particular case. Early in his career, one of the leading Chancery judges of the twentieth century, Mr Justice Megarry, wrote[6]:

> 'The cynical truth about interpretation in England seems to be that the Bench has been provided with some dozens of "principles" from which a judicious selection has been made to achieve substantial justice in each individual case. From time to time, all the relevant principles point in the same direction and leave the court no choice, but in most of the cases susceptible of any real dispute, the function of counsel is merely to provide sufficient material for the court to perform its task of selection.'

In fairness to the courts, they are required to be consistent with previous court decisions whilst doing justice in the individual case. Strict adherence to so-called rules or principles of interpretation does not always enable this to be achieved. An even more vivid comment appears in a judgment of Lord Denning in a leading case concerned with an exclusion clause in a contract[7]:

> 'Faced with this abuse of power, by the strong against the weak, by the use of the small print of the conditions, the judges did what they could to put a curb on it. They still had before them the idol, "freedom of contract". They still knelt down and worshipped it, but they concealed under their cloaks a secret weapon. They used it to stab the idol in the back. This weapon was called "the true construction of the contract". They used it with great skill and ingenuity. They used it to depart from the natural meaning of the words of the exemption clause and to put on them a strained and unnatural construction.'

Faced with comments like these, the reader may wonder whether it is worthwhile spending much time considering the many principles of interpretation which have been developed by the English courts. None the less, it is suggested that it is very important to do so because:

---

[5]   For a fuller understanding of how the courts interpret contracts, the reader is referred to the leading contract law texts, particular the excellent work by Kim Lewison (now a judge of the High Court), *The Interpretation of Contracts* (5th Edn) 2011 Sweet and Maxwell. This book is recommended for all serious legal drafters.

[6]   *Review* (1945) 61 LQR 102.

[7]   *George Mitchell (Chesterhall) Ltd v Finney Lock Seeds Ltd* [1983] QB 284, CA.

- In many situations the principles lead to a consistent, predictable interpretation. In such situations, the drafter must take account of the principles in order to achieve the interpretation he intends.

- Even where the courts have been accused of manipulating the principles to suit the 'merits' of the case, they have generally proceeded within the general framework of those principles. Although the drafter may not be able to ensure a particular interpretation by the courts, he can at least try to make sure the drafting is as watertight as possible, so that the court is not obliged to stretch the principles to achieve the intended purpose.

These comments may sound cynical. The problem is that contractual interpretation is not an exact science, no matter how many principles of interpretation are developed. The best that can be said for such principles is that they provide a broad framework for interpreting individual contracts, and are a guide to the drafter (and to the courts). Past cases can only provide a general guide to how a court will interpret particular wording, not least because the facts of contract disputes will rarely coincide exactly with the facts of previous, reported cases. Applying the same legal principle may lead to a different result if the facts in each case differ.

Despite these limitations, it is important for the drafter to be aware of and understand the main principles of interpretation which the courts apply when deciding contract disputes. It is recommended that contracts are drafted in the expectation that the court will interpret the words used strictly, particularly if the drafter is legally trained or the contracting parties take legal advice. Some of the principles described in this chapter may provide a 'safety valve' where drafting is unclear, ambiguous or otherwise defective. But the court's view of how those mistakes should be corrected may differ from what one or both of the parties intended; the best course is to make the drafting as clear and unambiguous as possible.

6.4   General approach of the courts to interpreting contracts

The methods used by the courts to interpret contracts can conveniently be thought of in two stages:

- *Stage 1* is to determine which terms form the contract, the meaning of the words used in those terms, and generally how the courts establish what the parties have agreed. This stage can be thought of as identifying the contract terms and their meaning;

- *Stage 2* is where the court applies detailed principles of interpretation (the 'canons of construction') to the contract terms which have been identified in stage 1.

The following sections consider stage 1.

6.4.1   *Reformulation of general principle to the interpretation of contracts*

The principal method for the interpretation of contracts by the courts for stage 1 in recent years has undergone some change. Many cases follow, as a starting point the five principles as set out in a case now considered the foundation for the modern interpretation of contracts[8]. In this case, Lord Hoffmann indicated that judges are to interpret contractual documents according 'to the common sense principles by which any serious utterance would be interpreted in ordinary life'. The case has been widely adopted in, and commented on by, the English courts[9]. But in many ways the principles are no more than a restatement of existing case law (but in more modern language). It would be easy to replace much of the commentary appearing in this chapter with a brief discussion of Lord Hoffmann's five principles. But this would not provide a useful guide for the drafter; it may be argued that the five principles do not provide a complete 'code' for interpreting contracts, nor do they provide sufficient practical detail to assist a person in attempting to interpret a contract as subsequent case law still continues to apply the older methods of interpreting contracts[10]. The five principles outlined by Lord Hoffmann are as follows[11]:

'(1) Interpretation is the ascertainment of the meaning which the document would convey to a reasonable person having all the background knowledge which would reasonably have been available to the parties in the situation in which they were at the time of the contract.

(2) The background was famously referred to by Lord Wilberforce as the "matrix of fact", but this phrase is, if anything, an understated description of what the background may include. Subject to the requirement that it should have been reasonably available to the parties and to the exception to be mentioned next,

---

[8]   See *Investors Compensation Scheme v West Bromwich Building Society* [1998] 1 All ER 98. Lord Hoffmann stated that there was a fundamental change in the courts' approach to the construction of documents following the speeches of Lord Wilberforce in *Prenn v Simmonds* [1971] 1 WLR 1381 at 1384–1886 and *Reardon Smith Line Ltd v Hansen-Tangen* [1976] 1 WLR 989 at 995–997.

[9]   A detailed analysis is beyond the scope of this book, but the approach suggested by Lord Hoffmann has not met universal acceptance or approval (despite it being a decision of the highest court in the United Kingdom). Some of the doubts about the principles being a new method for the interpretation of contracts, and the limits on the usefulness of some of the principles can be found in K Lewison, *Interpretation of Contracts* (5th Edn) 2011 Sweet and Maxwell, 1.02–1.08. Irrespective of the criticism, its wholesale and widespread adoption by English courts is not in doubt. Many of the cases which are mentioned in this chapter which are added for this third edition refer to the case (or other cases where Lord Hoffmann further elaborates on the principles).

[10]   See *KG Bominflot Bunkergesellschaft für Mineralole mbH & Co v Petroplus Marketing AG (The Mercini Lady)* [2010] EWCA Civ 1145, [2011] 2 All ER (Comm) 520 for a recent example where the court explicitly debated whether to follow the principles outlined by Lord Hoffmann or to follow older precedent. The court held that if it was not for older precedents it would have made a different decision using the approach of Lord Hoffmann (see para 61).

[11]   *Investors Compensation Scheme v West Bromwich Building Society* [1998] 1 All ER 98 at 114–115.

it includes absolutely anything which would have affected the way in which the language of the document would have been understood by a reasonable man[12].

(3) The law excludes from the admissible background the previous negotiations of the parties and their declarations of subjective intent. They are admissible only in an action for rectification. The law makes this distinction for reasons of practical policy and, in this respect only, legal interpretation differs from the way we would interpret utterances in ordinary life. The boundaries of this exception are in some respects unclear. But this is not the occasion on which to explore them.

(4) The meaning which a document (or any other utterance) would convey to a reasonable man is not the same thing as the meaning of its words. The meaning of words is a matter of dictionaries and grammar; the meaning of the document is what the parties using those words against the relevant background would reasonably have been understood to mean. The background may not merely enable the reasonable man to choose between the possible meanings of words which are ambiguous but even (as occasionally happens in ordinary life) to conclude that the parties must, for whatever reason, have used the wrong words or syntax (see *Mannai Investment Co Ltd v Eagle Star Life Assurance Co Ltd* [1997] 3 All ER 352, [1997] 2 WLR 945).

(5) The "rule" that words should be given their "natural and ordinary meaning" reflects the common sense proposition that we do not easily accept that people have made linguistic mistakes, particularly in formal documents. On the other hand, if one would nevertheless conclude from the background that something must have gone wrong with the language, the law does not require judges to attribute to the parties an intention which they plainly could not have had. Lord Diplock made this point more vigorously when he said in *Antaios Cia Naviera SA v Salen Rederierna AB, The Antaios* [1984] 3 All ER 229 at 233, [1985] AC 191 at 201:

> "... if detailed semantic and syntactical analysis of words in a commercial contract is going to lead to a conclusion that flouts business common sense, it must be made to yield to business common sense.'"

6.4.2   Intentions of the parties

When interpreting contractual obligations, the courts try to ascertain the parties' intentions as expressed in the words they have used. In other words

---

[12] Lord Hoffmann, in a later case, qualified this principle by stating that: 'I said that the admissible background included "absolutely anything which would have affected the way in which the language of the document would have been understood by a reasonable man", I did not think it necessary to emphasise that I meant anything which a reasonable man would have regarded as *relevant*. I was merely saying that there is no conceptual limit to what can be regarded as background. It is not, for example, confined to the factual background but can include the state of the law (as in cases in which one takes into account that the parties are unlikely to have intended to agree to something unlawful or legally ineffective) or proved common assumptions which were in fact quite mistaken. But the primary source for understanding what the parties meant is their language interpreted in accordance with conventional usage: "... we do not easily accept that people have made linguistic mistakes, particularly in formal documents". I was certainly not encouraging a trawl through "background" which could not have made a reasonable person think that the parties must have departed from conventional usage.' See *Bank of Credit and Commerce International SA (in liq) v Ali* [2001] UKHL 8, [2002] 1 AC 251 at [40].

they look objectively at the words used in the contract, and do not generally consider what one or other party privately intended when it agreed to those words[13]. This is the general principle, although there are exceptions, as will be discussed later. This may mean that the courts consider what reasonable people would have intended by the terms which were agreed. If the words used are clear, they may be applied even if this contradicts the commercial purpose of the contract.

In one case[14], Staughton LJ said that:

(1)   there is in general no law against people making unreasonable contracts if they wish;

(2)   whether they have done so is to be decided by ascertaining their intention (which of course has to be found in the language they used, read in the light of the surrounding circumstances); and

(3)   it is a matter of degree in two respects. The more unreasonable the result, the clearer the language needed. Therefore it would seem that if one intends to achieve a particularly illogical result, one must draft the wording of the contract so clearly that one is left in no doubt that the result was indeed intended.

6.4.2.1   Drafting and negotiating issues

The objective, rather than subjective, approach which the courts take has a number of implications for the drafter and negotiator, for example:

- *Consider how the court might interpret the parties' intentions from the words used.* It is necessary to think beyond what you intend by particular words, or what your client or commercial colleagues intend, or even what both parties to the contract intend, and consider what the court would regard as the likely intention of the parties using those words. If the words can be interpreted in several ways, consider which way the court is likely to interpret them. 'Clever' interpretations of the contract may be unlikely to succeed; if an unusual meaning is intended, it is better to spell it out in clear terms in the contract, so that the court will not misinterpret it. Even if both parties are in agreement as to their intentions, if these intentions are not clear from the wording of the contract, the court may reach a different conclusion;

---

[13]   Consider the words of Lord Wilberforce in *Reardon-Smith Line v Hansen-Tangen* [1976] 1 WLR 989: 'When one speaks of the intention of the parties to the contract one speaks objectively—the parties cannot themselves give direct evidence of what their intention was—and what must be ascertained is what is to be taken as the intention which reasonable people would have had if placed in the situation of the parties.' See also above, the first principle outlined by Lord Hoffmann in *Investors' Compensation Scheme Ltd v West Bromwich Building Society* [1998] 1 All ER 98.

[14]   *Charter Reinsurance Co Ltd (in liq) v Fagan* [1996] 1 All ER 406, CA.

- *Make it intelligible to the non-businessperson.* Increasingly, the courts are prepared to consider the underlying commercial purpose of contractual obligations. However, this should not be assumed. Make the contract intelligible to the outsider, not just to people who are familiar with industry practice.

6.4.3   Relevance of past court decisions

The English courts have considered some types of contract on many occasions so that a body of case law has built up as to how contracts of the same type are to be interpreted. This is particularly true in the case of contracts concerned with real property (such as leases) or construction. In other areas there is relatively little case law, for example, in relation to some types of intellectual property agreement (such as the licensing of patents). Where a large body of case law has built up, the courts may be inclined to follow the general approach taken in past decisions, unless they are persuaded that the parties to the contract before them intended something different. The implications for the drafter are as follows.

6.4.3.1   Drafting and negotiating issues

- *Ideally, the drafter will be aware of how similar contracts have been interpreted in reported cases.* Alternatively, take specialist advice. The general ways in which the courts interpret contracts are discussed in this book, but there may be specific interpretations for particular types of contract (eg rent review clauses in leases[15]) which are beyond the scope of this book. If particular words have acquired a particular meaning, and this is not the meaning you intend, use different words or specifically state the meaning intended.

- *If in doubt, state obligations specifically.*

6.5   Which terms comprise the contract

6.5.1   The terms set out in the contractual documents

Before considering how the courts will interpret particular terms of a contract, it is first necessary to be clear as to which terms the courts will consider. Where the parties have signed a written agreement, the terms set out in that

---

[15]   See further, *Encyclopaedia of Forms and Precedents* LANDLORD AND TENANT 'Business Leases' (5th Edn) LNUK, Vol 22(3)A.

agreement may be the main, or only, terms that the court will consider[16]. Almost certainly, those written terms will be binding on the parties who sign the agreement, even if they have not read the agreement[17].

Similarly, documents incorporated into the main agreement by reference will be binding on the parties. For example, the contract might include wording such as the following to ensure that the provisions of schedules form part of the agreement:

> The provisions of Schedules 1, 2 and 5 to this Agreement shall form part of this Agreement as if set out here.

If a document is attached to the main agreement (eg as a schedule to it) but it is not made clear in the agreement whether provisions of the attachment form part of the contract, the legal position will be unclear. For example, parties sometimes put details of work to be done under a contract in a schedule, and include in the agreement an obligation on one of the parties to 'perform the work set out in the schedule'. In the course of negotiations the parties include in that schedule other provisions and obligations, not concerned with the work to be done. Are those other obligations part of the contract between the parties[18]? In most cases they probably are, but the matter can be put beyond doubt with a provision in the agreement stating that provisions in the schedule form part of the agreement.

Where an agreement is stated to be supplemental to an earlier agreement, the two documents are read as a whole, so that terms of the earlier agreement can be considered in interpreting terms of the later agreement. To avoid any uncertainty, this might be stated in the agreement. For example, in an agreement which amends an earlier agreement, words such as the following are sometimes used:

> Except as expressly varied by the terms of this Agreement, the provisions of the agreement between the Parties dated 9th February 1960 ('Prior Agreement') shall remain in full force and effect in accordance with its terms. This Agreement shall be read in conjunction with, and as an amendment to, the Prior Agreement. Words defined in the Prior Agreement shall have the same meaning in this Agreement, unless the context requires otherwise.

Where several documents are executed as part of the same transaction, when interpreting one of those documents, it may be permissible to consider

---

[16] Whether the court will consider other terms, not set out in the written agreement, is considered in later sections of this chapter.

[17] In the absence of fraud or misrepresentation. See further Chapter 5, *Chitty on Contracts* (30th Edn) 2010 Sweet and Maxwell.

[18] In *Youell v Bland Welch & Co Ltd* [1990] 2 Lloyd's Rep 423, underwriters subscribed to a contract of reinsurance. In accordance with usual practice, the reinsurance was initially agreed in the form of a slip. A policy was subsequently issued. It was held by the Court of Appeal that the slip was inadmissible in construing the policy.

provisions of the other documents to assist the interpretation[19]. The relationship between those several documents could be stated specifically in the agreements. For example, the contractual documents for the sale of a business might include a main agreement and several ancillary documents, such as intellectual property assignments, novations of contracts with third parties, conveyances and leases of land and buildings. The main agreement might include an obligation on the parties to execute the ancillary documents. In such a case these ancillary documents might include wording such as the following, perhaps in a recital.

> This Assignment is made pursuant to an Agreement between the Parties dated 1 January 2012.

6.5.1.1   Drafting and negotiating issues

- *State the relationship of one agreement to another.* In appropriate cases, state clearly in the agreement:

  o   whether it is supplemental to, or to be read in conjunction with, another agreement;

  o   whether it has higher or lower priority then another agreement;

  o   the extent to which one agreement amends or varies another agreement;

  o   whether words and expressions used in one agreement have the same meaning in another agreement; and

  o   whether it comes into force or operation subject to certain obligations taking place under another agreement[20]

- *Expressly incorporate ancillary documents into the contract, where appropriate.* Ensure that all attachments, schedules and ancillary documents which are intended to have contractual effect are expressly incorporated into the main agreement, using wording such as that quoted above in relation to schedules.

---

[19]   See, eg, *Smith v Chadwick* (1882) 20 Ch D 27 at 62. For recent examples, see *Peacock v Custins* [2001] 2 All ER 827 and *Holding & Barnes Plc v House Hamond Ltd (No 1)* [2002] L&TR 7, CA.

[20]   Where there is a sale of a business, the main sale and purchase agreement may require the purchaser to pay a sum by a certain date and the ancillary documents may include provisions that they will come into effect only when this payment is made. Such provisions could further state that if the purchase price is not paid by a certain date then the agreement will automatically terminate on that date.

6.5.2   Drafts of the agreement and deleted provisions

Drafts of an agreement are generally not considered by the court when interpreting the signed version of the agreement[21]. To understand why a party might wish to produce to the court evidence of what was discussed in negotiations, consider the following fictional example.

A dispute is heard in the High Court, in which a breach of contract is alleged. The contract in question concerns the supply of software to be used to calculate the standard daily charges to be made by a private hospital for the use of beds. The purchaser is a national chain of private hospitals, the supplier a computer software company. During the negotiation of the contract, the purchaser tries to include in the contract a warranty to be given by the supplier that the software is fit for the purpose of calculating standard charges for use of hospital facilities. The supplier rejects this proposed term and it is not included in the signed contract. The software proves to be defective, but this is only discovered after several months of charging patients (or their insurers) too little. As a result of the defects in the software, the hospital chain loses several million pounds in revenue.

The purchaser sues the supplier for breach of contract, including breach of an implied term that the software would be fit for the purpose of calculating standard charges for use of hospital facilities. The supplier wishes to bring evidence of the fact that the hospital chain tried to negotiate such a term as an express term of the contract, but eventually agreed to sign a contract which did not include such a term. The supplier's argument is that such a term cannot be implied because it was specifically agreed in negotiations that such a term would not be included in the contract. The court decides that:

- it will not admit evidence of what was discussed in negotiations;

---

[21] See *National Bank of Australasia v Falkingham & Sons* [1902] AC 585. For example, in *Lola Cars International Ltd v* Dunn [2004] EWHC 2616 (Ch), [2004] All ER (D) 247 (Nov), the judge refused to consider various drafts of an agreement to help him interpret the meaning of the definition of a 'business': 'At one stage in his submissions [the advocate for the applicant] asked me to consider the various travelling drafts of the Agreement that passed between the parties' solicitors prior to the execution of the Agreement. He wanted me to examine these documents in order to show the changes that had taken place to the definition of "Business". In my view this is not an appropriate approach to questions of construction. Just as the Court will not have regard to the subjective intentions of the parties or to evidence of the negotiations leading up to the making of a contract it should not, in my view, admit evidence of drafts which do not represent the final consensus between the parties: see *National Bank of Australasia v Falkingham & Sons* [1902] AC 585 at 591 (per Lord Lindley); Lewison "The Interpretation of Contracts" (2004) at para 3.05. I have reached my conclusion on the meaning of the term "Business" without regard to this material' (para 20).

- the contract includes an implied term of fitness for purpose, and the supplier was in breach of that term[22].

The supplier (who was not properly advised when he negotiated the contract) is surprised by this decision. He assumed, wrongly, that the parties' negotiations would be taken into account by the court. Had he known that the court would take this approach, he would have included a term in the contract stating that no warranty for fitness for purpose was being given[23].

The reasons why the courts will not normally consider pre-contract negotiations or drafts of an agreement are various. The main reason seems to be that pre-contract negotiations and drafts do not record an agreed position; therefore it is unhelpful to consider them when interpreting the final version of the agreement[24]. Recently the principle that pre-contract negotiations are not admissible has been restated by the most senior UK court in strong terms. That court held that to take account of pre-contract negotiations would be to step away from the purpose of the law of contract which is:

> 'an institution designed to enforce promises with a high degree of predictability and that the more one allows conventional meanings or syntax to be displaced by inferences drawn from background, the less predictable the outcome is likely to be.'[25]

---

[22] If this sounds unlikely, consider the judgment of Sir Iain Glidewell in the Court of Appeal in the case of *St Albans City and District Council v International Computers Ltd* [1996] 4 All ER 481, in which he stated that there was an implied term in a contract for the supply of software that it was fit for its purpose.

[23] As to whether such a disclaimer would be upheld by a court, see the discussion of exemption clauses later in this chapter.

[24] See judgment of Lord Wilberforce in *Prenn v Simonds* [1971] 1 WLR 1381. See also *Itoh (C) & Co Ltd v Republica Federativa do Brasil, The Rio Assu (No 2)* [1999] 1 Lloyd's Rep 115 at 124, CA. But although the extent of this principle was not clear following the decision in *Investors' Compensation Scheme Ltd v West Bromwich Building Society* [1998] 1 All ER 98 and *Bank of Credit and Commerce International SA (in liq) v Ali* [2001] UKHL 8, [2002] AC 251, see [31] of the later judgment, the position is now beyond doubt following the case of *Chartbrook Ltd v Persimmon Homes Ltd and Another* [2009] UKHL 38, [2010] 1 All ER (Comm) 365 which approved the approach of *Prenn v Simonds*. The position does however appear different in civil law countries, see the European Principles of Contract Law (para 5.102(a)) where regard can be had to the parties' preliminary negotiations.

[25] *Chartbrook Ltd v Persimmon Homes Ltd and Another* [2009] UKHL 38, [2010] 1 All ER (Comm) 365 from para 37. Another strand from this judgment is the focus on objectivity, which is not likely to be available from statements, etc made during the course of negotiations: 'But pre-contractual negotiations seem to be capable of raising practical questions different from those created by other forms of background. Whereas the surrounding circumstances are, by definition, objective facts, which will usually be uncontroversial, statements in the course of pre-contractual negotiations will be drenched in subjectivity and may, if oral, be very much in dispute. It is often not easy to distinguish between those statements which (if they were made at all) merely reflect the aspirations of one or other of the parties and those which embody at least a provisional consensus which may throw light on the meaning of the contract which was eventually concluded. But the imprecision of the line between negotiation and provisional agreement is the very reason why in every case of dispute over interpretation, one or other of the parties is likely to require a court or arbitrator to take the course of negotiations into account', from para 38.

While a court will not normally consider drafts of an agreement or communications between the parties, it can look at the *objective* factual background known to the parties at or before the date of the contract[26]. Given the restatement of the principle that pre-contract negotiations are not admissible, there still exist a number of limited 'exceptions':

- to demonstrate that the parties were aware of a fact which is relevant as background;

- to help a party who wishes to bring a claim for rectification of a contract;

- estoppel[27].

Despite the clear view of the most senior court that pre-contract negotiations are not of use in looking at the meaning of a contract, the position is slightly different where concluded agreements are concerned. These can be used in interpreting a contract[28], but the assistance derived from doing so may be limited:

> '83. In principle, it would seem to me that it is always admissible to look at a prior contract as part of the matrix or surrounding circumstances of a later contract. I do not see how the parol evidence rule can exclude prior contracts, as distinct from mere negotiations. The difficulty of course is that, where the later contract is intended to supersede the prior contract, it may in the generality of cases simply be useless to try to construe the later contract by reference to the earlier one. Ex hypothesi, the later contract replaces the earlier one and it is likely to be impossible to say that the parties have not wished to alter the terms of their earlier bargain. The earlier contract is unlikely therefore to be of much, if any, assistance.

---

[26] See the second principle outlined by Lord Hoffmann in *Investors' Compensation Scheme Ltd v West Bromwich Building Society* [1998] 1 All ER 98. This is the modern restatement of the general proposition that a court is able to construe a written document so that 'even where the words are in themselves plain and intelligible, and even where they have strict legal meaning, it is always allowable, in order to enable the Court to apply the instrument to its proper object, to receive evidence of the circumstances by which the testator or founder was surrounded at the date of the execution of the instrument in question, not for the purpose of giving effect to any intention of the writer not expressed in the deed, but for the purpose of ascertaining what was the intention evidenced by the expressions used; to ascertain what the party has said; not to give effect to any intention he has failed to express': in *Shore v Wilson* (1842) 9 Cl & Fin 355 at 512.

[27] *Chartbrook Ltd v Persimmon Homes Ltd and Another* [2009] UKHL 38, [2010] 1 All ER (Comm) 365 from para 42. Strictly these are not exceptions but operate outside the principle of the non-admissibility of pre-contract negotiations. A claim for rectification in essence means that one or more provisions in a contract (or other document) needs correction (as the contract does not record the parties' intentions). Estoppel has a number of meanings, but can include for example, where the parties have negotiated a contract on the basis of an assumption, but if later on one of the parties wishes to assert that the assumption meant something different they will be prevented (estopped) from doing so.

[28] See *HIH Casualty and General Insurance Ltd v New Hampshire Insurance Co and Others* [2001] All ER (D) 258 (May). Followed in *Standard Life Assurance Ltd v Oak Dedicated Ltd and Others* [2008] EWHC 222 (Comm), [2008] 2 All ER (Comm) 916.

Where the later contract is identical, its construction can stand on its own feet, and in any event its construction should be undertaken primarily by reference to its own overall terms. Where the later contract differs from the earlier contract, prima facie the difference is a deliberate decision to depart from the earlier wording, which again provides no assistance. Therefore a cautious and sceptical approach to finding any assistance in the earlier contract seems to me to be a sound principle. What I doubt, however, is that such a principle can be elevated into a conclusive rule of law.

84. Where, however, it is not even common ground that the later contract is intended to supersede the earlier contract, I do not see how it can ever be permissible to exclude reference to the earlier contract. I do not see how the relationship of the two contracts can be decided without considering both of them. In essence there are, it seems to me, three possibilities. Either the later contract is intended to supersede the earlier, in which case the above principles apply. Or, the later contract is intended to live together with the earlier contract, to the extent that that is possible, but where that is not possible it may well be proper to regard the later contract as superseding the earlier. Or the later contract is intended to be incorporated into the earlier contract, in which case it is prima facie the second contract which may have to give way to the first in the event of inconsistency.'

The following are specific situations when courts have been prepared to look at other agreements:

- where a contract forms part of a series of documents all in relation to one transaction;[29]

- where a contract forms part of a series of linked transactions;[30]

- where a contract is preceded by antecedent agreements.[31]

Where words are deleted from a contract, it seems that the courts *may* take account of them in interpreting the contract, but there are conflicting judgments. In one recent case, it was held that where a printed form is used then the deleted words may be used to deal with ambiguity in non-deleted

---

[29] See eg *Smith v Chadwick* (1882) 20 Ch.D. 27, *Encia Remediations Ltd v Canopius Managing Agents Ltd* [2007] SGCA 36.

[30] See *Temple Legal Protection Ltd* v *QBE Insurance (Europe) Ltd* [2008] EWHC 843 (Comm). In this case, where there is a series of linked contracts, the provisions of the other contract 'must be considered together with the commercial context'; however the starting point is to consider of the provisions the contract at the centre of the dispute.

[31] See eg *Ladbroke Group Plc v Bristol City Council* [1988] 1 EGLR 126; *KPMG LLP v Network Rail Infrastructure Ltd* [2007] EWCA Civ 363, [2007] All ER (D) 245 (Apr). For example, an agreement may include a draft lease attached to it, but the executed lease may contain an error etc. In such a case it would be permissible to look at the draft lease to discover the intentions of the party.

words and also to demonstrate 'if the fact of deletion shows what it is the parties agreed that they did not agree and there is ambiguity in the words that remain'[32]. However, case law indicates that there is considerable doubt as to the worth of such an exercise.

6.5.3   Amendments to standard form agreements in common use

As an exception to the general principle just stated, it seems the courts may be prepared to consider deletions from commonly used printed forms of contracts (eg the standard forms of contract used in the construction industry, such as the Institution of Civil Engineers ('ICE') Standard Terms) which are made prior to signing the agreement[33]. For example, the parties might cross through a provision of a printed form of contract and initial the deletion. The deleted words are still visible when the contract comes before the court. This seems to be a very specific exception to the general rule that drafts of agreements are not considered, and it has not been universally applied. A possible reason for the exception is that when a standard contract is in general use, and has perhaps been considered by the courts on many occasions, it is unrealistic to expect the courts to ignore the fact of the deletion.

6.5.4   Post-execution amendments

It seems that a different principle is applied to words which are deleted from a contract after it has been executed. In this situation the court may be prepared to look at the deleted words, as an aid to interpreting the contract. In the software supply example referred to above, if the parties had signed a contract including an express warranty of fitness for purpose, and had subsequently agreed to delete that provision, it is possible that the court might be prepared to interpret this deletion as meaning that the parties agreed that there would be no warranty of fitness for purpose, express or implied[34].

6.5.4.1   Drafting and negotiating issues

• *Consider words used in final agreement, not words used in negotiations.* Although sometimes easier said than done, the drafter should ensure that the words used in the final agreement state his party's intentions. Do not rely on 'understandings' between the negotiators, developed during the

---

[32] See *Mopani Copper Mines Plc v Millennium Underwriting Ltd* [2008] EWHC 1331 (Comm), [2008] 2 All ER (Comm) 976. Quote from para 120.

[33] See *Bravo Maritime (Chartering) Est v Baroom, The Athinoula* [1980] 2 Lloyd's Rep 481.

[34] See *Punjab National Bank v de Boinville* [1992] 1 WLR 1138, per Staughton LJ.

negotiations, as to what the words mean, as evidenced by deletions from drafts. Do not assume that because a party has agreed not to include a provision in a contract, that the same provision will not be implied into the contract by the court. If in doubt, include a specific disclaimer in the contract. Consider all provisions without reference to the negotiations which led to the final provisions being agreed.

- *Consider the words or phrases used which have a particular meaning.* Negotiations between parties (and the agreements prepared based on the negotiations) are often replete with particular phrases or business or other jargon. Although the parties may each assume they understand the meaning of the phrase, their understanding may be different. Consider whether any meaning can be derived adequately for any documentation exchanged between the parties and whether a common meaning can be derived. If not, then phrases should be properly defined in the final agreement.

- *Standard form contracts in common use.* When using standard contracts which are in common use, be aware that different rules may operate. Consider the effect of a deletion upon other provisions of the contract. Consider whether the court is likely to be influenced by the fact that the term was deleted, and whether additional wording is needed to clarify the parties' intentions.

6.5.5   *The parol evidence rule, collateral contracts and misrepresentations*

Where a contract is made in writing, the court will not normally consider evidence of oral terms which vary the written terms. The courts assume that where parties enter into a written agreement, that agreement sets out all the terms of the agreement. This is known as the parol evidence rule. A party may be able to prove that the parties did, in fact, intend to enter into an oral agreement in addition to the terms set out in the written agreement but he is likely to have an 'uphill struggle' in view of the parol evidence rule.

The courts sometimes avoid the parol evidence rule by making use of other legal principles, for example, that a collateral oral contract exists, or that one party is guilty of fraud or misrepresentation[35]. At this point, Mr Justice Megarry's comments (quoted at **6.3**) about the courts selecting the legal principle to apply is particularly apt. In this area of the law the courts have a number of principles of interpretation to choose from, and the outcome to a case may depend on which principle is used.

---

[35]   A detailed discussion of the law on misrepresentation, fraud and collateral contracts is beyond the scope of this book. For further information consult the standard texts, eg Chapters 6 and 12 in *Chitty on Contracts* (30th Edn) 2010 Sweet and Maxwell.

In practice, detailed written agreements often include provisions which seek to address most if not all of these principles of interpretation. An example of such a clause follows: it can be broken down into several elements, namely (1) this is the complete agreement (implicitly, there are no collateral contracts); (2) all previous agreements are cancelled; (3) the parties are not relying on any prior representations; and (4) this agreement cannot be varied orally (ie supporting the parol evidence rule).

> This Agreement, including its Schedules, sets out the entire agreement between the Parties [relating to its subject matter].
>
> It supersedes all prior oral or written agreements, arrangements or understandings between them [relating to such subject matter]. The Parties acknowledge that they are not relying on any representation, agreement, term or condition which is not set out in this Agreement. However, nothing in this Agreement purports to exclude liability for any fraudulent statement or act[36].
>
> To be legally binding, any amendment to this Agreement must be in writing signed by authorised representatives of the Parties.

The drafter will generally wish to discuss with colleagues or clients whether such a clause is in their commercial interests. For example, if during the negotiation of the contract the supplier's salesman made over-optimistic promises about the quality of the goods being supplied, the supplier might want to try to ensure that such promises were not part of the contract, whilst the purchaser might be happy for them to be part of the contract. But if the promises are not specifically included in the written agreement, they may not be legally binding anyway[37]. In many cases the only certain way of ensuring that an undertaking forms part of the contract is to set out that undertaking in the written agreement.

6.5.5.1   Drafting and negotiating issues

- *Reproduce prior representations, etc in the contract.* Check whether there are any other terms or understandings which have not been incorporated into the contractual documents. If so, consider whether these need to be expressly included in, or excluded from, the written contract.

- *Put all terms and amendments in writing.* Where the contract is made in writing, make sure that the contract terms, including any variation of those terms, are recorded in the contract document or in a written amendment

---

[36]   Often called an 'entire agreement clause'. For recent case law see **6.5.22.10**.

[37]   Putting aside whether there is a clause in a contract such as one illustrated here, the law distinguishes between statements which are merely enthusiastic sales talk and those which induce a person to enter into a contract. Those latter statements are called representations and where they include inaccurate or false information, they are called misrepresentations.

to it. Do not assume that other terms which the parties have agreed orally will be considered by the court.

- *Evaluate other agreements related to the subject matter of the contract.* If there are other agreements which relate to the subject matter of the contract, evaluate their effect on the contract; are the agreements to continue (co-exist) or supersede the contract? If other agreements are to be superseded or have no effect on the contract, then do not rely on an 'entire agreement' clause, but introduce clear wording which explicitly states the relationship between the agreement and the contract[38].

- *Consider including an 'entire agreement' clause, clarifying which terms have legal effect.* For example, consider including some or all of the wording quoted above in an attempt to (1) exclude collateral contracts, (2) exclude prior representations, and (3) reinforce the parol evidence rule. Bear in mind that in 'deserving cases' the court may decide to ignore such wording.

6.5.6   *The meaning of words used in contract terms*

6.5.6.1   **The golden rule of interpretation**

Having established which terms comprise the contract, a next stage is to establish what the words used in that contract mean, or would be considered by the court to mean.

Over the years the courts have applied different methods of interpreting the words used in contracts and other instruments. Some of these methods have jostled for supremacy, as in the battle between the so-called golden rule of interpretation and its rivals, for example, literal interpretation of the words used, and purposive construction[39]. The golden rule developed in the nineteenth century and was described by one leading judge[40] as follows:

> 'In construing all written instruments, the grammatical and ordinary sense of the words is to be adhered to, unless that would lead to some absurdity, or some repugnance or inconsistency with the rest of the instrument, in which case the grammatical and ordinary sense of the words may be modified, so as to avoid that absurdity and inconsistency, but no further.'

This rule allows some limited deviation from the strict meaning of the words actually used in the contract, but not much. If the wrong words are used in the

---

[38]   Such as providing details of the other agreements (name of the agreement, date entered into) and also which clauses are to continue in effect, which clauses are to be disapplied compared to the contract under consideration, etc.

[39]   Literal interpretation means strictly applying the words used in the contract, however absurd the outcome, the golden rule of interpretation takes a fairly strict approach, as discussed in this section, whilst the purposive approach to interpretation allows the court to consider the underlying intentions of the parties and ignore the strict language used.

[40]   Lord Wensleydale in *Grey v Pearson* (1857) 6 HL Cas 61 at 106.

contract, and have a different meaning to the intended meaning, the golden rule will not normally allow the court to substitute the intended meaning[41]. The parties to the contract may be bound by what they agreed, not what they intended to agree. The golden rule is generally applied by the courts, with some exceptions. In particular, in recent years the courts have given increasing attention to the underlying commercial purpose of the contract, even if the words used in the contract do not reflect that commercial purpose. However, it cannot be assumed that this will be done in an individual case. In some cases, the court may apply the golden rule very strictly. In one case, Hobhouse J said[42]:

> '... it has to be borne in mind that commercial contracts are drafted by parties with access to legal advice and in the context of established legal principles as reflected in the decisions of the courts. Principles of certainty and indeed justice, require that contracts be construed in accordance with the established principles. The parties are always able by the choice of appropriate language to draft their contract so as to produce a different legal effect. The choice is theirs.'

6.5.6.2   Drafting and negotiating issues

- *Careful use of language.* Care should be taken to use words correctly and grammatically. If this is not done, and the intended meaning is different to that expressed in the words used, the courts are unlikely to interpret the words used in the way the drafter intended.

6.5.7   Ordinary, dictionary meaning of words

The court will generally interpret words according to their ordinary 'popular' meaning, unless it considers that a word is being used as a legal term of art, or in accordance with a statutory definition, or in a scientific sense, or in accordance with some special meaning given to the word in the 'industry' in which the parties are engaged, or in accordance with a special meaning given by the parties (eg, but not only, if they have included a definition of the word's

---

[41] The position is no different, in reality, following the decision of *Investors Compensation Scheme v West Bromwich Building Society* [1998] 1 All ER 98. For example, Lord Hoffmann stated in *BCCI v Ali* [2002] 1 AC 251 at 269: 'the primary source for understanding what the parties meant is their language interpreted in accordance with conventional usage".

[42] *EE Caledonia Ltd v Orbit Valve Co Europe* [1993] All ER at 173.

meaning in the contract)[43]. Where the court applies the ordinary meaning of a word, it will sometimes refer to dictionaries to help it to ascertain that ordinary meaning[44].

Difficulties can arise if a word has several meanings. In general, the ordinary meaning is to be preferred over specialist meanings, unless it is established that the parties intended the specialist meaning. If there are several ordinary meanings, the court will attempt to find the correct meaning from the context in which the word is used. If the contract has clearly been badly drafted, the court may be less inclined to adopt a strict dictionary definition than if the contract appears to have been written by a specialist drafter. As Lord Bridge commented in one case[45]:

> 'But the poorer the quality of the drafting, the less willing any court should be to be driven by semantic niceties to attribute to the parties an improbable and unbusinesslike intention, if the language used, whatever it may lack in precision, is reasonably capable of an interpretation which attributes to the parties an intention to make provision for contingencies inherent in the work contracted for on a sensible and businesslike basis.'

---

[43] For example, *Sunport Shipping Ltd v Tryg-Baltica International (UK) Ltd* [2003] EWCA Civ 12; [2003] 1 All ER (Comm) 586 for a discussion of the meaning of a phrase 'customs ... regulations', the phrase had to be to construed in its context, having regard to its place in the contract and construed in the context of the surrounding circumstances, which in this case meant the Institute of War and Strike Clauses (Hulls-Time) of 1 October 1983 used worldwide in insurance of shipping. It was not appropriate to consider that the phrase held only a meaning limited to that found in the EU.

[44] See *Durham Tees Valley Airport Ltd v BMI Baby Ltd and Another* [2009] EWHC 852 (Ch), [2009] 2 All ER (Comm) 1083 at para 79 where the word 'summer' needed interpretation as it was undefined in a contract and uses of the word were considered by reference to the meanings found in the Shorter Oxford English Dictionary. The provision is reproduced at **6.5.11** Special meanings 'in the industry' below. See also in *Heronslea (Mill Hill) Ltd v Kwik-Fit Properties Ltd* [2009] EWHC 295 (QB), [2009] All ER (D) 75 (Mar), where it was stated that a '...Court is entitled to have regard dictionary definitions as an aid to construction to ascertain the natural and ordinary meaning of the words in their relevant context. It is also clear that words are to be interpreted in the way in which a reasonable commercial person would construe them; and the standard of the reasonable commercial person is hostile to technical interpretations, undue emphasis on niceties of language or literalism ...' (from para 19).

[45] *Mitsui Construction Co Ltd v A-G of Hong Kong* (1986) 33 BLR 1 at 14, PC. It is suggested that this case should not be used as justification for preferring to engage a poor-quality drafter over a skilled drafter. See also *Oxonica Energy Ltd v Neuftec Ltd* [2009] EWCA Civ 668, [2009] All ER (D) 13 (Sep) for a recent example which concerned a poorly drafted patent and know-how licence agreement, where the extract from *Mitsui Construction* was followed, and Jacob LJ stated '...faced with such a [poorly drafted agreement] fine arguments based upon supposed consistency of language or even thought throughout the document, will carry less or no weight than with an obviously carefully and well-drafted document—one obviously drafted by someone who knew what he was about' from para 11.

6.5.8   *Commercial contracts*

In commercial contracts, the courts may allow some latitude from the strict dictionary meaning, particularly if the dictionary meaning leads to an uncommercial result, but this will not allow the courts to rewrite the contract or ignore the meaning of the words used[46]. As Lord Diplock commented in one case[47]:

> '… if detailed semantic and syntactical analysis of words in a commercial contract is going to lead to a conclusion that flouts business commonsense, it must yield to business commonsense.'

However, neither of the last two quoted comments should be understood as allowing the court to depart significantly from the words as used in the contract; rather they suggest that some limited relaxation of the strict meaning of the words would be allowed, which would not be allowed if the document was not a commercial contract. Indeed, the courts, in considering the meaning of contractual terms within the surrounding context, can look beyond the bare meaning of the words used. Where the surrounding context is commercial, the courts have applied commercial principles. In one case, Steyn LJ said[48]:

> 'Dictionaries never solve concrete problems of construction. The meaning of words cannot be ascertained divorced from their context. And part of the contextual scene is the purpose of the provision.'

Finally[49], it is apparently the case that the courts interpret words according to the situation or the person. It has been held that an obligation to carry out work 'efficiently' should be interpreted according to the resources of the party which was required to carry out the work[50].

---

[46] For example, see the words for Peter Gibson LJ in *Kazakstan Wool Processors (Europe) Ltd v Nederlandsche Credietverzekering Maatschappij NV* [2000] 1 All ER (Comm) 708 at [49]: 'The court is entitled to look at [the] consequences [of taking an over literal approach of giving words their natural and ordinary meaning where the consequences can be seen to be so extravagant] because the more extreme they are, the less likely it is that commercial men will have intended an agreement with that result. But the court is not entitled to rewrite the bargain which they have made merely to accord with what the court thinks to be a more reasonable result, and the best guide to the parties' intentions remains the words which they have chosen to use in the contract.'

[47] *Antaios Cia Naviera SA v Salen Rederierna AB, The Antaios* [1985] AC 191 at 201, HL. See the fifth principle in the *Investors' Compensation Scheme Ltd v West Bromwich Building Society* [1998] 1 All ER 98 (at **6.4.1**) above, where Lord Hoffmann cited this case.

[48] *Arbuthnott v Fagan* [1996] LRLR 135, CA. See *Sunport Shipping Ltd v Tryg-Baltica International (UK) Ltd* [2003] EWCA Civ 12; [2003] 1 All ER (Comm) 586 for a recent illustration of this point.

[49] Further principles of interpretation are mentioned in the leading contract law texts, but the ones mentioned in this chapter are the main principles, and the ones most likely to affect the drafting of contract wording.

[50] *West London Rly Co v London and North Western Rly Co* (1853) 11 CB 327 at 356, Ex Ch.

However, the courts will assume that the parties have used the words in a contract in an intended way and to achieve a sensible commercial purpose and will only introduce other wording in limited circumstances[51]:

> 'It is not for a party who relies upon the words actually used to establish that those words effect a sensible commercial purpose. It should be assumed, as a starting point, that the parties understood the purpose which was effected by the words they used; and that they used those words because, to them, that was a sensible commercial purpose. Before the court can introduce words which the parties have not used, it is necessary to be satisfied (i) that the words actually used produce a result which is so commercially nonsensical that the parties could not have intended it, and (ii) that they did intend some other commercial purpose which can be identified with confidence. If, and only if, those two conditions are satisfied, is it open to the court to introduce words which the parties have not used in order to construe the agreement. It is then permissible to do so because, if those conditions are satisfied, the additional words give to the agreement or clause the meaning which the parties must have intended.'

6.5.8.1   Drafting and negotiating issues

- *Avoid ambiguous words.* Some words are clearly ambiguous; to take an extreme example, 'sanction' is sometimes used to mean 'allow' and sometimes used to mean 'prohibit'[52]. A more subtle example is 'immediate' which can mean 'without delay' (ie immediate in time) or 'nearest; not separated by others' (ie immediate in space). Avoid, where possible, words that could be ambiguous in the context in which they are used[53].

- *'Constructive ambiguity'.* Commercial parties sometimes adopt vague or ambiguous wording in contracts as a deliberate commercial decision. This might be done to avoid a major disagreement over a point, to keep the momentum of the negotiations going, or in the hope that the other side will miss the true meaning of a term. It might be thought commercially preferably to resolve any ambiguity by negotiation at a later date, after the agreement has been signed. This is sometimes referred to as 'constructive ambiguity'. It places the drafter in a difficult position; if the drafter cannot

---

[51]   *City Alliance Ltd v Oxford Forecasting Services Ltd* [2000] 1 All ER (Comm) 233 at [13], CA.

[52]   The *Concise Oxford Dictionary* (8th Edn) states the following meanings for 'sanction' when used as a transitive verb: '1. authorize, countenance or agree to; 2. ratify; *attach a penalty* or reward to; make binding' (emphasis added). Another example is 'I doubt' which is sometimes used, particularly by Scots, to mean 'I suspect' (which may reflect the influence of the Auld Alliance with France—*douter* in French meaning, to suspect). This can lead to almost an opposite meaning to the more conventional meaning of doubt, eg when used in a phrase such as 'I doubt ... that X is true'.

[53]   Another example encountered by the authors was where the phrase 'on completion of this contract' was used by a (non-lawyer) drafter. In the context there was some ambiguity about whether the phrase referred to the coming into effect of the contract or the completion of work under the contract.

(or does not consider it appropriate to) persuade the drafter's principal to adopt unambiguous wording, the principal should be warned that the ambiguous wording is unlikely to be interpreted in the way the principal hopes, particularly if it was drafted for the benefit of that principal (ie applying the *contra proferentem* rule, see **6.5.18**) and the other side has a different understanding of its meaning.

- *If in doubt as to the meaning of a word, consider the dictionary meaning.* Sometimes words are used inaccurately (ie not in any of the senses given in the dictionary) and without intending any special legal or technical meaning (as to which see below). Use of a good dictionary can assist the drafter. In international contracts, such as those made with US companies, bear in mind that the parties may use the same word to mean something different[54].

6.5.9   Legal terms of art and lawyers' jargon

Some words, when used in contracts, will be interpreted according to their meaning in law unless a different meaning is clearly given by the parties. These words can conveniently be divided into a number of categories.

- *Liability and litigation terms:* for example, negligence, tort, arbitration, mediation, proceedings, legal action, the parties submit to the jurisdiction of the [English] courts, exclusive jurisdiction, non-exclusive jurisdiction, expert, 'without prejudice' negotiations, entire agreement.

- *Special types of legal obligation:* for example, time shall be of the essence, condition/condition precedent/condition subsequent, warranties, representations, covenants, undertakings, guarantees, with full title guarantee, with limited title guarantee, beneficial owner.

- *Transfer and termination of obligations:* for example, assignment and novation, conveyance, indemnity, hold harmless, breach, material breach, insolvency, liquidators, receivers.

- *Expression of time:* for example, year, month, week, day, from and including, until, from time to time, for the time being, forthwith, immediately.

- *Other terms defined by legislation:* for example, person, firm, subsidiary, United Kingdom, European Union.

- *Other terms interpreted by the courts:* for example, best endeavours, due diligence, set-off, consent not to be unreasonably withheld, material, consult, penalty, nominal sum, subject to.

---

[54] For example, the word 'schedule' which is commonly used in the sense of 'timetable' in the United States, but less commonly used in this sense in the United Kingdom, although this usage is increasing.

Some of the terminology used in contracts falls into yet another category, namely lawyers' jargon, which is sometimes still in Latin or medieval French[55]. On other occasions the words used are English but are very old-fashioned and are no longer used in ordinary speech. Most of this jargon has disappeared from commercial contracts[56], but some is still encountered.

Examples include:

- *mutatis mutandis*;

- *prima facie*;

- aforesaid, hereinafter;

- to the intent that;

- whatsoever;

- hereby[57];

- procure;

- provided that;

- including without limitation;

- unless the context requires otherwise;

- without prejudice to the generality of the foregoing;

- notwithstanding.

In some cases it may be unfair to call these words jargon where they serve a specific legal purpose (and they are correctly used). For example, in the above list, 'including without limitation' has an important purpose and the words themselves are not particularly unusual, although 'limitation' could perhaps be replaced by 'limit'. In other cases, although the idea being expressed is important, the jargon used to express the idea could be avoided. For example, *mutatis mutandis* should, in the authors' view, be avoided and another way found of expressing the intended meaning.

---

[55]   Many of the 'canons of constructions' originally were expressed in Latin.

[56]   Due, probably, to the influence of business people on the terms of such contracts. By contrast, conveyancing documents, which are not subject to the same commercial pressures, are sometimes drafted in a very old-fashioned way, despite the standard models of conveyancing contract available.

[57]   But 'hereby' can sometimes be useful. For example, in the grant clause of an intellectual property contract it may be important to establish whether the IP owner *grants* a licence or merely *undertakes to grant* a licence at a future date. In some cases the licence should be registered with, eg, the Patent Office within six months of the date of grant (eg see s 68 of the Patents Act 1977). If the grant is intended to take place immediately, use of the phrase 'X hereby grants a licence' can make this clear. Special cases apart, use of 'hereby' is often redundant, as in 'X hereby undertakes to ...'.

In view of their importance in contracts, legal terms are discussed in detail, together with lawyers' jargon, in Chapter 8.

6.5.10   Scientific and technical terms

It seems that the courts take a different approach to interpreting scientific and technical terms to the approach taken with ordinary English words. With non-technical words the court is prepared to decide for itself what the ordinary meaning of the word is, assisted perhaps by the judge's dictionary. With technical words the court may require the parties to bring expert evidence of the meaning of the term, particularly if the meaning is in dispute. In complex patent infringement actions, the court sometimes even engages its own scientific adviser to assist it with the technicalities of the dispute, but this is unlikely to happen in most contract disputes even if the contract concerns technical subject matter, as in the case of a patent licence. In a few situations, case law has developed as to the meaning of technical terms[58].

6.5.10.1   Drafting and negotiating issues

• *Define any technical or scientific expressions.* If terms are not defined, and their meaning is disputed, each party may be put to the cost of engaging an expert witness to explain the meaning of the term used, and the court may decide on a different meaning to the one intended by one or both parties. If a technical or scientific word or phrase is or must be used then the parties should provide an agreed definition or use a reputable third party definition[59].

• *Avoid using technical or scientific jargon.* Lawyers are sometimes rightly criticised for using jargon, but at least their jargon usually has a specific meaning. Some scientific or technical jargon, particularly in the computer industry, is used in a very loose way, and should therefore be avoided

---

[58]   For example, the term 'improvement'. It has been held in an old case that: 'an improvement of a patented machine includes any machine which, while retaining some of those essential or characteristic parts of the machine which are the subject of the monopoly claims, yet by addition, omission or alteration better achieves the same or better results, whether such improvement infringes the monopoly claims for the patented machine or not.' See *Linotype and Machinery Ltd v Hopkins* (1910) 27 RPC 109, HL; quoted words come from Court of Appeal judgment.

[59]   For example, a permanent source of information published by a recognised scientific or technical body; and most probably not a source such as Wikipedia (which anyone can potentially change).

in contracts[60]. In other situations it may be better to state the intended meaning in simple English rather than use a technical expression[61].

6.5.11 Special meanings 'in the industry'

Sometimes words acquire a special meaning in a particular trade, industry or profession[62].

An example relates to a frequently cited nineteenth century case[63], which concerned the lease of a rabbit warren[64] in Suffolk. The agreement included a provision that 10,000 rabbits would be left in the warren at the end of the lease term. In a dispute over the agreement, evidence was brought (and admitted) to show that, in Suffolk, it was the custom that 1,000 rabbits meant 1,200. Thus a special meaning in the trade was accepted as overriding the ordinary dictionary meaning. Other reported cases on words which have a special meaning include a case concerning the delivery of a 'weekly account' of work done by a builder[65]. A more recent example concerned an agreement (regarding the use by an airline of an airport) where the following clause came in for consideration:

> 'Operation: Initial "lead-in" flying programme (to an agreed number of destinations) to commence no later than 31 October 2003 to support the establishment of a minimum x2 based aircraft operation (initially B737) operating exclusively from TIAL by Summer 2004'.

and in particular, the word 'exclusively'. After the calling of expert evidence, this word was found to have a meaning particular to the aviation industry, referring to an aircraft flying only from and to a particular airport (and not to an aircraft flying from an airport to a destination, then to a third destination and then returning to the airport, whether directly or indirectly)[66].

---

[60] For example, the term 'interface' (as in graphical user interface) is used in a variety of ways.

[61] For example, in a computer software licence, there may be situations in which it would be better to use ordinary English words such as 'temporary memory' and 'permanent memory' rather than 'RAM', 'Random Access Memory', 'CDROM' or 'Compact Disc Read Only Memory'.

[62] A recent example of the court considering whether words had a specific meaning in a particular industry can be found in *Confetti Records (a firm) v Warner Music UK Ltd (trading as East West Records)* [2005] EWHC 1274 (Ch), [2003] All ER (D) 61 (Jun) where the court held that the words 'subject to contract' did not have a special meaning within the music industry.

[63] *Smith v Wilson* (1832) 3 B & Ad 728.

[64] Working rabbit warrens are rarely encountered nowadays. They were often manmade constructions, specially designed for the commercial breeding and farming of rabbits, and included elaborate tunnels.

[65] *Myers v Sarl* (1860) 3 E & E 306.

[66] *Durham Tees Valley Airport Ltd v BMI Baby Ltd and Another* [2009] EWHC 852 (Ch), [2009] 2 All ER (Comm) 1083 at para 30.

Moreover, in some circumstances trade usage has become enshrined in statute. Under the Costs of Leases Act 1958, s 1, for the purpose of this Act, the meaning of 'lease' includes an underlease or an agreement for a lease; the meaning of 'costs' includes fees, charges, disbursements, expenses and remuneration[67].

6.5.11.1   Drafting and negotiating issues

- *State any special meanings in the contract.* Rather than rely on the court accepting that a word was understood as having a special meaning in the trade or is willing to look at pre-contractual documentation[68], it will generally be much safer to define any word which is to have a special meaning.

6.5.12   Special meanings given by the parties

The clearest way in which contracting parties can give a special meaning to a word, is to include a definition of that word in the contract. The court will generally apply any definitions given by the parties, no matter how different the definition may be to the ordinary meaning of the word unless the effect of so doing leads to an absurd result (set against its background)[69] This approach is likely to apply even where a definitions clause includes wording such 'unless the context provides otherwise'; wording sometimes included in the definitions section of agreements to allow for the possibility that a definition may carry another meaning. Where this wording appears, it will be used very sparingly and not merely simply to produce a better meaning[70].

Even where a word is not specifically defined, the court might decide that the parties have used the word in a special sense, and not in accordance with the ordinary dictionary meaning. However, in coming to such a conclusion, the court will only look at evidence to be found in the contract itself (ie the particular context in which the words are used). As has already been mentioned, the court will generally not consider evidence from the parties as to what they intended a word to mean.

---

[67]   See further 12 *Halsbury's Laws* (4th Edn) paras 482–500.
[68]   Such as in *ProForce Recruit Ltd v Rugby Group Ltd* [2006] EWCA Civ 69; [2006] All ER (D) 246 (Feb) at [28].
[69]   See comments of Jacob LJ in *City Inn (Jersey) Ltd v Ten Trinity Square Ltd* [2008] EWCA Civ 156, [2008] All ER (D) 76 (Mar), and *Oxonica Energy Ltd v Neuftec Ltd* [2009] EWCA Civ 668, [2009] All ER (D) 13 (Sep).
[70]   See *Hammonds (a firm) v Danilunas and Others* [2009] EWHC 216 (Ch), [2009] All ER (D) 174 (Feb) at para 44.

6.5.12.1   Drafting and negotiating issues

- *Use definitions or use ordinary dictionary meaning.* The same drafting point is made here as in the discussion of technical terms and legal terms of art: if a special meaning is intended, it should be defined in the contract

- *Use of defined words other than in their defined meaning.* If a word is used in way other than its defined meaning then at a minimum include 'unless the context otherwise requires' or include clear wording that there is a definite meaning.

6.5.13   Interpreting express[71] contract terms

Earlier sections of this chapter have discussed how the courts establish:

- the general intentions of the parties to a contract;

- which are the terms of that contract; and

- the intended meaning of the words used in that contract.

As was mentioned at the beginning of this chapter, this can be regarded as stage 1 in the interpretation of a contract. Once the terms of the contract have been fully established, the scene is set for detailed 'construction' (ie interpretation) of those terms, to establish their legal effect. The following sections consider this second stage, in which the courts apply the so-called 'canon of construction'. The headings to the following sections summarise the main principles which are followed by the courts, or at least those which have significant drafting implications. Clauses should not be considered in isolation, but instead should be considered in the context of the document as a whole. In one case[72] Lord Watson referred to the general principle that:

> '… a deed ought to be read as whole, in order to ascertain the true meaning of its several clauses; and that the words of each clause should be so interpreted as to bring them into harmony with the other provisions of the deed, if that interpretation does no violence to the meaning of which they are naturally susceptible.'

Although he was discussing deeds, the same principles apply to contracts executed under hand. Problems can arise if one provision of a contract is inconsistent with another, for example, if a similar obligation is expressed in

---

[71] Express terms are those which have been specifically agreed ('expressed') by the parties. In a written contract they are the terms set out in the written contract. They can be contrasted with implied terms which form part of the contract but have not been written into the contract. For example, the Sales Goods Act 1979, s 14(2): 'Where the seller sells goods in the course of a business, there is an implied term that the goods supplied under the contract are of satisfactory quality.'

[72] *Chamber Colliery Co v Hopwood* (1886) 32 Ch D 549, CA.

a different way in two different clauses: is the difference deliberate (or merely sloppy drafting)? As Lord Diplock put it in one case[73]:

> '... the habit of a legal draftsman is to eschew[74] synonyms. He uses the same words throughout the document to express the same thing or concept and consequently if he uses different words the presumption is that he means a different thing or concept.'

Whilst this may be thought of as an ideal, it is not always followed in practice, even by the best drafter. Moreover, where a contract has been prepared using a number of different templates or precedents, and the clauses have been 'cut and pasted' together, they may have used slightly different words to express similar ideas on different subjects[75]. Unless the drafter is very careful, some of these inconsistencies may remain in the final contract. For example, one clause may refer to an obligation being performed 'forthwith', whilst another clause is silent as to the time of performance—is this intended to mean that the time for performance of the latter obligation is less urgent than in the clause which includes the word 'forthwith'?

The requirement that a contract should be interpreted 'as a whole' concerns more than just the inconsistent use of individual words. When considering the meaning of one clause of a contract, the court may consider all the remaining provisions to enable them to understand what that one clause means. For example, one reported case concerned a contract to charter a ship for several voyages. The ship owners were stated to be entitled to substitute a ship of similar size at any time. The court was asked whether this provision entitled them to substitute only once, or more than once. The court held that the words of the clause in question were ambiguous but, in the context of the contract as a whole, it was clear that substitutions could be made more than once[76].

This principle may not sound particularly surprising; what may be more surprising is the limited extent of the principle. If the wording of the clause under consideration is clear, it seems the court will not override the words used by the drafter, unless other words, elsewhere in the contract, indicate a clearly different intention[77].

---

[73]   *Prestcold (Central) Ltd v Minister of Labour* [1969] 1 WLR 89, CA.

[74]   'Eschew', meaning 'avoid', is not a good 'plain English' word to use in a contract—the *Concise Oxford Dictionary* describes it as 'literary'.

[75]   This is more likely to occur nowadays, not only because everyone has their own computer, but also because so many companies have their terms and conditions of business on their website. It is possible for someone to assemble a set of terms and conditions from copying the sections they like from a selection of websites. This only increases the chances that there will be inconsistent use of wording to express the same concepts and ideas. This is, of course, leaving aside the question of breach of copyright in 'drafting' in this way.

[76]   *Maritime et Commerciale of Geneva SA v Anglo-Iranian Oil Co Ltd* [1954] 1 WLR 492, CA.

[77]   See comments of Leach V-C in *Hume v Rundell* (1824) 2 Sim & St 174.

A further application of the principle that contracts should be interpreted as a whole, is that it is not necessary for definitions and interpretation provisions to appear at the beginning of the contract, although conventionally that is where they do appear. In this respect contracts, and the way judges interpret them, is more flexible than a computer would be in understanding a computer program.

6.5.14   Give effect to all parts of the document

The courts will generally assume that all words and provisions of the contract have been deliberately included, and will try to give effect to them[78]. So, if one provision appears to contradict another provision, the court will try to find an interpretation which reconciles the two provisions[79]. If a mistake has been made in the drafting, this may have adverse consequences to both the mistaken clause and the other clause which it contradicts.

This is a general approach rather than a hard rule which the courts must always follow. There is authority to suggest that the court will not follow this approach in standard form agreements such as leases which are drafted in a traditional, wordy way[80].

6.5.15   Special conditions override standard conditions

Sometimes contracts consist of a short agreement to which are attached (1) a set of standard conditions, and (2) extra clauses which are agreed by the parties (sometimes known as special conditions). This practice is common, for example, in residential conveyancing[81], in the construction industry[82] and

---

[78]   See the comments at para 13 in *DWR Cymru Cyfyngedig v Corus UK Ltd and Another* [2007] EWCA Civ 285, [2007] All ER (D) 515 (Mar) that the inclusion of a clause in a contract means that 'One starts, therefore, from the presumption that [the clause] was intended to have some effect on the parties' rights and obligations'. See also *Bindra v Chopra* [2009] EWCA Civ 203, [2009] All ER (D) 219 (Mar) at paras 22–23.

[79]   See *Re Strand Music Hall Co Ltd* (1865) 35 Beav 153.

[80]   See comments on Hoffmann J in *Tea Trade Properties Ltd v CIN Properties Ltd* [1990] 1 EGLR 155 and in *Beaufort Developments (NI) Ltd v Gilbert-Ash (NI) Ltd* [1999] 1 AC 266.

[81]   Using the Law Society's Standard Conditions of Sale and the Standard Commercial Property Conditions.

[82]   For example, using one of the published sets of conditions such as those produced by the JCT (Joint Contracts Tribunal Limited), ICE (Institution of Civil Engineers, Association of Consulting Engineers and Civil Engineering Contractors Association), or NEC Engineering and Construction Contract.

in the advertising industry[83], using published forms of contract. A similar practice is sometimes adopted by large companies which have standard purchase and supply contracts. It is also common in contracts between government departments and companies and organisations giving grants for research purposes.

The long-established principle followed by the courts is that, if there is any conflict between the terms set out in the standard document and the 'special' conditions, the latter will override the former[84]. The reason for this principle seems to be that the courts are prepared to regard the printed conditions as a 'general formality adapted equally to their case and that of all contracting parties upon similar occasions and subjects'[85]. Put another way, the standard terms have not been prepared specially for the contract in question and may not be entirely appropriate for that contract. By contrast, the special conditions have been specially prepared for the contract in question. Therefore a provision in the standard conditions which contradicts a special condition can perhaps be ignored or at least interpreted more loosely than would otherwise be permissible[86]. Special conditions or tailor-made clauses will normally only override standard conditions where there is a conflict between the two types of clauses[87]:

> '... I accept that tailor-made clauses will normally prevail over typed clauses, that is in my judgment only so if there is indeed a "conflict" between the two (as this charterparty also expressly provides). The courts will, however, seek to construe a contract as a whole and if a reasonable commercial construction of the whole can reconcile two provisions (whether typed or printed) then such a construction can and in my judgment should be adopted. The "conflict" can of course be found either as a matter of language or effect.'

What is less clear, though, is whether this principle allows the courts to override the wording of standard conditions which are inconsistent with the

---

[83]   For example, the Incorporated Society of British Advertisers, the Chartered Institute of Purchasing and Supply and the Institute of Practitioners in Advertising providing a set of precedents for use between advertising agents and their clients (see *Encyclopaedia of Forms and Precedents* (5th Edn) Volume 1, Advertising and Marketing.

[84]   See words of Lord Ellenborough CJ in *Robertson v French* (1803) 4 East 130, and applied recently in *Hombourg Houtimport BV v Agrosin Private Ltd, The Starsin* [2003] UKHL 12, [2004] 1 AC 715. Consider the words of Lord Bingham at [13]: '... it is common sense that greater weight should attach to terms which the particular contracting parties have chosen to include in the contract than to pre-printed terms probably devised to cover very many situations to which the particular contracting parties have never addressed their minds. It is unnecessary to quote the classical statement of this rule by Lord Ellenborough in *Robertson v French* (1803) 4 East 130 at 136; 102 ER 779 at 782 ...'

[85]   See *Bravo Maritime (Chartering) Est v Baroom, The Athinoula* [1980] 2 Lloyd's Rep 481.

[86]   See *Hombourg Houtimport BV v Agrosin Private Ltd, The Starsin* [2003] UKHL 12, [2004] 1 AC 715 for a recent illustration of this point in the speech of Lord Hoffmann where the words on the front of a bill of lading were 'determinative and overriding' other clauses (at [83]).

[87]   *Bayoil SA v Seawind Tankers Corp* [2001] 1 All ER (Comm) 392 at 397, per Langley J.

commercial purpose of the contract but which are not clearly contradicted by any provision of the special conditions[88].

The reported cases mostly refer to the standard conditions being in 'printed' form, but it is suggested that the same principle would apply where there are two distinct sections of a contract comprising 'standard' terms and 'special' terms, each generated on a word processor, provided it could be established that the standard conditions were genuinely in standard form and applied generally, and had not been 'tailored' for the contract in question. It seems unlikely that this principle would be of assistance where all the terms of the contract, standard and special, are 'intermingled' in a single document[89].

6.5.16   Hierarchy of clauses

Where the contract consists of several parts which may have conflicting provisions, one technique adopted by draftsmen is to include a clause stating which parts have priority in the event of conflict.

If there is any conflict in meaning between any provision of this Agreement, its Schedules and the Standard Conditions respectively, effect shall be given to the main body of this Agreement in preference to its Schedules or the Standard Conditions, and to the Schedules in preference to the Standard Conditions.

6.5.16.1   If some things are mentioned in a contract, and similar things are not mentioned, it may be assumed that the omission was deliberate

For example, if a contract states that party A will reimburse party B's legal costs associated with party B taking part in an application by a third party to overturn planning permission in a local authority hearing but no mention of reimbursing party B's costs where party B is involved in a planning hearing before an inspector the court might assume that party A is not required to reimburse the planning hearing costs[90]. Some of the reported cases on this

---

[88]   In such a situation a court which wished to override a standard term might have more difficulty; it might seek to apply the principle mentioned earlier, that the contract should be interpreted 'as a whole'.

[89]   See *Leonie's Travel Pty Ltd v International Air Transport Association* [2009] FCA 280 where the judge noted that the principle is less likely to apply where both the primary contract and incorporated terms were in standard terms. Also it appears that nowadays a court will try to arrive at a way to interpret them 'as parts of one coherent contractual document', see *Alchemy Estates Ltd v Astor* [2008] EWHC 2675 (Ch), particularly if they have adopted them as one contractual document and not indicated which has primacy (see para 35 of the judgment).

[90]   For example, by (loose) analogy with *Tropwood AG v Jade Enterprises Ltd, The Tropwind* [1977] 1 Lloyd's Rep 397.

principle suggest that it is less rigidly applied than some of the other principles mentioned in this section, because the omission may be accidental[91].

If, taking the above example, party A had a more general obligation to reimburse B's legal costs, the clause dealing with the planning hearing might include wording such as the following to try to ensure that the general principle would not be overridden by the specific obligation.

> Without prejudice to the generality of A's obligations to [reimburse H's legal costs [as set out in clause X]], A shall …

6.5.16.2   If the contract includes express terms on a topic, it is unlikely that the court will imply terms on the same topic

If the parties have expressly provided for a subject matter, then the courts will not normally allow for a term to be implied which deals with the same subject matter[92]. For example, it seems the courts may be prepared to imply a term into a contract for the supply of computer software that it will be fit for its purpose[93]. If a contract for the supply of computer software includes an express term on the subject of fitness for purpose, it is unlikely, following this principle, that any term would be implied on the same subject. However, if an implied term is capable of co-existence with an express term without conflict, then the court may accept the implied term as well as the express term, although the express term may narrow the ambit of the implied term[94].

6.5.17   The ejusdem generis[95] ('of the same kind') rule

Where the contract includes a list of similar items followed by words such as 'or other [items]', the 'others' will be interpreted as being limited to items

---

[91] See comments of Lopes LJ in *Colquhoun v Brooks* (1888) 21 QBD 52 and Lord Hoffmann in *National Grid v Mayes* [2001] [2001] UKHL, [2001] 2 All ER 417.

[92] See eg *Aspdin v Austin* (1844) QB 671; *Mills v United Counties Bank Ltd* [1912] 1 Ch 231, and more recently, *Waterman v Boyle* [2009] EWCA Civ 115, [2009] All ER (D) 285 (Feb).

[93] See comments of Sir Iain Glidewell in *St Albans City and District Council v International Computers Ltd* [1996] 4 All ER 481, CA in relation to a common law implied term of fitness for purpose, in addition to the terms implied by the Sale of Goods Act 1979 and the Supply of Goods and Services Act 1982.

[94] See the judgment of Sir Nicolas Browne-Wilkinson V-C in *Johnstone v Bloomsbury Health Authority* [1992] QB 333, CA and the speech of Lord Steyn in *Equitable Life Assurance Society v Hyman* [2000] All ER (D) 1026.

[95] Several of the principles stated in this chapter have Latin names associated with them. In most cases the Latin names have been ignored in this chapter, as adding little to one's understanding of the principle. For some reason the *ejusdem generis* rule is still given the name by practitioners, perhaps because there is no obvious alternative name—the 'of the same kind rule' sounds clumsy.

which are of the same kind, or similar, to the listed items. This is regarded by the courts as a guide to interpretation rather than a hard rule, but nevertheless is frequently applied[96].

Rather than discuss the subtleties of the many cases in which the principle has or has not been applied, it may be useful to give a practical example. For example, consider the following examples.

Example 1

Neither party shall have any liability to the other party for any delay or failure in performance of this Agreement resulting from floods, fires, accidents, earthquakes, riots, explosions, war or other events beyond the control of that party.

Example 2

Neither party shall have any liability to the other party for any delay or failure in performance of this Agreement resulting from circumstances beyond the reasonable control of that party, including without limitation labour disputes involving that party.

Both examples deal with what is known as *force majeure*[97]. In Example 1, there is a list of events followed by the phrase 'or other events beyond the control of that party'. Although the list is quite lengthy, it is not uncommon to find much longer lists of *force majeure* events in some contracts. For example, there is no reference to labour disputes; many *force majeure* clauses make a specific reference to labour disputes, as there is authority to suggest that disputes involving one's own workforce are not beyond one's control[98]. There is a significant risk that, by omitting to mention labour disputes, they would not be covered by the wording of the first clause, despite the concluding words 'or other events beyond the control of that party'.

Example 2 does not give a long list of *force majeure* events. Instead, it sets up a general principle—'circumstances beyond the reasonable control of that party' and then gives the example of labour disputes in order to remove any doubt over whether these would be covered by the clause. To ensure that this example does not inadvertently narrow the types of circumstance which would be covered by the clause (ie in light of the *ejusdem generis* rule), the

---

[96]   See, eg, comments of Devlin J in *Chandris v Isbrandtsen-Moller Co Inc* [1951] 1 KB 240. In *BOC Group Plc v Centeon LLC* [1990] 1 All ER (Comm) 970, despite the judgment in *Investors Compensation Scheme v West Bromwich Building Society* [1998] 1 All ER 98, this principle is still relevant: 'What cannot be denied, in my view is that the consideration which underlie [the *ejusdem generis* rule] are ones which a reasonable man would take into account as a matter of commonsense. It is perhaps better now to refer to it as a factor which, when it is relevant, cannot be properly ignored.'

[97]   See **5.12.2** for a discussion of *force majeure* clauses. These examples are incomplete—a typical *force majeure* clause will deal with a number of other issues beyond those addressed here.

[98]   For example, if the dispute is over pay, the employer can solve the dispute by paying the employees what they demand.

example is introduced by the words 'including without limitation'. This is not the only phrase which can be used to disapply the rule. As Devlin J commented in one case[99], phrases such as 'whether or not similar to the foregoing' and 'without prejudice to the generality of the foregoing' would have the same effect. Sometimes lists of examples are followed by words such as 'or any other [item] whatsoever'; use of the word 'whatsoever' has been held to have the effect of disapplying the rule[100] although it is not clear that this word will always have this effect. It is suggested that words such as 'including without limitation' are better. Also relevant is whether the items in the list are of the same type. In a case involving the interpretation of an insurance contract, the following came in for consideration: 'fire or intruder alarm switch gear control panel or machinery'. It was held that 'machinery' was a distinct category to the other items in the list (in the context of the contract regarding that of fire protection equipment)[101].

6.5.18   Unclear contract wording will be construed against the interests of the grantor or the party which benefits from the wording

This is sometimes known as the *contra proferentem* rule. There seem to be two main strands to the rule:

- in agreements concerned with the grant of rights to property, unclear wording is construed against the grantor[102];

- in agreements generally, unclear wording in a clause is construed against the party in whose favour the clause is made[103] (ie the party which 'proffered' (proposed) the wording).

The *contra proferentem* rule is sometimes understood as meaning that wording will be construed against the party which drafted the wording or the wording is interpreted against the party who benefits from the wording[104]; often the party who benefits will have drafted the wording.

---

[99]   See the *Chandris* case, cited above.

[100]   See *Earl of Jersey v Neath Poor Law Union Guardians* (1889) 22 QBD 555.

[101]   See *Reilly v National Insurance and Guarantee Corporation Ltd* [2008] EWHC 722 (Comm), [2008] 2 All ER (Comm) 612.

[102]   See comments of Romilly MR in *Johnson v Edgware, etc Rly Co* (1866) 35 Beav 480.

[103]   See comments of Sterling LJ in *Savill Bros Ltd v Bethell* [1902] 2 Ch 523.

[104]   See comments of Staughton LJ in *Pera Shipping Corpn v Petroship SA, The Pera* [1984] 2 Lloyd's Rep 363 at 356 and in *Youell v Bland Welch & Co Ltd* [1992] 2 Lloyd's Rep 127 at 134. See also *Kleinwort Benson Ltd v Malaysian Mining Corpn BM* [1988] 1 WLR 799, where Hirst J held that the rule did not apply to a joint drafting effort.

If the wording is clear, the rule will not be applicable[105]. It seems that if the wording does not clearly benefit one party, or benefits both parties equally[106] or is the result of joint drafting effort[107], the rule will not be applicable. Concerning grants from the Crown, it appears that unclear wording is construed against the grantee (ie the rule is reversed and the Crown has the benefit of the doubt); but apparently this exception only applies to grants concerned with land[108].

6.5.19   The court is unlikely to interpret the contract so as to allow a party to take advantage of his own wrongdoing unless clear wording is used

The principle was stated by Lord Diplock as follows[109]:

> '... except in the unlikely event that the contract contains clear express provisions to the contrary, it is to be presumed that it was not the intention of the parties that either party should be entitled to rely upon his own breaches of his primary obligations as bringing the contract to an end.'

This principle seems to be one of public policy, and is not limited to termination provisions in contracts[110]. An example which comes to mind concerns restrictive covenants in employment contracts. It has been held that an obligation on an employee not to compete with his employer after termination of the contract of employment is not enforceable if the termination arose from the employer's breach of contract[111]. There is conflicting case law as to whether a party is able to take advantage of his own wrongdoing; some of this case law suggests that there is a principle of law (and therefore a party cannot do so) while other cases suggest that it is a matter of interpretation (and the party can if there

---

[105] See *London and Lancashire Fire Insurance Co Ltd v Bolands Ltd* [1924] AC 836 at 848, HL, and also more recently in *Quest 4 Finance Ltd v Maxfield and Others* [2007] EWHC 2313 (QB), [2007] All ER (D) 180 (Oct), see para 35: '...However, before [the *contra proferentem*] principle comes into play there must be a true ambiguity. If the meaning which the document would convey to a reasonable person having all the background knowledge which could reasonably have been available to the parties in the situation in which they were at the time of the contract (see *Investors Compensation Scheme v West Bromwich Building Society* [1998] 1 WLR 896 at 912) is clear then there is no ambiguity and there is no room for the *contra proferentem* to come into play (see *Static Control Components v Egan* [2004] 2 LI Rep 429 at para 37)'.

[106] See eg *Steria Ltd v Sigma Wireless Communications Ltd* [2008] BLR 79.

[107] *Levison v Fairn* [1978] 2 All ER 1149; *Kleinwort Benson Ltd v Malaysian Mining Corp Berhad* [1988] 1 WLR 799.

[108] *Earl of Lonsdale v A-G* [1982] 1 WLR 887.

[109] See *Cheall v Association of Professional, Executive, Clerical and Computer Staff* [1983] 2 AC 180, HL.

[110] For example, see *Alghussein Establishment v Eton College* [1988] 1 WLR 587, HL.

[111] See *D v M* [1996] IRLR 192; and *Living Design (Home Improvements) Ltd v Davidson* [1994] IRLR 69.

are clear words). The current view appears to be that the approach of Lord Diplock is correct[112].

It is not entirely clear what kind of 'clear express provisions' Lord Diplock had in mind; perhaps something along the following lines.

> The Parties acknowledge and agree that this Agreement shall be interpreted so as to allow a Party to rely on, or take advantage of, his own wrongdoing (including without limitation any wilful default, negligence, breach of contract or other misconduct or failing) when exercising any rights or avoiding any obligations under this Agreement.

No doubt this wording could be improved. It would be a very rare situation where all parties to a contract agreed to include wording along these lines. In practice there may be little one can do as drafter or negotiator to address this principle of interpretation.

The courts prefer interpretations which result in lawful, valid, reasonable contracts which are capable of performance.

- If there are two possible interpretations, one lawful and one unlawful, the court will apply the lawful interpretation[113].

- If by one interpretation the contract is valid, and by the other the contract is invalid, and the two interpretations are equally plausible, the valid interpretation will be preferred[114].

- An interpretation which leads to a reasonable result may be preferred over one which leads to an unreasonable result[115].

- An interpretation which requires a party to do something which is possible will be preferred over a requirement to do something which is impossible[116].

---

[112] See *Micklefield v SAC Technology Ltd* [1991] 1 All ER 275; *Decoma UK Ltd v Haden Drysys International Ltd* [2006] EWCA Civ 723. Although the starting point appears to be that 'it will be presumed that the parties intended that neither should be entitled to rely on his own breach of duty to obtain a benefit under a contract, at least where the breach of duty is a breach of an obligation under that contract', from para 17, *Petroplus Marketing AG v Shell Trading International Ltd* [2009] EWHC 1024 (Comm), [2009] 2 All ER (Comm) 1186.

[113] *Faussett v Carpenter* (1831) 2 Dow & Cl 232. For a more recent consideration of this principle see *Landlord Protect Ltd v St Anselm Development Co Ltd* [2008] EWHC 1582 (Ch), [2008] All ER (D) 89 (Jul), at para 12.

[114] *Hillas & Co v Arcos Ltd* (1932) 147 LT 503, per Lord Wright. In *Anglo Continental Educational Group (GB) Ltd v Capital Homes (Southern) Ltd* [2009] EWCA Civ 218, [2009] EWCA Civ 218 in relation to a badly drafted agreement Arden LJ stated (at para 13): 'In that situation, a principle which has particular potency and resonance is that, if the agreement is susceptible of an interpretation which will make it enforceable and effective, the court will prefer that interpretation to any interpretation which would result in its being void. The court will also prefer an interpretation which produces a result which the parties are likely to have agreed over an improbable result'.

[115] *Schuler (L) AG v Wickman Machine Tool Sales Ltd* [1974] AC 235, per Lord Reid.

[116] *Eurico SpA v Philipp Bros, The Epaphus* [1987] 2 Lloyd's Rep 215.

It is perhaps not surprising that the courts will tend to favour a lawful interpretation over an unlawful interpretation. In most cases it may be thought unlikely that any advantage would be gained by wording the contract so as to try to contradict this presumption.

These principles may allow the court to interpret a contract a little more broadly than the golden rule (see **6.5.6.1**) would normally allow. Few drafting issues would seem to arise. If the drafter intends to include a provision which requires an unlawful, invalid or unreasonable result, or requires a party do something which is impossible, it would be prudent: (a) to make the wording as clear as possible; and (b) perhaps also to signpost the fact that such an interpretation is intended. This would make it more difficult for the court to misinterpret the wording, although this probably only helps in borderline cases where the obligation is not too extreme. If the court was really hostile to the provision it would probably find another way to make it unenforceable, on public policy grounds.

6.5.19.1   Drafting and negotiating issues in relation to the interpretation of express contract terms

- *Consistent use of words.* Take care to use the same language to express the same ideas throughout the contract.

- *Consistency generally.* More generally, check the contract for consistency, for example, between the obligations of different clauses[117].

- *Avoid unnecessary or redundant words.*

- *State hierarchy of parts of agreement.* If the contract consists of several parts, for example, a main agreement, standard conditions, special conditions, schedules, or other attachments, consider including a clause which states the order of priority (see suggested wording above).

- *Avoid partial or incomplete obligations.* If issues of particular concern are to be mentioned in the contract, consider whether similar issues need to be mentioned (as in the planning example given above). Sometimes clauses are included on topics of immediate concern which repeat or overlap with more general provisions. If so, consider including wording in the specific clause such as 'without prejudice to the generality of clause X'.

- *State general principles, make clear examples are 'without limitation'.* Rather than just list examples, state the general principle to which the examples relate (if this benefits your client). If it is useful then to state examples of that principle, introduce them with words such as 'including without limitation'.

---

[117] See also Chapter 9 for more on checking of agreements before signing them.

6.5.20   Implied terms

The expression 'implied terms' can cover a variety of different types of term, including:

- *Terms implied because of the general relationship of the parties:* for example, as buyer and seller of goods, or as solicitor and client, or as employer and employee. Such terms may be implied under common law (eg an employee's duty of 'fidelity' to his employer) or by statute (eg the warranty for title in a contract for the sale of goods, as provided for in s 12 of the Sale of Goods Act 1979).

- *Terms implied into the particular transaction:* in other words, terms which the parties have not expressed in their contract but which the court decides are nevertheless a part of their particular bargain. For example, a term might be implied (a) under the 'business efficacy' principle (ie without it the contract would not be workable)[118], or (b) because the contract does not address an issue which needs to be addressed[119], or (c) under the 'officious bystander test', because the term[120]:

  > '… is something so obvious that it goes without saying; so that if, while the parties were making their bargain, an officious bystander were to suggest some express provision for it in the agreement, they would testily suppress him with a common "oh, of course".'[121]

Terms in these categories are to be implied only where strictly necessary[122] and only where the agreement 'does not expressly provide for what is to happen when some event occurs'[123].

---

[118] See judgment of Bowen LJ in *The Moorcock* (1889) 14 PD 64. See also the speech of Lord Steyn in *Equitable Life Assurance Society v Hyman* [2002] 1 AC 408, [2000] All ER (D) 1026.

[119] For example, as to the duration of the contract—in some situations, particularly in distribution agreements, if the contract does not include a provision for termination it may be implied that the contract may be terminated by either party on reasonable notice. See, eg, *Martin-Baker Aircraft Co Ltd v Canadian Flight Equipment Ltd* [1955] 2 QB 556 at 578.

[120] See *Shirlaw v Southern Foundries (1926) Ltd* [1939] 2 KB 206 at 227, CA.

[121] These various methods are not independent methods of determining whether to imply a term. See *Attorney General of Belize and Others v Belize Telecom Ltd and Another* [2009] UKPC 10, [2009] 2 All ER 1127: The methods are 'best regarded, not as series of independent tests which must each be surmounted, but rather as a collection of different ways in which judges have tried to express the central idea that the proposed implied term must spell out what the contract actually means, or in which they have explained why they did not think that it did so' (from para 27). See also *Mediterranean Salvage and Towage Ltd v Seamar Trading and Commerce Inc; The Reborn* [2009] EWCA Civ 531, [2010] 1 All ER (Comm) 1 at para 15.

[122] See speech of Lord Steyn in *Equitable Life Assurance Society v Hyman* [2002] 1 AC 408, [2000] All ER (D) 1026 and *Mediterranean Salvage and Towage Ltd v Seamar Trading and Commerce Inc; The Reborn* [2009] EWCA Civ 531, [2010] 1 All ER (Comm) 1 at para 15.

[123] *Attorney General of Belize and Others v Belize Telecom Ltd and Another* [2009] UKPC 10, [2009] 2 All ER 1127, from para 17. This case provides a thorough review of the different methods of implying terms set out under this bullet point, against the background of the principles outlined in *Investors' Compensation Scheme Ltd v West Bromwich Building Society* [1998] 1 All ER 98.

6.5.21   Terms implied by statute

A detailed discussion of the cases in which terms have been implied into a contract is beyond the scope of this book. For a discussion of that subject, the reader is referred to the standard contract law texts[124].

It may, though, be helpful to include here a summary of the main terms implied under the Sale of Goods Act 1979 and the Supply of Goods and Services Act 1982. Although terms are implied by other statutes[125], they are not of such general application as those in the Sale of Goods Act and the Supply of Goods and Services Act.

6.5.21.1   Terms implied by the Sale of Goods Act 1979

1. Implied terms about title, etc[126]: an implied condition that the seller has the right to sell the goods; an implied warranty that the goods are free from any charge or encumbrance not disclosed or known to the buyer before the contract is made; and an implied warranty that the buyer will enjoy quiet possession of the goods, except for disturbance by a person holding a charge or encumbrance over the goods which was disclosed or known to the buyer before the contract was made.

However, the above terms are not implied where there appears from the contract or is to be inferred from its circumstances an intention that the seller should transfer only such title as he or a third person may have. Instead, there is an implied warranty that all charges or encumbrances known to the seller and not known to the buyer have been disclosed to the buyer before the contract is made; and an implied warranty that the seller or other person transferring title to the buyer, and anyone claiming through or under such person (other than a holder of a charge or encumbrance known to the buyer before the contract is made), will not disturb the buyer's quiet possession.

It has been held that the implied term of quiet possession is breached if the product is subject to third-party patent rights[127] or trade mark rights[128].

2. Implied terms about quality[129]: where the goods are sold in the course of a business, an implied term that the goods are of satisfactory quality. Goods are

---

[124] For example, Chapter 13 *Chitty on Contracts* (30th Edn) 2010 Sweet and Maxwell.

[125] For example, under the Package Travel, Package Holiday and Package Tours Regulations 1992, SI 1992/3288; Consumer Protection (Distance Selling) Regulations 2000, SI 2000/2334; Sale and Supply of Goods to Consumers Regulations 2002, SI 2002/3045, reg 2.

[126] Sale of Goods Act 1979, s 12.

[127] *Microbeads AC v Vinhurst Road Markings Ltd* [1975] 1 All ER 529, CA.

[128] *Niblett Ltd v Confectioners' Materials Co Ltd* [1921] 3 KB 387, CA.

[129] Sale of Goods Act 1979, s 14.

of satisfactory quality for the purposes of the Act if 'they meet the standard that a reasonable person would regard as satisfactory, taking account of any description of the goods, the price (if relevant) and all the other relevant circumstances'[130]. The quality of goods is further defined[131] as follows:

> '(2B) For the purposes of this Act, the quality of goods includes their state and condition and the following (among others) are in appropriate cases aspects of the quality of goods
> (a)   fitness for all the purposes for which goods of the kind in question are commonly supplied,
> (b)   appearance and finish,
> (c)   freedom from minor defects,
> (d)   safety, and
> (e)   durability.'

However, the implied term of satisfactory quality does not apply to any matter which is drawn to the buyer's attention before the contract is made or, where the buyer examined the goods before the contract was made, any matter which that examination ought to have revealed or, in the case of a sale by sample, any matter which would have been apparent on a reasonable examination of the sample[132].

3. *Implied terms about fitness for purpose*[133]: where the goods are sold in the course of a business, and the buyer expressly or by implication makes known any particular purpose for which the goods are being bought[134], an implied condition that the goods are reasonably fit for that purpose, except where the circumstances show that the buyer does not rely, or that it is unreasonable for him to rely, on the skill and judgment of the seller.

4. *Implied terms about sale by sample*[135]: an implied condition that (i) the bulk will comply with the sample in quality and (ii) the goods will be free from any defect making their quality unsatisfactory, which would not be apparent on reasonable examination of the sample.

5. *Implied terms about sale by description*[136]: where there is a sale of goods by description, an implied condition that the goods will correspond with the description.

---

[130]   Sale of Goods Act 1979, s 14(2A). There is an additional category to add to this list if the purchaser is a consumer: 'any public statements on the specific characteristics of the goods made about them by the seller, the producer or his representative (particularly in advertising or on labelling)'.

[131]   Sale of Goods Act 1979, s 14(2B).

[132]   Sale of Goods Act 1979, s 14(2C).

[133]   Sale of Goods Act 1979, s 14.

[134]   If goods have only one purpose, it is not necessary to specify it for this implied term to be engaged: *Priest v Last* [1903] 2 KB 148, CA.

[135]   Sale of Goods Act 1979, s 15.

[136]   Sale of Goods Act 1979, s 13.

Under the Unfair Contract Terms Act 1977 ('UCTA 1977'), it is not possible to contract out of liability for breach of the terms referred to in (1) above; nor, in the case of a consumer sale, to contract out of liability for breach of the terms referred to in (2)–(5) above. In the case of non-consumer sales, any exclusion or limitation of liability for breach of (2)–(5) above must be reasonable[137]. In the case of non-consumer sales, the buyer's right to reject the goods for breach by the supplier of ss 13, 14 and/or 15 of the Sale of Goods Act 1979 is to be treated as a breach of warranty rather than a breach condition if the breach is so slight it would be unreasonable for the purchaser to reject the goods[138].

6.5.21.2   Terms implied by the Supply of Goods and Services Act 1982

The Supply of Goods and Services Act is concerned with three main types of contract:

- contracts for the transfer of property in goods;
- contracts for the hire of goods; and
- contracts for the supply of services.

As is discussed in more detail below, the Supply of Goods and Services Act implies certain terms into such contracts, including conditions or warranties as to title, freedom from encumbrances, quiet possession, correspondence with description or sample, quality, fitness for purpose, right to transfer possession and, in relation to the supply of services, that the service will be carried out with reasonable care and skill, in a reasonable time and for a reasonable charge.

6.5.21.3   Contracts for the transfer of property in goods

This category of contract is broader than a sale of goods[139], and covers, for example, a contract where the consideration is something other than money. As with contracts for the sale of goods, if property in the goods is not transferred, the relevant provisions of the Supply of Goods and Services Act will not operate. The terms implied into contracts for the transfer of property in goods are very similar to those implied into contracts for the sale of goods, as to which see above.

---

[137] UCTA 1977, s 6.

[138] Sale of Goods Act 1979, s 15A.

[139] See Supply of Goods and Services Act 1982, s 1: excluded from the definition are certain categories, eg hire-purchase agreements and mortgages.

6.5.21.4   Contracts for the hire of goods

Such contracts are defined for the purposes of the Supply of Goods and Services Act as follows[140]:

> 'In this Act a "contract for the hire of goods" means a contract under which one person bails or agrees to bail goods to another by way of hire, other than … (a) a hire purchase agreement; [or] … (b) a contract under which goods are (or are to be) bailed in exchange for trading stamps on their redemption.'

Where a supply of materials is a contract for the hire of goods as defined by the Supply of Goods and Services Act, a number of terms may be implied into the contract. These may be summarised as follows.

- *Implied terms about right to transfer possession, etc:* an implied condition that the bailor has the right to transfer possession of the goods; and an implied warranty that the bailee will enjoy quiet possession of the goods for the period of the bailment except for disturbance by the holder of charge or encumbrance which was disclosed or known to the bailee before the contract is made.

- *Implied terms about quality:* where the bailor bails goods in the course of a business, an implied condition that the goods supplied are of satisfactory quality, except for defects specifically drawn to the bailee's attention before the contract is made or, if the bailee examines the goods before the contract is made, except for defects which the examination ought to reveal.

- *Implied terms about fitness for purpose:* where the bailor bails goods in the course of a business and the bailee makes known, expressly or by implication, any particular purpose for which the goods are being bailed, an implied condition that the goods supplied are reasonably fit for that purpose, unless the bailee does not rely, or it is unreasonable for him to rely, on the skill and judgment of the bailor.

- *Implied terms where hire is by sample:* where the bailor bails goods by reference to a sample, an implied condition (i) that the bulk will correspond with the sample in quality, (ii) that the bailee will have a reasonable opportunity of comparing the bulk with the sample, and (iii) that the goods will be free from any defect rendering them unmerchantable, which would not be apparent on reasonable examination of the sample.

- *Implied terms where hire is by description:* where the bailor bails the goods 'by description', an implied condition that the goods will correspond with the description.

---

[140]   Supply of Goods and Services Act 1982, s 6.

These terms may be 'negatived or varied by express agreement, or by the course of dealing between the parties, or by such usage as binds both parties to the contract' (unless this is prohibited under UCTA 1977[141]). In addition to these statutory terms, terms may also be implied[142] under the common law of bailment.

6.5.21.5   Contracts for the supply of services

Such contracts are defined[143] for the purposes of the Supply of Goods and Services Act as 'a contract under which a person ("the supplier") agrees to carry out a service'. This may or may not also involve a transfer or hire of goods. However, certain contracts are excluded[144].

Where a contract for the supply of services exists, the Supply of Goods and Services Act provides that certain terms are implied into the contract. These may be summarised as follows.

- *Implied term about care and skill:* where the supplier is acting in the course of a business, an implied term that the supplier will carry out the service with reasonable care and skill.

- *Implied term about time for performance:* where the supplier is acting in the course of a business and the time for the service to be carried out is not (i) fixed by the contract, (ii) left to be fixed in a manner agreed by the contract, or (iii) determined by the course of dealing between the parties, an implied term that the supplier will carry out the service within a reasonable time.

- *Implied term about reasonable charges:* where the consideration for the service is not (i) determined by the contract, (ii) left to be determined in a manner agreed by the contract, or (iii) determined by the course of dealing between the parties, an implied term that the party contracting with the supplier will pay a reasonable charge.

Such terms may be 'negatived or varied by express agreement, or by the course of dealing between the parties, or by such usage as binds both parties to the contract', unless this is prohibited by UCTA 1977[145].

---

[141] Supply of Goods and Services Act 1982, s 11.

[142] Other than in relation to quality of fitness—see Supply of Goods and Services Act 1982, ss 11(3) and 9(1).

[143] Supply of Goods and Services Act 1982, s 12.

[144] A contract of service (ie employment) or apprenticeship is excluded. The Secretary of State may by statutory instrument exclude categories of service from one or more of the implied terms under the Act. A number of categories of service have been excluded by the Secretary of State in relation to the implied term of care and skill, eg the services of an advocate in court or before an arbitrator, building society directors and arbitrators.

[145] Supply of Goods and Services Act 1982, s 16.

6.5.21.6   Drafting and negotiating issues

If a court decides that a term should be implied into a contract, it will also decide what the scope of that implied term will be; in many cases this will be beyond the control of the contract drafter. However, there are some things a drafter can do to try to ensure that the contract will be interpreted in the way the drafter's clients or colleagues intend, particularly the following:

- *Include general disclaimer of implied terms.* It is common to include in detailed contracts a provision that the contract contains no terms other than those stated in the contract document. Typical wording for such a clause[146] (which also seeks to exclude prior representations) follows:

    > Each of the Parties acknowledges that, in entering into this Agreement, it does not do so in reliance on any representation, warranty or other provision except as expressly provided in this Agreement, and any conditions, warranties or other terms implied by statute or common law are excluded from this Agreement to the fullest extent permitted by law. Nothing in this Agreement excludes liability for fraud.

- *Consider what terms might be implied/include specific disclaimers.* A general disclaimer may not be legally effective, particularly if a term needs to be implied in order for the contract to work. As discussed below, it may be desirable to include express terms to ensure contractual certainty and to avoid the risk that the court will imply terms which you do not want. In addition, it may be useful to consider whether the court might imply terms for any of the following reasons, and if so whether specific disclaimers should be included (or whether terms should be included to avoid having the court imply terms):

    - terms implied by statute[147];

    - terms implied at common law[148];

    - terms implied by trade usage or custom;

    - terms implied from previous course of dealing of the parties;

    - terms implied from recitals, which need to be stated in the operative terms of the contract[149].

---

[146] See discussion of entire agreement below at **6.5.22.10**.

[147] Particularly under the Sale of Goods Act 1979; the Supply of Goods and Services Act 1982; the Law of Property (Miscellaneous Provisions) Act 1989; the Package Travel, Package Holiday and Package Tours Regulations 1992, SI 1992/3288; the Sale and Supply of Goods to Consumers Regulations 2002, SI 2002/3045; the Consumer Protection (Distance Selling) Regulations 2000, SI 2000/2334; and under consumer credit legislation.

[148] Too numerous to mention here—see standard contract law texts such as *Chitty on Contracts* (30th Edn) 2010 Sweet and Maxwell.

[149] See **2.6** in relation to the status of recitals.

- *Include express terms.* Consider whether express terms need to be added to the contract to ensure that it deals with all the important issues which are likely to arise in the operation of the contract. For example, do the express terms address when particular obligations are to be performed, the duration of the obligations, the standard or manner of their performance, and the price to be paid, bearing in mind that failure to state these things may (depending on the facts) lead the court to imply terms which do not coincide with what you want the obligations to be, or may cause the contract to be void for uncertainty?

6.5.22   Special rules for exemption clauses

There are many reported cases in which the courts have been asked to decide whether exemption clauses—clauses excluding or limiting liability—are legally effective. Over time, different principles have emerged from the cases[150], and it is quite possible that aspects of the current law may change as more cases come before the courts[151]. A discussion of the many reported cases in which exemption clauses have been considered is beyond the scope of this book. This section will focus mainly on drafting issues.

There are two main areas to be considered when drafting exemption clauses: (a) the general approach of the courts when interpreting such clauses, and (b) the effect of legislation upon such clauses, particularly UCTA 1977 and the Unfair Terms in Consumer Contracts Regulations 1999[152]. For the purposes of considering the drafting and negotiating issues which arise in relation to exemption clauses, it is useful to highlight some of the main issues which the courts consider when interpreting exemption clauses.

6.5.22.1   General hostility of the courts to exemption clauses

The courts tend to look much more critically at exemption clauses than they do at other types of contract clause. This is particularly true where the

---

[150] For example, there was a series of cases in which it was decided that exemption clauses could not apply to fundamental breaches of contract, but these are no longer considered to be good law.

[151] For example, see the case law since the first edition of this book on whether pre-contractual misrepresentations are covered by 'entire agreement' clauses (an illustration on how the view of the courts change over time): *Thomas Witter Ltd v TBP Industries* [1996] 2 All ER 573 to more recent case law such as *Watford Electronics v Sanderson CFL Ltd* [2001] EWCA Civ 317; [2001] 2 All ER (Comm) 696 and *Exxonmobile Sales and Supply Corpn v Texaco Ltd, The Helene Knutsen* [2003] EWHC 1964 (Comm)), [2004] 1 All ER (Comm) 435. See **6.5.22.10** on the Misrepresentation Act 1967.

[152] SI 1999/2083.

contract is between a commercial company and a consumer, or (no matter who the parties are) where the clause seeks to exclude all liability even for serious breaches of contract. However, the law is more indulgent towards clauses limiting liability rather than those excluding it completely[153]. The wording of exemption clauses is scrutinised closely, and if it does not 'beyond the possibility of misunderstanding'[154] cover the type of liability which is the subject of the dispute, it will often not be found to be exempt such liability. If the wording is ambiguous or unclear, it will be interpreted against the interests of the party seeking to rely on it. Whilst this approach is taken to all types of contract clause (see discussion of the *contra proferentem* rule, above) the approach is particularly strict in the case of exclusion clauses[155].

At one time the courts seemed to be developing a principle of interpretation which stated that parties could not exclude or limit liability for 'fundamental' breaches of contract. However, it is now settled law that no such principle of interpretation should be applied. It is[156]:

> '... a question of contractual intention whether a particular breach is covered or not and the courts are entitled to insist, as they do, that the more radical the breach the clearer must be the language be if it is to be covered.'

and[157]:

> '... the question whether, and to what extent, an exclusion clause is to be applied to a fundamental breach, or a breach of a fundamental term, or indeed to any breach of contract, is a matter of construction of the contract.'

In practice, a court may well find that the proper construction of the contract is that the parties did not intend the exemption clause to apply to fundamental breach, or to complete non-performance by a party of its obligations. But this is a rather different matter to saying that one cannot exempt liability for such breach or non-performance. If the words of the exemption clause are clear enough, it seems that any and all types of liability may be excluded (subject to statutory constraints on exclusion clauses, discussed below). But very clear

---

[153]   See *Ailsa Craig Fishing Co Ltd v Malvern Fishing Co Ltd and Securicor (Scotland) Ltd* [1983] 1 All ER 101, HL; *EE Caledonia Ltd v Orbit Valve Plc* [1995] 1 All ER 174, CA. See also *Frans Maas (UK) Ltd v Samsung Electronics (UK) Ltd* [2004] EWHC 1502 (Comm); [2005] 2 All ER (Comm) 783.

[154]   See judgment of Denning LJ in *White v John Warwick & Co Ltd* [1953] 1 WLR 1285.

[155]   In *Tai Hing Cotton Mill Ltd v Liu Chong Hing Bank Ltd* [1984] 1 Lloyd's Rep 555, Judge Kingham said: 'Such [limitation] clauses will of course be read contra proferentem and must be clearly expressed, but there is no reason why they should be judged by the specially exacting standards which are applied to exclusion [clauses].'

[156]   See judgment of Lord Wilberforce in *Suisse Atlantique Société d'Armement Maritime SA v Rotterdamsche Kolen Centrale NV* [1967] 1 AC 361, HL.

[157]   See leading judgment of Lord Wilberforce in *Photo Production Ltd v Securicor Ltd* [1980] AC 827.

words will be needed[158]. For example, in a contract for the supply of goods, if the supplier is to exclude liability for supplying completely different goods to those ordered, this would need to be stated explicitly, using words which might well be commercially off-putting to any purchaser:

> We may supply you with completely different goods to those you have ordered, or supply you with no goods at all, and we will have no liability to you for doing so.

Language of this kind goes well beyond the typical 'legal' language of many exclusion clauses and is rarely encountered. It may have the effect of making the contract merely a statement of intent rather than a legally binding contract.

6.5.22.2   Liability for breach of condition(s) implied by the Sales of Goods Act 1979 cannot not be excluded unless explicitly stated

If a party wishes to exclude liability for conditions implied by the Sale of Goods Act 1979 then the exclusion clause needs to expressly use the word 'condition'. No other word will do (such as warranty or guarantee). In one of the leading cases (made by the House of Lords) on this point, the contract provided:

> 'Sellers give no warranty, express or implied, as to growth, description, or any other matters, and they shall not be held to guarantee or warrant the fitness for any particular purpose of any grain, seed, flour, cake, or any other article sold by them, or its freedom from injurious quality or from latent defect.'[159]

In this case the distinction between the breach of condition and a breach of warranty was clearly distinguished; and the above wording was held only to exclude liability for breach of warranty. This case has been followed such that an exclusion of liability clause worded as:

---

[158] It appears that the courts are more willing to set an exclusion clause in the context of the agreement, and there is a greater recognition that 'parties to commercial contracts are entitled to apportion the risk of loss as they see fit and that provisions which limit or exclude liability must be construed in the same way as other terms' (from para 46 in *Tradigrain SA and Others v Intertek Testing Services (ITS) Canada Ltd and Another* [2007] EWCA Civ 154, [2007] All ER (D) 376 (Feb). However there is still a requirement that clear wording is used, see *Stocznia Gdynia SA v Gearbulk Holdings Ltd* [2009] EWCA Civ 75, [2009] 2 All ER (Comm) 1129, from para 23: '...It is important to remember that any clause in a contract must be construed in the context in which one finds it, both the immediate context of the other terms and the wider context of the transaction as a whole. The court is unlikely to be satisfied that a party to a contract has abandoned valuable rights arising by operation of law unless the terms of the contract make it sufficiently clear that that was intended. The more valuable the right, the clearer the language will need to be'.

[159] *Wallis, Son and Wells v Pratt and Haynes*, HL [1911] AC 394, [1911–13] All ER Rep 989.

'The foregoing guarantee is accepted, instead of and expressly excludes any other guarantee or warranty express or otherwise'

did not exclude an implied condition[160] and similarly a clause which guaranteed goods against 'defective material and workmanship' for a specified period (but otherwise did not include any exclusion of liability) also did not exclude the statutory implied condition of fitness for purpose[161].

This position has remained unchanged in a recent case[162] even where exclusion of liability wording more closely mirrored the wording found in the Sales of Goods Act:

'There are no guarantees, warranties or misrepresentations, express or implied, [of] merchantability, fitness or suitability of the oil for any particular purpose or otherwise which extend beyond the description of the oil set forth in this agreement.'

Wording such as 'merchantability' (the old word used in the Sale of Goods Act 1979 for what is now 'satisfactory quality') and 'for any particular purpose' was not enough to cover a breach of condition under a contract. The leading judgment in the case clearly emphasised, and restated the continuing validity, of the established principle in this area:

'In the present case, it is not a question of whether the exclusion is unreasonable or not. Either submission of the parties would be perfectly acceptable as long as the position was clear. It is, however, a case where the implied obligations which it is said on behalf of the seller have been excluded are not only fundamental obligations of English law, long enshrined in our Sale of Goods Acts, but there has also been a judicial consensus that such obligations can only be excluded by language which expressly refers (or perhaps one may add which must necessarily be taken to refer) to conditions: and that such language as has been used in our case falls within that consensus and principle.'[163]

---

[160] *Baldry v Marshall Ltd* [1925] CA, 1 KB 260, [1924] All ER Rep 155. '… [I]n Wallis *v* Pratt and, to my mind, it is quite plain that in that case the learned Law Lords also based their decision upon the express difference drawn in the Sale of Goods Act between "condition" and "warranty" and treated the condition that goods were to be equal to description—which is a condition just as the condition of fitness in the present case is a condition—as not being excluded by a clause which excluded warranty. In my opinion, the … [the judge at first instance] was right in treating the word "guarantee" or "warranty" as being different from, certainly as not including, a condition. I think another way of looking at it is this, … that if a person wishes in a contract of sale to exclude what would be the ordinary statutory rights of a purchaser, he must do so in plain and unambiguous terms. In the present case the words are very, very far from being plain.'

[161] *Cammell Laird & Co, Ltd v Manganese Bronze and Brass Co Ltd* [1934] AC 402, [1934] All ER Rep 1.

[162] See *KG Bominflot Bunkergesellschaft für Mineralole mbH & Co v Petroplus Marketing AG (The Mercini Lady)* [2010] EWCA Civ 1145, [2011] 2 All ER (Comm).

[163] Ibid, from para 62 of the judgment.

6.5.22.3   Liability for negligence will not be excluded unless this is made clear

It is now clearly established under English law[164] that an exemption clause will not relieve a party from liability for his own negligence (or that of his 'servants'), unless this is stated specifically or is clearly intended by implication. If the exemption clause does not refer to negligence, it may nevertheless be interpreted as exempting liability for negligence if the clause uses words which imply that negligence is covered, such as 'all losses however caused'[165], or 'from any cause whatsoever'[166]. If the only possible basis of liability is negligence, it may not be necessary to refer to negligence specifically[167], unless there are a 'number of far from fanciful examples not involving negligence'[168]. The reported cases suggest that, where the word 'negligence' is not used, the courts have some flexibility in deciding whether to interpret the exemption clause as covering negligent liability; therefore the drafter will generally wish to mention negligence specifically. It may also be desirable to mention liability for breach of statutory duty, if it is intended that this should be exempted[169].

6.5.22.4   Indemnity clauses, time limits on making claims, and clauses defining obligations very narrowly

These are interpreted in a similar way to exemption clauses. These principles are explicitly stated in UCTA 1977, but they apply also under common law. A clause which requires party A to indemnify party B against losses caused by party B's wrongdoing is in effect a type of exclusion clause, if it covers

---

[164] See judgment of Lord Morton of Henryton in *Canada Steamship Lines Ltd v R* [1952] AC 192, PC, a Canadian case, approved in *Gillespie Bros & Co Ltd v Roy Bowles Transport Ltd* [1973] QB 400, CA, per Buckley LJ, and more recently in *HIH Casualty and General Insurance Ltd v Chase Manhattan Bank* [2003] UKHL 6, [2003] 1 All ER (Comm) 349.

[165] See comments of Scrutton LJ in *Gibaud v Great Eastern Rly Co* [1921] 2 KB 426, CA.

[166] *A E Farr Ltd v Admiralty* [1953] 1 WLR 965.

[167] *Lamport and Holt Lines Ltd v Coubro and Scrutton (M and I) Ltd, The Raphael* [1982] 2 Lloyd's Rep 42, CA.

[168] See *Casson v Ostley PJ Ltd* [2001] EWCA Civ 1013, [2001] All ER (D) 340 (Jun), where the following clause 'works covered by this estimate, existing structures in which we shall be working, and unfixed materials shall be at the sole risk of the client as regards loss or damage by fire and the client shall maintain a proper policy of insurance against that risk in an adequate sum. If any loss or damage affecting the works is so occasioned by fire, the client shall pay to us the full value of all work and materials then executed and delivered' was interpreted by the court as being wide enough to cover the consequences of the builder's negligence, but there were a number 'far from fanciful examples in which, without negligence, a builder might be held liable for a fire resulting from goods supplied and work done by him'. In such a case, applying wording from *Canada Steamship Lines v R* [1952] 1 AC 192 at 208, the wording used in the clause was able to support a head of damage based on some ground other than that of negligence and that other ground was not so fanciful or remote so that the builder cannot be supposed to have desired protection against it.

[169] *EE Caledonia Ltd v Orbit Valve Plc* [1994] 1 WLR 1515, CA.

losses suffered by party A. If, however, the clause merely requires party A to indemnify against third-party losses, different considerations may apply.

A clause which sets a strict time limit on a party's remedies (eg a clause in a contract for the sale of goods which requires the purchaser to notify the supplier of any damaged goods within seven days of delivery) will be interpreted in a similar way to an exemption clause[170].

Similarly, a clause which purports to define a party's obligations in a narrow way or which states that one party will bear the risk of liability[171] will also be interpreted as a type of exclusion clause. A clause which defines what a party is responsible (or not responsible) for doing under the contract may have the same effect as an exemption clause.

6.5.22.5   Liability for own fraud cannot be excluded

On public policy grounds, a contracting party cannot exclude liability for its own fraud in inducing the other party to enter into a contract[172]. Also a party cannot exclude liability for its own fraud during the course of the agreement[173].

It may be possible to exclude the fraud or deceit of a party's *agent* in inducing a contract, but general wording will not be sufficient. Where there is such an intention then 'such intention must be expressed in clear and unmistakable terms on the face of the contract'[174]. It is possible to exclude liability for the deliberate wrongdoing of a party's agent arising from the performance of the agreement[175].

6.5.22.6   Liability for own repudiation cannot be excluded except with clear words

If a party deliberately decides not to perform its obligations (whether before or at the time the party is due to perform the obligations) then it causes a

---

[170] See judgment of Lord Wilberforce in *Suisse Atlantique*, cited above.

[171] *Dorset County Council v Southern Felt Roofing Co Ltd* (1989) 48 BLR 96, CA.

[172] *HIH Casualty and General Insurance Ltd v Chase Manhattan Bank* [2003] UKHL 6, [2003] 1 All ER (Comm) 349.

[173] *Frans Maas (UK) Ltd v Samsung Electronics (UK) Ltd* [2004] EWHC 1502 (Comm), [2005] 2 All ER (Comm) 783.

[174] *HIH Casualty and General Insurance Ltd v Chase Manhattan Bank* [2003] UKHL 6, [2003] 1 All ER (Comm) 349, at [16], although the House of Lords did not come to a final view on this point.

[175] *Frans Maas (UK) Ltd v Samsung Electronics (UK) Ltd* [2004] EWHC 1502 (Comm), [2005] 2 All ER (Comm) 783. In this case it was held that the following wording, as a matter of construction rather than law, was capable of covering deliberate wrongdoing: 'the Company's liability howsoever arising and notwithstanding that the cause of the damage be unexplained shall not exceed …'

repudiatory breach of the contract. For a repudiatory breach to occur, the effect of the breach must in effect stop or destroy the purpose of the contract[176]. The effect of the breach allows the party not in breach either to treat the contract as ended, or to have a claim in damages.

In a recent case, it was held that where a party wishes to exclude liability for its own repudiatory breach, then the clearest words must be used[177]. The judge in this case held it was not possible for there to be a rule of law to exclude such personal wrongdoing, and it was a matter of construction to see whether a clause covered repudiatory breach[178]. The judge summarised the relevant principles concerning this type of breach and what is necessary to exclude it:

'… (1) There is no rule of law applicable and the question is one of construction. (2) There is a presumption, which appears to be a strong presumption, against the exemption clause being construed so as to cover deliberate, repudiatory breach. (3) The words needed to cover a deliberate, repudiatory breach need to be very "clear" in the sense of using "strong" language such as "under no circumstances". (4) There is a particular need to use "clear", in the sense of "strong", language where the exemption clause is intended to cover deliberate wrongdoing by a party in respect of a breach which cannot, or is unlikely to be, covered by insurance. Language such as "including deliberate repudiatory acts by [the parties to the contract] themselves" would need to be used in such a case. (5) Words which, in a literal sense, cover a deliberate repudiatory breach will not be construed so as to do so if that would defeat the "main object" of the contract. (6) The proper function between commercial parties at arm's length and with equal bargaining power of an exemption clause is to allocate insurable risk, so that an exemption clause should not normally be construed in such cases so as to cover an uninsurable risk or one very unlikely to be capable of being insured, in particular deliberate wrongdoing by a party to the contract itself (as opposed to vicarious liability for others). (7) Words which in a literal sense cover a deliberate repudiatory breach cannot be relied upon if they are "repugnant" …'

6.5.22.7   Statutory control of exemption clauses

Exemption clauses are controlled by several statutes and regulations. It may be helpful to summarise briefly the provisions of the most frequently encountered

---

[176] A mere failure to perform an obligation at a stated time is not enough normally for a repudiatory breach. The details and conditions for fulfilling, and consequences of, a repudiatory breach are beyond the scope of this book. Users should consult a contract textbook such as *Chitty on Contracts*. Each case will turn on its own facts, but as an example, if a party fails to pay a deposit, this can amount to a repudiation (*Damon Cia Naviera SA v Hapag-Lloyd International SA, The Blankenstein, The Bartenstein, The Birkenstein* [1985] 1 All ER 475, [1985] 1 WLR 435, CA.

[177] *Internet Broadcasting Corporation Ltd (trading as NETTV) and Another v MAR LLC (trading as MARHedge)* [2009] EWHC 844 (Ch), [2010] 1 All ER (Comm) 112.

[178] The judge felt bound by the decisions of *Suisse Atlantique Société d'Armement Maritime SA v Rotterdamsche Kolen Centrale NV* [1967] 1 AC 361, HL and *Photo Production Ltd v Securicor Ltd* [1980] AC 827.

of these statutes and regulations, UCTA 1977, the Misrepresentation Act 1967 and the Unfair Terms in Consumer Contracts Regulations 1999[179].

6.5.22.8   Unfair Contract Terms Act 1977 (as amended)

UCTA 1977 is described in its preamble as 'an Act to impose further[180] limits on the extent to which under the law of England and Wales and Northern Ireland civil liability for breach of contract, or for negligence or other breach of duty, can be avoided by means of contract terms and otherwise, and under the law of Scotland civil liability can be avoided by means of contract terms'. In very brief summary, the Act imposes limits on the extent to which one can exclude or limit liability, including certain limits in the following situations.

- *Negligence:* under s 2 of UCTA 1977 it is not permitted to exclude or restrict liability, by a contract term or notice, for death or personal injury caused by one's negligence. In the case of other loss or damage caused by negligence, any exclusion or restriction of liability will not be effective unless it 'satisfies the requirement of reasonableness'[181].

- *Standard terms of business/consumer transactions:* under s 3 of UCTA 1977 where a contract is made on a party's written standard terms of business[182],

---

[179] Further statutory controls on exemption clauses cover the following subjects: fair trading (Fair Trading Act 1973, Part II); consumer protection (Consumer Protection Act 1987, ss 7, 41); doorstep selling (eg under the Cancellation of Contracts made in a Consumer's Home or Place of Work, etc Regulations 2008, SI 2008/1815; Distance Selling (Consumer Protection (Distance Selling) Regulations 2000, SI 2000/2334); contractually binding guarantees (Sale and Supply of Goods to Consumers Regulations 2002, SI 2002/3045, reg 4); regulated agreements (Consumer Credit Act 1974, s 173); and compulsory warranties (eg relating to the sale of intoxicating liquor, motor vehicles, agricultural machinery, seeds, fertilisers, horticultural produce, farm and garden chemicals, gold, silver and platinum articles, endangered species of wild flora and fauna, pollution, game laws and deer): (see further *Encyclopaedia of Forms and Precedents,* Sale of Goods (5th Edn) LNUK, Vol 34 [399] onwards.)

[180] The impact of the common law: see *Boomsma v Clark and Rose Ltd* (1983) SLT 67, and other legislation upon exclusion clauses should not be overlooked, including the provisions of the Unfair Terms in Consumer Contracts Regulations 1999, SI 1999/2083 and the Consumer Protection Act 1987.

[181] As to which see UCTA 1977, s 11 and Sch 2 (reproduced in Appendix 2).

[182] For UCTA 1977 to apply it was not necessary for the whole of the contract to be 'on the other's written standard terms of business', see *Pegler Ltd v Wang (UK) Ltd* [2000] All ER (D) 260. For case law as to the meaning of 'written standard terms of business' (which is not otherwise defined in UCTA 1977), see, eg, *Salvage Association v CAP Financial Services Ltd* [1995] FSR 654, *Fillite (Runcorn) Ltd v APV Pasilac Ltd The Buyer,* July 1995 and *St Albans City and District Council v International Computers Ltd* [1996] 4 All ER 481, CA. The *Salvage Association* case provides a useful non-exhaustive list for deciding whether the provisions of a contract are on 'written standard terms of business'. In *British Fermentation Products Ltd v Compair Reavell Ltd* [1999] 2 All ER (Comm) 389 the court held that the burden of proof was on the party who wished to argue that a contract was on written standard terms of business and for a trade association's terms and conditions to be considered written standard terms of business depended on the frequency they were used by a party.

or where the other party 'deals as consumer'[183], that party may not, inter alia, exclude or restrict liability for breach of contract, unless the contract term satisfies the requirement of reasonableness.

- *Unreasonable indemnity clauses:* under s 4 of UCTA 1977 a person dealing as consumer cannot by reference to any contract term be made to indemnify another person in respect of liability incurred by the other for negligence or breach of contract, except in so far as the contract term satisfies the requirement of reasonableness.

- *Terms implied by the Sale of Goods Act and the Supply of Goods and Services Act:* under ss 6 and 7 of UCTA 1977 it is not possible to exclude liability for breach of the implied terms as to title nor (in the case of consumer sales) the other terms implied by these statutes (satisfactory quality, description, sample). In the case of non-consumer sales, any exclusion of the other implied terms must be reasonable in order to be effective.

UCTA 1977 also includes specific provisions concerning liability relating to consumer guarantees[184]. Certain types of contract, listed in Sch 1 to the Act (eg concerned with the creation and transfers of interests in land, intellectual property or securities, and contracts of insurance) are excluded from certain provisions of the Act[185]. The Act does not apply to certain contracts which are agreed to be made under the law of a part of the United Kingdom[186] if, in the absence of such agreement, the contract would not be subject to the law of any part of the United Kingdom[187]. On the other hand it is not possible to evade the operation of the Act by agreeing to apply another country's laws[188].

Also certain contracts for the international supply of goods are exempted from some of the provisions of the Act[189]. This exclusion can have greater application than the specific ones mentioned in the previous paragraph. Where this occurs, the limits that UCTA places on a person as to the extent

---

[183] For example, not in a business context—see definition in UCTA 1977, s 12. Note that the meaning of a consumer under UCTA 1977 is substantially different to that of Unfair Terms in Consumer Contracts Regulations 1999. Under UCTA 1977 a 'consumer' has been held to mean a business who purchases goods partly for business use and partly for non-business use, see *R & B Customs Brokers Co Ltd v United Dominions Trust Ltd* [1988] 1 All ER 847, CA. The business in this case was a limited company.

[184] UCTA 1977, s 5. Note that there is now a second type of guarantee which applies to transactions with consumers under the Sale and Supply of Goods to Consumers Regulations 2002, SI 2002/3045, see reg 15. This newer form of guarantee has contractual effect and is worded in a different way to that found in UCTA 1977. See further below.

[185] UCTA ss 2, 3 and 4 do not apply to these contracts. Note: the disapplication of these sections for some of the areas mentioned here does not extend to the whole contract but only to provisions which deal with that particular area.

[186] Under the law of (a) England and Wales, or (b) Northern Ireland, or (c) Scotland.

[187] UCTA 1977, s 27(1).

[188] UCTA 1977, s 27(2).

[189] UCTA 1977, s 26.

to which they can exclude or restrict liability by reference to a contract term does not apply to liability arising under a contract. Also, any requirement of reasonableness under UCTA ss 3 and 4 do not apply. An international supply of goods contract is one where:

- there is a contract of sale of goods or it is a contract where the possession or ownership of goods passes; and

- the contract is made by parties based in territories of different states[190].

A contract comes within the above definition when one of the following conditions is applied:

- the goods involved at the time of the conclusion of the contract, are in the course of carriage, or will be carried, from the territory of one state to that of another[191]; or

- the acts of making the offer and acceptance to create the contract have to be done in different states; or

- the goods need to be delivered to a third state[192].

More generally, it is perhaps worth stating that UCTA applies only where a contract or its provisions attempt to exclude or limit liability. This is not the same as where the parties in a contract seek to define what is being provided (and the conditions on which they will provide it). A clause in a contract that:

> 'simply define[s] the basis upon which services will be rendered and confirm[s] the basis upon which parties are transacting business are not subject to section 2 of UCTA. Otherwise, every contract which contains contractual terms defining the extent of each party's obligations would have to satisfy the requirement of reasonableness.'[193]

---

[190] Unfair Contract Terms Act 1977 s 26(3). Concerning the requirement that the contract is made by parties based in territories of different states, this is a reference to the parties themselves not their agents, see *Ocean Chemical Transport Inc and Another v Exnor Craggs Ltd*.

[191] *Trident Turboprop (Dublin) Ltd v First Flight Couriers Ltd* [2009] EWCA Civ 290 where this was interpreted as being 'directed to any case in which the parties contemplate at the time of entering into the contract that the goods in question will be transported across national boundaries, not necessarily in order to fulfil the terms of the contract, but in order to achieve its commercial object. In my view if a person who carries on business abroad hires equipment from a supplier in this country in circumstances where both know that the intention is for it to be used abroad, the lease is one pursuant to which the goods will be carried from the territory of one state to the territory of another within the meaning of s 26(4)(a) and can sensibly be described as an international supply contract', from para 28.

[192] See *Amiri Flight Authority v BAE Systems Plc* [2003] EWCA Civ 1447, despite the wording in UCTA (which is less then ideally clear), it was held that for delivery to take place there needed to be an international movement of the goods. In this case one party was based in Abu Dhabi and the other in another country; they signed a contract in Abu Dhabi for goods to be manufactured and delivered in England, and consequently there was an international supply contract.

[193] *JP Morgan Chase Bank and Others v Springwell Navigation Corp* [2008] EWHC 1186 (Comm),]2008] All ER (D) 167 (Jun) at para 602. Following *IFE Fund SA v Goldman Sachs International* [2006] All ER (D) 268 (Nov), [2006] EWHC 2887 (Comm).

6.5.22.9   Unfair Terms in Consumer Contracts Regulations 1999[194]

These Regulations[195] were introduced as a UK statutory instrument pursuant to the EC Directive on Unfair Contract Terms[196] There is some overlap with the provisions of UCTA 1977 and some significant differences, in that:[197]

- contract terms which are 'unfair' as defined by the Regulations are void; in contrast, the Act makes terms to which the Act applies subject to the requirement of reasonableness (except for clauses which exclude certain provisions of the Sale of Goods Act or the Sale and Supply of Goods Act);

- the Regulations only apply to contractual terms; the Act applies to both contractual and non-contractual notices (eg excluding liability for non-contractual negligence);

- the Regulations cover a wider range of contract clauses than the Act—the Act is only concerned with clauses which seek to limit or exclude liability and not with unfair terms generally (despite the title of the Act); the Regulations apply to all contractual provisions (eg one-sided termination clauses and other clauses that are unduly favourable to one party)[198];

- the Regulations only apply to contracts with 'consumers' (defined as 'a natural person who, in making a contract to which these Regulations apply, is acting for purposes which are outside his business'); the Act applies to both consumers and business-to-business contracts.

The main requirements of the Unfair Contract Terms in Consumer Contracts Regulations 1999 can briefly be summarised as follows[199].

- *Standard form consumer contracts.* The Regulations apply to terms in contracts with consumers which have not been 'individually negotiated' (ie where the contract has been drafted in advance and the consumer

---

[194] This legislative measure, and its practical implications in drafting consumer contracts, is considered further in Chapter 7.

[195] SI 1999/2083.

[196] Council Directive 93/13/EEC of 5 April 1993.

[197] Except those concerning the definition of the main subject matter of the contract or the price, reg 6(2) of the 1999 Regulations.

[198] A copy of the Regulations appears in Appendix 2.

[199] For the meaning of 'good faith' see *Director General of Fair Trading v First National Bank Plc* [2001] UKHL 52, [2002] 1 AC 481, [2002] 1 All ER 97, where it was held to mean 'fair and open dealing'. Openness requires that the terms of the contract are 'expressed fully, clearly and legibly, containing no concealed pitfalls or traps', and that the terms state predominantly those 'which might operate disadvantageously to the customer'. Fairness concerns the substance of the contract so that the supplier does not deliberately or unconsciously, take advantage of the consumer's necessity, intelligence, lack of experience, unfamiliarity with the subject matter of the contract, or weak bargaining position.'

has not been able to influence the substance of the terms). Even if a specific term has been individually negotiated the Regulations will still apply to the remainder of the contract if the remainder consists of a pre-formulated standard contract.

- *Meaning of unfair terms and good faith.* A contractual term which has not been individually negotiated is to be regarded as unfair if, contrary to the requirement of good faith[200], it 'causes a significant imbalance in the parties' rights and obligations arising under the contract to the detriment of the consumer'. Schedule 2 to the Regulations provides a non-exhaustive list of unfair terms (and terms which exclude or limit liability are included in the list).

- *Unfair terms not binding.* Unfair terms are not binding on the consumer, although this does not apply to terms in 'plain, intelligible language' which concern the 'definition of the main subject matter of the contract' or 'the adequacy of the price or remuneration, as against the goods or services sold or supplied'[201].

- *Requirement to draft terms in plain, intelligible language.* A seller or supplier shall ensure that 'any written term of a contract is expressed in plain, intelligible language', and 'if there is doubt about the meaning of a written term, the interpretation most favourable to the consumer shall prevail'[202].

The Regulations apply even if the contract is made under the law of a country which is not part of the European Union if the contract has 'a close connection with the territory of [the European Union)]'. The Office of Fair Trading ('OFT')[203] has powers to bring proceedings against any person using or recommending unfair terms in contracts with consumers. The Regulations do not apply to contracts concerned with employment, the incorporation and organisation of companies and/or partnerships, and certain other matters[203].

---

[200] These exceptions to the assessment of fairness of a term are likely to be given a restrictive meaning. See *Bairstow Eves London Central Ltd v Smith and Darlingtons (a firm)* [2004] EWHC 263 (QB), [2004] All ER (D) 354 (Feb). In this case a price escalation clause was not protected from scrutiny under the Regulations and that the assessment of fairness of terms not relating to the adequacy of the price or remuneration, as against the goods or services supplied in exchange is to be given a restrictive meaning. The burden of proof of showing a term is unfair is on the consumer (under UCTA 1977, the burden is on the party that is relying on a clause to show that clause is reasonable).

[201] In other words, the *contra proferentem* rule applies.

[202] And certain other organisations (known as 'qualifying bodies') which are specified in Sch 1 to the 1999 Regulations.

[203] These are listed in Council Directive 93/13/EEC (recital 14), but not in the 1999 Regulations.

6.5.22.10 Misrepresentation Act 1967

Section 3 of the Misrepresentation Act 1967 (as substituted by s 8 of UCTA 1977) limits the ability of a person to contract out of liability for misrepresentation. The section reads as follows:

> 'If a contract contains a term which would exclude or restrict
> (a) any liability to which a party to a contract may be subject by reason of any misrepresentation made by him before the contract was made; or
> (b) any remedy available to another party to the contract by reason of such a misrepresentation,
>
> that term shall be of no effect except in so far as it satisfies the requirement of reasonableness as stated in section 11(1) of the Unfair Contract Terms Act 1977; and it is for those claiming that the term satisfies that requirement to show that it does.'

This provision significantly restricts a party's ability to contract out of liability. The test for reasonableness is the same one that is applied under UCTA 1977, in the case of exclusion clauses in standard terms of business[204]. Factors to be taken into account (among others mentioned in that Act) include the relative bargaining power of the parties; whether a contract without such an exclusion clause was available; whether the customer knew of the existence and extent of the exclusion clause; whether the goods were specially made or adapted for the customer; and (in the case of financial limits on liability) the resources available to the party limiting liability and the availability of insurance.

Recent case law has highlighted the difficulties of enforcing exclusion clauses in this area[205], particularly in relation to entire agreement clauses. It seems that clauses which exclude liability for fraudulent representations are unlikely to satisfy the test for reasonableness under s 3[206]. As for the exclusion of liability for pre-contractual misrepresentations the position is less clear. However, in more recent cases, there has been a recognition that the parties to a contract should be able to negotiate and decide the terms of a contract and that the language used in the final agreement fulfils those intentions[207].

---

[204] See summary above.

[205] See *St Albans City and District Council v International Computers Ltd* [1995] FSR 686.

[206] See *Thomas Witter Ltd v TBP Industries* [1996] 2 All ER 573 at 598, where wording in an entire agreement clause did not explicitly exclude fraudulent misrepresentation—the width of the clause was too great, and therefore unreasonable and unenforceable. It also held that the clause did not specifically exclude remedies for pre-contractual misrepresentation (but see footnote 175 below).

[207] See, eg, *National Westminster Bank v Utrecht-America Finance Company* [2001] EWCA Civ 658, [2001] 2 All ER (Comm) 7. In *Watford Electronics v Sanderson CFL Ltd* [2001] EWCA Civ 317, [2001] 2 All ER (Comm) 596, which involved similar wording coming under consideration to that of the *Thomas Witter* case, such wording was sufficient to exclude liability for pre-contract misrepresentation: 'Liability in damages under the Misrepresentation Act 1967 can arise only where the party who has suffered the damage has relied upon the representation. Where both parties to the contract have acknowledged, in the document itself, that they have not relied upon any pre-contract representation, it would be bizarre (unless compelled to do so by the words which they have used) to attribute to them an intention to exclude a liability which they must have thought could never arise', from the judgment of Chadwick, LJ in the *Watford* case.

Parties may now be able to exclude pre-contractual representations without explicitly stating that such liability is being excluded (unlike in the *Thomas Witter* case[208]), this is not the case where a clause attempts to exclude liability for misrepresentation. Clear wording is necessary[209].

Another area of difficulty with entire agreement clauses is whether the provisions of other agreements will be effectively excluded by such clauses. In one case, despite an entire agreement clause existing in one agreement, the judge was able to find after looking at the background that another collateral agreement was not superseded as the parties had proceeded on the basis that it would be honoured[210]. In other cases, judges have taken account of other agreements by construing the other agreements as being part of a package of agreements or that the other agreements where not covered by the specific wording of the entire agreement clause; for example in a case the entire agreement clause read:

> 'Entire Agreement: This Agreement together with its Annexures set forth and shall constitute the entire Agreement between [the parties] with respect to the subject hereof, and shall supersede any and all agreements, understandings, promises and representations made by one party to the other concerning this subject matter herein and the terms and conditions applicable hereto. Also, in case of any inconsistency between the documents constituting the Entire Agreement, this Agreement together with its Annexures would supersede all other documents.'

---

[208]   See footnote 174 above.

[209]   See *BSkyB Ltd v HP Enterprise Services UK Ltd* [2010] EWHC 86 (TCC), [2010] All ER (D) 192 (Jan) where the entire agreement clause read: 'Subject to Clause 1.3.2, this Agreement and the Schedules shall together represent the entire understanding and constitute the whole agreement between the parties in relation to its subject matter and supersede any previous discussions, correspondence, representations or agreement between the parties with respect thereto notwithstanding the existence of any provision of any such prior agreement that any rights or provisions of such prior agreement shall survive its termination. The term "this Agreement" shall be construed accordingly. This clause does not exclude liability of either party for fraudulent mis-representation.' The judge in this case held that there was no wording in this clause which indicated that the parties had agreed, so 'that representations are withdrawn, overridden or of no legal effect so far as any liability for misrepresentation may be concerned. The provision is concerned with the terms of the Agreement. It provides that the Agreement represents the entire understanding and constitutes the whole agreement. It is in that context that the Agreement supersedes any previous representations. That is, representations are superseded and do not become terms of the Agreement unless they are included in the Agreement. If it had intended to withdraw representations for all purposes then the language would, in my judgment, have had to go further' (from para 382 of the judgment). The additional wording necessary to exclude misrepresentations would be contractually binding wording indicating that the parties were not relying on a representation made outside of the contract.

[210]   *Ryanair Ltd v SR Technics Ireland Ltd* [2007] EWHC 3089 (QB), [2007] All ER (D) 345 (Dec), where the judge held that the collateral agreement was not a 'previous … agreement' for the purposes of the entire agreement clause which read: 'This Contract represents the entire agreement of the parties hereto and supersedes all previous negotiations, statements or agreements whether written or oral'.

but another agreement was found to be inconsistent with the above entire agreement clause and therefore not to be 'concerning this subject matter herein'[211].

Faced with these issues the contract drafter might consider it impossible to draft an entire agreement clause which will work so that its primary purpose is achieved[212]. It is suggested that the problem falls into two categories; (1) where there are other agreements and (2) where there are statements/representations. In the first category, the contract drafter has an easier task as these agreements are more likely to be known and, except in a more complex deal, if general wording in the entire agreement clause cannot be agreed then the specific agreements can be listed or at least examined by the contract drafter to determine the effect on the entire agreement clause[213]. Where representations are concerned, the contract drafter has a bigger problem as they may not be aware of what has been said, by whom and when it was said. In this regard the comments of the judge in the *BSkyB Ltd v HP Enterprise Services UK Ltd* [2010] EWHC 86 (TCC), [2010] All ER (D) 192 (Jan) should be considered.

6.5.22.11   Drafting and negotiating issues

The following comments assume that the drafter's objective is to limit or exclude liability to the maximum extent possible[214].

- *Decide whether the statutory controls on limitation and exclusion of liability apply.* For example:

  o UCTA 1977 does not apply to some types of contract (eg contracts of insurance, contracts to the extent that they relate to the creation, transfer or termination of an interest in intellectual property; contracts relating to the formation or dissolution of a company, etc; contracts relating to the creation or transfer of securities or of any right or interest in securities; and contracts relating to the creation,

---

[211] *Satyam Computer Services Ltd v Upaid Systems Ltd* [2008] EWCA Civ 487, [2008] 2 All ER (Comm) 465, paras 55 to 58.

[212] Particularly when the contract drafter is faced with judicial comment about entire agreement clauses such as 'the court should not approach [the entire agreement clause] with the pre-conceived idea that its sole intention is to ensure that the parties cannot subsequently contradict the wording of the agreement by reference to agreements or understandings supposedly arrived at in the course of negotiations (which is undoubtedly normally the main object of such clauses)' from para 55 in *Satyam Computer Services Ltd v Upaid Systems Ltd* [2008] EWCA Civ 487, [2008] 2 All ER (Comm) 465.

[213] Or at least that the parties are asked specifically to consider, negotiate and agree on the status of other agreements in relation to the one they are dealing with at the moment.

[214] None of what follows should be taken as being applicable to contracts with consumers except as explicitly indicated.

transfer or termination of an interest in land (UCTA 1977, s 1(2), Sch 1));

    ○   for consumer transactions, the 1999 Regulations do not apply to contractual provisions which are individually negotiated (reg 5(2)), the main definition of the main subject matter of the contract, nor the adequacy of the price (reg 6(2), employment contracts, etc).

- *Draft explicitly and precisely.* Exemption clauses are not the place to engage in 'constructive ambiguity' (see **6.5.8.1**). It is very important that the language be made clear and unambiguous. Liability clauses deal with technical legal subjects and some legal language (eg references to negligence and breach of statutory duty—see below) may be inevitable, although this should be minimised in consumer contracts in view of the requirement for 'plain, intelligible language' under the 1999 Regulations[215]. If it is intended to exempt liability for what were once called 'fundamental' breaches of contract, this should be stated as explicitly as possible.

- *Mention liability for negligence.* For example, include in the exemption clause words such as:

  > A's liability under or in connection with this Agreement, whether in contract, tort, negligence, breach of statutory duty or otherwise shall be limited to ...

- *Correlate level of liability and insurance.* If the party limits liability to a set sum, consider whether this sum is sufficient in light of the amount of insurance and resources available to that party. It may be difficult to justify a lower level of liability than the limit of a party's insurance, although offering this level of liability may not be commercially attractive, particularly in small value contracts[216].

- *Separate treatment in exclusion/limitation of liability clauses if different things/ services to be provided.* If the agreement is to cover the provision of different things and/or services, consider whether the limitation of liability is suitable for all the things/services being provided. An exclusion/ limitation of liability clause may have been drafted to cover the provision

---

[215] A different approach is required for drafting the wording of exemption clauses in the case of consumer contracts.

[216] In *St Albans City and District Council v International Computers Ltd* [1996] 4 All ER 481, CA, the level of liability was capped at £100,000 by ICL, but their insurance policy was £50 million. There is explicit provision for this in UCTA 1977, s 11(4). Whether insurance is available will not by itself be a determining factor as to the reasonableness of the exclusion clause, and the guidelines found in Sch 2 to UCTA 1977. See, eg, *Overseas Medical Supplies Ltd v Orient Transport Services Ltd* [1999] 2 Lloyd's Rep 273, [1999] 1 All ER (Comm) 981, CA, and *Watford Electronics Ltd v Sanderson CFL Ltd* [2001] EWCA Civ 317; [2001] 1 All ER (Comm) 696; [2001] IP&T 588.

of one type of service, but the agreement may cover other services, for which the clause is not appropriate or suitable[217].

- *Sufficient time to notify a breach.* Are any of the stated time limits in an agreement within which a party is to act or notify in regard to a breach by another party too short?[218]

- *Consider limitations of liability rather than complete exclusions.* The reported cases suggest that limitations of liability are construed less strictly than total exclusions of liability. Moreover, it will generally be easier to satisfy the test of 'reasonableness' under UCTA 1977 (eg ss 2(3) and 3) if liability is limited to a reasonable amount rather than excluded entirely. What is a reasonable amount will be considered by the court on a case-by-case basis, and (in the context of UCTA 1977) will take into account ss 11, 24 (in Scotland) and Sch 2[219] to UCTA 1977[220].

- *Separate treatment of direct and consequential losses.* It is fairly common in contracts to deal separately with so-called 'direct' losses and 'indirect' or 'consequential' losses, and to seek to exclude all liability for the latter types of loss. Whether such an exclusion would normally be regarded as 'reasonable' under UCTA 1977 is not clear. It is also not entirely clear from reported cases where the boundary lies between these different categories of loss, and it is usual to include wording to clarify what is meant by indirect and consequential losses, as in the following example:

> Neither party shall be liable to the other party in contract, tort, negligence, breach of statutory duty or otherwise for any loss, damage, costs or expenses of any nature whatsoever incurred or suffered by that other party (a) of an indirect or consequential nature or (b) which consists of any economic loss or other loss of turnover, profits, business or goodwill.

---

[217] *Overseas Medical Supplies Ltd v Orient Transport Services Ltd* [1999] 2 Lloyd's Rep 273, [1999] 1 All ER (Comm) 981, CA, where it was held that a limitation of liability clause which limited liability for the delivery of items was reasonable for a courier to include, but that those same limitations of liability terms were not appropriate, and therefore unreasonable, where the courier was also to effect insurance.

[218] See *Granville Oil and Chemicals Ltd v Davies Turner and Co Ltd* [2003] EWCA Civ 570; [2003] 1 All ER (Comm) 819.

[219] These provisions may give other opportunities to the party seeking to limit liability, eg if he offers to contract without the exemption clause but at a higher contract price—see UCTA 1977, Sch 2, para (b). Please refer to the specialist texts for a discussion of this and other aspects of limitation of liability, eg *Yates on Exclusion Clauses*.

[220] The authors' personal view is that a limit to the amount of one's insurance cover (assuming that limit is a reasonable one) is the most likely to succeed, although a lower level may be justifiable in the case of some contracts. The drafter should bear in mind that professional liability, eg consultancy advice or the supply of software, may be excluded from public and products liability policies, and will instead by covered under a professional indemnity policy. Not all companies have professional indemnity insurance.

Best practice might suggest that in order to ensure that a total exclusion of liability for consequential or indirect loss is not considered unreasonable, a sum should be set for which liability for direct losses will be met.

- *Be very explicit about the loss that is to be excluded or limited.*

- *Do not attempt to exclude liability for fraud.* In any wording which seeks to exclude some or all liability include wording which states specifically that liability for fraud is not excluded such as:

  Nothing in this agreement excludes liability for a Party's fraud.

- *Offer something positive and exclude implied terms.* A clause which offers some redress for failure to perform the contract may be more likely to be found reasonable by the court than one which merely excludes all liability. A clause which offers a reasonable but limited 'warranty' and seeks to exclude all other liability may provide the best solution for a party seeking a legally enforceable exemption clause. For example, the following clause appears in the Conditions of Sale for machinery equipment (exclusive of erection): United Kingdom, published by BEAMA[221]:

  'DEFECTS AFTER DELIVERY—We will make good, by repair or the supply of a replacement, defects which, under proper use, appear in the goods within a period of twelve calendar months after the goods have been delivered and arise solely from faulty design (other than a design made, furnished or specified by you for which we have disclaimed responsibility in writing), materials or workmanship: provided always that defective parts have been returned to us if we shall have so required. We shall refund the cost of carriage on such returned parts and the repaired or new parts will be delivered by us free of charge as provided in clause 11 (Delivery).

  Our liability under this clause shall be in lieu of any warranty or condition implied by law as to the quality or fitness for any particular purpose of the goods, and save as provided in this clause we shall not be under any liability, whether in contract, tort or otherwise, in respect of defects in goods delivered or for any injury (other than personal injury caused by our negligence as defined in section 1 of the Unfair Contract Terms Act 1977) damage or loss resulting from such defects or from any work done in connection therewith.'

- *Include 'safety valve' wording.* The most obvious example of this is that (in appropriate cases) the clause should state that the exemption of liability

---

[221] The Federation of British Electrotechnical and Allied Manufacturers' Associations. The Conditions are reproduced with their permission in 34 *Forms and Precedents*, Sale of Goods (5th Edn) [747]. The authors are grateful to Dan Graham, who was involved in drafting the Conditions, for his guidance in contract drafting in past years, when he and one of the authors were at the same firm.

does not apply to death or personal injury caused by negligence[222]. It may also be useful to include in the clause a more general statement that the exemption does not apply where liability may not be excluded or limited under applicable law. For example, consider adding wording to the exclusion clause to read:

> Except to the extent that liability may not be so excluded under applicable law ...

- *Third party indemnities.* Indemnity clauses are sometimes drafted very broadly, and it is not always clearly stated that they apply only to third-party losses, and not losses suffered by the other party to the contract. It may improve the chances of such a clause being upheld if this is made clear. Generally, bear in mind that indemnity clauses may be caught by s 4 of UCTA 1977, and are interpreted by the courts in a similar way to exemption clauses. In some cases it may be appropriate to state that the limits of liability set out in other clauses do not apply to the indemnity clauses.

- *Do not contract on 'standard' terms.* The restrictions set out in s 3(1) of UCTA 1977 apply to consumer contracts and 'where one of [the contracting parties] deals ... on the other's written standard terms of business'. If it can be established that the wording of the exemption clause was specifically negotiated, s 3(1) will not apply[223]. However, there does not seem to be clear authority on this point, and UCTA 1977 appears to make no such requirement.

  However, the meaning of 'written standard terms of business' is not defined or explained in the Act, and it has been held that even though some terms may have been negotiated and agreed in an agreement, a contract may still be regarded as on written standard terms[224].

  It appears that it will be a matter of fact and degree as to whether the terms agreed were standard terms of the party putting them forward[225] although it may be that if the exclusion or limitation of liability clause

---

[222] See UCTA 1977, s 2.

[223] *Fillite (Runcorn) Ltd v APV Pasilac Ltd, The Buyer* July 1995.

[224] *St Albans City and District Council v International Computers Ltd* [1996] 4 All ER 481, CA, both at first instance and at appeal. Consider also the definition provided in *McCrone v Boots Farm Sales Ltd* 1981 SLT 103: 'A "standard form contract" cannot be confined to written contracts in which both parties use standard forms. It is wide enough to include any contract, whether wholly written or partly oral, which includes a set of fixed terms or conditions which the proponer applies, without material variation, to contracts of the kind in question.' This definition was adopted in *Salvage Association v CAP Financial Services Ltd* [1995] FSR 654.

[225] *Salvage Association v CAP Financial Services Ltd* [1995] FSR 654 at 674.

is not amended, then the agreement may be considered to be standard. In another case[226], although a case not directly about the use of standard terms, the fact that standard terms were used was not a deciding fact in whether the exclusion and limitation of liability clauses were held to be unreasonable.

From another case[227], some guidelines were laid down as to whether terms provided by one party are to be considered as standard terms:

○ the degree to which the 'standard terms' are considered by the other party as part of the process of agreeing the terms of the contract;

○ the degree to which the 'standard terms' are imposed on the other party by the party putting them forward;

○ the relative bargaining power of the parties;

○ the degree to which the party putting forward the 'standard terms' is prepared to entertain negotiations with regard to the terms of the contract generally and the standard terms' in particular;

○ the extent and nature of any agreed alterations to the 'standard terms' made as a result of the negotiations between the parties; and

○ the extent and duration of the negotiations.

• *Be aware that the exemption clause may be held to be invalid despite the most careful of drafting.* This is particularly true in the case of contracts with consumers, in light of the 1999 Regulations, but is also true in relation to contracts between commercial parties. The most the drafter can do is make an educated guess as to the limits in amount and types of liability the court will find acceptable and try to draft clear language to reflect these limits. At a minimum where specific terms and conditions are not drafted for a consumer contract the following should be included in a contract with a consumer:

---

[226] *Watford Electronics Ltd v Sanderson CFL Ltd* [2001] EWCA Civ 317, [2001] 1 All ER (Comm) 696. This case marks a step back from the approach found in *St Albans City and District Council v International Computers Ltd* (see above), and in particular *South West Water Services Ltd v International Computers Ltd* [1999] BLR 420. In the *Watford Electronics* case the court, in effect, appears to be stating that parties, which are equal, should be allowed to decide the terms for themselves. In the *South West Water case*, the fact that the concluded contract contained terms from each party's standard contracts, and that there had been extensive negotiations on terms and some changes to the limitations clauses (from an ICL contract and including South West Water, it appears, putting its own terms forward for exclusion and limitation of liability clauses), did not save ICL from the finding that they had used standard terms.

[227] Laid down by the Official Referee in *Overseas Medical Supplies Ltd v Orient Transport Services Ltd* 1999 2 Lloyd's Rep 273, [1999] 1 All ER (Comm) 981, CA

1. Any provision in this Agreement which seeks to or does exclude liability of the Supplier for breach of the terms implied by the [Sale of Goods Act 1979]

[Supply of Goods and Services Act 1982] shall not apply where the Customer is a consumer.

2. Any provision in this Agreement where delivery is stated to be made by delivery to a courier shall not apply to a Customer who is a consumer.

Chapter 7

Drafting Consumer Contracts

Key points

The main topics covered in this chapter are:

- an introduction to the Unfair Terms in Consumer Contracts Regulations (the Regulations);

- a checklist of when the Regulations do not apply to a provision or the whole of a consumer contract;

- a checklist of basic factors to consider when preparing terms and conditions;

- a checklist of other relevant legislation when drafting consumer contracts;

- an outline comparison between the Regulations and the Unfair Terms in Contracts Act 1977 (UCTA), as the latter overlaps in some places with the Regulations;

- general points about the applicability of the Regulations;

- key issues in the Regulations, including:

  - what is a consumer;

  - whether contracts are individually negotiated;

  - assessing fairness;

  - use of plain, intelligible language;

- words that should not appear in a consumer contract.

7.1   Introduction

This chapter concentrates on issues which are particular to contracts between a business and a consumer and which are distinct from the general run of commercial contracts.

Most legislation governing commercial transactions does not specify or control the content of a contract[1]. However, the Regulations do so in certain areas.

---

[1]   For example, the Consumer Protection (Distance Selling) Regulations 2000, Electronic Commerce (EC Directive) Regulations 2002 or the Provision of Services Regulations 2009 do not require contractual wording to deal with the issues they raise.

The Regulations specify the type of language a contract drafter should use and also require that a contract term must not create a significant imbalance in the rights and obligations between the parties (ie that it should be fair).

Consequently, it is necessary to use a different approach for the drafting of consumer contracts compared to the approach used for contracts between commercial parties. This difference goes beyond a mere choice of the words used. Although consumer contracts need to be expressed in plain intelligible language, this requirement in itself is not enough to distinguish it from agreements made between commercial parties, as the latter are nowadays often expressed in plain and simple language. The key distinguishing factor is perhaps the requirement on the trader to use good faith towards a consumer, so that the consumer knows the terms and conditions on which they are contracting and understands the significance and consequence of these terms and conditions before entering into the contract[2]. This is perhaps best summed up in the following passage from one of the leading cases concerning the Regulations:

> 'The requirement of good faith ... is one of fair and open dealing. Openness requires that the terms should be expressed fully, clearly and legibly, containing no concealed pitfalls or traps. Appropriate prominence should be given to terms which might operate disadvantageously to the customer. Fair dealing requires that a supplier should not, whether deliberately or unconsciously, take advantage of the consumer's necessity, indigence, lack of experience, unfamiliarity with the subject matter of the contract, weak bargaining position or any other factor listed in or analogous to those listed in Schedule 2 of the regulations. Good faith in this context is not an artificial or technical concept .... It looks to good standards of commercial morality and practice[3].'

Since the first edition of this book, it is noticeable that many suppliers of goods and services to consumers have simplified their terms and conditions, not only in the wording they use but also in how they often do not seek to finesse or interpret (or restrict) the law providing rights to consumers.

Creating a 'fair' contract does not mean that the contract has to treat the parties equally. It is still possible to create a one-sided contract in favour of the supplier. However, such a contract should not create a significant imbalance between the rights and obligations of the parties[4].

---

[2]   Or at least have a real opportunity to do so.

[3]   From the speech of Lord Bingham in *Director General of Fair Trading v First National Bank Plc* [2001] UKHL 52, [2002] 1 AC 481, [2002] 1 All ER 97.

[4]   For example, most traders on the internet selling standard goods control (at their discretion) the moment the contract comes into existence and also do not commit themselves to any firm delivery date or time. Many traders 'balance' these provisions with the consumer not needing to pay until the trader is ready to make a binding contract and if there is no delivery within a reasonable period then the consumer can cancel the contract and get their money back.

7.2   The Regulations—an introduction

It is possible briefly to summarise the Regulations as follows.

- *Standard form consumer contracts.* The Regulations apply to terms in contracts with consumers which have not been 'individually negotiated' (ie where the contract has been drafted in advance and the consumer has not been able to influence the substance of the terms). Even if a specific term is individually negotiated, the Regulations will still apply to the remainder of the contract if the remainder consists of a pre-formulated standard contract.

- *Meaning of unfair terms and good faith.* A contractual term which is not individually negotiated is unfair if, contrary to the requirement of good faith[5], it 'causes a significant imbalance in the parties' rights and obligations arising under the contract to the detriment of the consumer'. Schedule 2 to the Regulations provides a non-exhaustive list of unfair terms (terms which exclude or limit liability are included in the list).

- *Unfair terms not binding.* Unfair terms are not binding on the consumer; although this does not apply to terms concerning the 'definition of the main subject matter of the contract' or 'the adequacy of the price or remuneration, as against the goods or services sold or supplied' as long as these are in plain, intelligible language[6].

- *Requirement to draft terms in plain, intelligible language.* A seller or supplier shall ensure that 'any written term of a contract is expressed in plain, intelligible language', and 'if there is doubt about the meaning of a written term, the interpretation most favourable to the consumer shall prevail'[7].

The Regulations apply even if the contract is made under the law of a country which is not part of the European Union if the contract has 'a close connection with the territory of [the European Union)]'. The Office of Fair Trading (OFT) has the power to bring proceedings against any person using or recommending unfair terms in contracts with consumers[8]. The Regulations do not apply to contracts concerned with employment, the incorporation and organisation of companies and/or partnerships, and certain other matters.

---

[5] For the meaning of 'good faith' see *Director General of Fair Trading v First National Bank Plc* [2001] UKHL 52, [2002] 1 AC 481, [2002] 1 All ER 97.

[6] See **7.5.3** below for consideration of this.

[7] In other words, the *contra proferentem* rule applies.

[8] And certain other organisations (known as 'qualifying bodies') which are specified in Sch 1 to the 1999 Regulations.

7.2.1   Checklist—when the Regulations do not apply

The Regulations will not apply at all in the following situations or will not apply to an individual provision in a contract with a consumer, if:

Will not apply at all

- a trader enters into a contract other than with an individual;

- the contract is between businesses;

- the consumer is entering into the contract primarily for a business purpose;

- the contract is between individuals who are not entering into a contract for the purposes of trade or business;

- the contract deals with an excluded subject matter relating to employment, contracts relating to succession rights, contracts relating to rights under family law and contracts relating to the incorporation and organisation of companies or partnership agreements[9]

Will not apply in relation to a specific contract term

- one or more provisions are individually negotiated (or the consumer has had a genuine chance to influence the substance of the provisions);

- one or more provisions deal with core provisions of the contract; those relating to the definition of the main subject matter of the contract, or to the adequacy of the price or remuneration, as against the goods or services supplied in exchange;

- one or more provisions reflect mandatory statutory or regulatory provisions or the principles of an international treaty.

7.2.2   Checklist—basic factors to consider when preparing terms and conditions

- Will the consumer have a genuine chance to consider the provisions of the contract before they enter into it (in particular not 'hiding' or failing to bring to the attention of the consumer significant, onerous or core provisions from the consumer)?

---

[9]   These topics are not mentioned in the current version of the Regulations, but are listed in the underlying EU Directive: Council Directive 93/13/EEC of 5 April 1993 on unfair terms in consumer contracts, recital 11.

- Will the contract drafter consider the guidance available from the OFT, such as:

  ○ the *Unfair contract terms guidance* (and its appendix)[10];

  ○ for particular industries and trades, including the guidance on unfair terms in tenancy agreements, health and fitness club agreements, consumer entertainment contracts, IT consumer contracts made at a distance, etc[11]?

- *Presentation:* If printed onto to paper, are the provisions:

  ○ printed legibly;

  ○ not printed in too small a type;

  ○ not printed in fancy colours or too faintly or onto highly coloured paper?[12]

- *Basic steps for writing the contract in 'plain intelligible language':* Has the contract drafter written the contract with the following points at the forefront of their mind:

  ○ Is the contract written in short sentences?

  ○ Are there plenty of short paragraphs and is there extensive use of meaningful sub-headings?

  ○ Does the contract avoid the use of 'legal' words?[13]

  ○ Does the drafting avoid:

    - double negatives;

    - references to statutory material (unless required to do so);

    - detailed definitions;

    - extensive use of cross-referencing?

---

[10]   OFT311, available from http://www.oft.gov.uk/OFTwork/publications/publication-categories/guidance/unfair-terms-consumer/. The OFT update this guidance from time to time. In the opinion of the authors, it is not too much to write that these documents should always be to hand when drafting a consumer contract. They provide detailed guidance as to the practical scope of the Regulations as well as wording which the OFT find unacceptable and their redrafted replacements.

[11]   Also available from http://www.oft.gov.uk/OFTwork/publications/publication-categories/guidance/unfair-terms-consumer/

[12]   The point here is what is printed onto paper. The OFT guidance does not speak about terms and conditions appearing on websites. In the latter case, the wording is often displayed in sometimes very small type. Here, there is an easy technical solution within the reach of the consumer: it is easy to increase the size of text and graphics use the feature built into most modern web browsers (Pressing the Control key and the '+' key).

[13]   See the list at **7.6** below.

- ○   Is there use of 'you' and 'we' when referring to the consumer and the trader?

- ○   For provisions where the consequences are not clear or the meaning may not be obvious to the consumer, has the contract drafter explained the consequences or provided a meaning?[14]

- *Basic commercial issues in preparing contract terms:*

  - ○   *Does the contract term meet the conditions to be assessed as 'unfair'?* has the contract drafter considered each of the elements under the Regulations which make up the definition of an unfair contract term:

    - Will the contract term be individually negotiated? If so, it will not be subject to assessment[15].

    - Is it contrary to good faith?[16]

    - If it is contrary to good faith, does the contract term create a significant imbalance in the parties' rights and obligations arising under the contract?[17] and

---

[14]   This calls for judgment as it is possible for any provision in a contract to require further explanation. However clauses that limit liability or relate to damage caused by a consumer may need particular attention. For example, a trader may hire equipment and wish to indicate that the consumer is responsible for damage caused due to the fault of the consumer. Rather than a bald statement to that effect, the limits or consequences of which may be unclear to the consumer, wording could approach this point in one of two ways such as: 'You shall be responsible for any loss or damage to the equipment if you (a) fail to operate the equipment in accordance with the instruction manual; (b) do not take reasonable care of the equipment while in your possession; or (c) deliberately damage the equipment etc', or 'You shall be responsible for any loss or damage to the equipment except for any loss or damage which (i) we (or our employees) have caused; (ii) is due to a manufacturing design or design fault, or (iii) results from fair wear and tear'.

[15]   See the comments below on the meaning of 'individually negotiated'.

[16]   As set out in *Director General of Fair Trading v First National Bank Plc* [2001] UKHL 52, in the speech of Lord Bingham at paragraph 17. There is an extract at the beginning of this chapter.

[17]   For the meaning of 'significant imbalance' see the following passage from the speech of Lord Bingham in *Director General of Fair Trading v First National Bank Plc* [2001] UKHL 52: 'The requirement of significant imbalance is met if a term is so weighted in favour of the supplier as to tilt the parties' rights and obligations under the contract significantly in his favour. This may be by the granting to the supplier of a beneficial option or discretion or power, or by the imposing on the consumer of a disadvantageous burden or risk or duty. The illustrative terms set out in Schedule [2] to the regulations provide very good examples of terms which may be regarded as unfair; whether a given term is or is not to be so regarded depends on whether it causes a significant imbalance in the parties' rights and obligations under the contract. This involves looking at the contract as a whole. But the imbalance must be to the detriment of the consumer; a significant imbalance to the detriment of the supplier, assumed to be the stronger party, is not a mischief which the regulations seek to address'.

- Does the contract term cause a detriment to the consumer?[18]

- Has the list of terms set out in Schedule 2 to the Regulations been consulted?[19]

  o *Does the contract contain any terms set out in Schedule 2 to the Regulations?* If there are provisions in a contract on the terms as set out in Schedule 2, they will always be unfair unless they are subject to qualifications or restrictions.

  o *For core terms, has the contract drafter used plain intelligible language to avoid assessment for fairness?* If these are not expressed in plain intelligible language then they will be subject to assessment as to whether they are fair[20].

  o *Has the contract drafter considered the factors for assessing the fairness of a contract term which is subject to such assessment?* If the contract drafter wishes to write a contract term which may be potentially unfair, have they considered the factors for assessing fairness in the Regulations being that:

    - the nature of the goods and services for which the contract was concluded are taken into account;

    - reference has been made, at the time of conclusion of the contract;

      o to all the circumstances attending the conclusion of the contract;

      o to all the other circumstances of the contract (or another contract) on which a contract term is dependant[21].

---

[18] Unfair Terms in Consumer Contracts Regulations 1999, reg 5(1). In *Director General of Fair Trading v First National Bank Plc* [2001] UKHL 52 the court discussed some of the facts to consider when deciding whether a contract is unfair: 'It is obviously useful to assess the impact of an impugned term on the parties' rights and obligations by comparing the effect of the contract with the term and the effect it would have without it. But the inquiry cannot stop there. It may also be necessary to consider the effect of the inclusion of the term on the substance or core of the transaction; whether if it were drawn to his attention the consumer would be likely to be surprised by it; whether the term is a standard term, not merely in similar non-negotiable consumer contracts, but in commercial contracts freely negotiated between parties acting on level terms and at arm's length; and whether, in such cases, the party adversely affected by the inclusion of the term or his lawyer might reasonably be expected to object to its inclusion and press for its deletion. The list is not necessarily exhaustive; other approaches may sometimes be more appropriate' (at para 57).

[19] Because of its importance, Schedule 2 is set out at the end of this chapter. Also for each term the contract drafter should consider the *Unfair contract terms guidance* and its annexes.

[20] Unfair Terms in Consumer Contracts Regulations, reg 5(2). This provision appears to make it clear that a clause which is unfair to a consumer (and which, by itself, might be non-binding on a consumer) cannot be looked at alone; it needs to be set in the context of the purpose of the contract.

[21] Unfair Terms in Consumer Contracts Regulations reg 6(1).

This appears to permit a term which is unfair to lose its 'unfairness' if other parts of the contract (or another contract) give rights or alleviate the unfairness of the unfair term[22].

○   *Does the contract attempt to exclude or limit liability for specific provisions which cannot be excluded or limited?* Although it may seem an obvious statement, traditional methods of limiting or excluding of liability are unlikely to work. For example, adding wording to limit the liability of a business for its breach of the implied term of satisfactory quality would be counterproductive (ie stating that the goods are satisfactory but then limiting the business's liability for a breach or limiting the liability to a sum of money, or excluding any warranties or liability (ie that the business/trader is not liable for damage which is its own fault)).

However, there is nothing to stop a supplier defining what 'satisfactory quality' means in relation to particular goods that are being sold or stating that they will not be liable for any damage etc caused by the consumer.

○   *Use the wording of the statutory provisions to indicate clearly matters affecting the goods (or services) being provided.* For example, Sale of Goods Act 1979, s 14(2A) and (2B) state the factors determining satisfactory quality as:

● description;

● price;

● fitness for all the purposes of which goods of the kind in question are commonly supplied;

● freedom from minor defects;

● safety;

● durability;

● public statements on the specific characteristics of the goods made by the seller, producer or his representative (particularly in advertising or on labelling).

---

[22]   For example, a consumer joins a club, and is required to pay a membership fee in advance. A term which states that the fee is non-refundable in any circumstances is likely to be unfair in all circumstances. However, if the contract contains other provisions which state that membership entitles a member to a certain number of hours of use of the club, or if where the particular services the club offers are withdrawn, the member would be entitled to the use of the same type of services of another club, this might be enough to prevent the offending term from being unfair.

○   *State clearly the 'strengths', 'weaknesses', 'limitations', and the requirements on a consumer of a product or service.* Providing a more descriptive meaning of the product or service can help to reduce or avoid liability[23].

7.3   Checklist of other relevant legislation when drafting consumer contracts

The following are additional points, which specifically apply to consumers and will generally form the background to any contract terms in a consumer contract:

- In favour of the consumer, a business cannot contract out of its liability concerning the implied terms of quality and fitness for purpose if there is a sale by sample or a sale by description under the Sale of Goods Act 1979[24].

- A consumer has the right to repair, replacement and reduction in price where goods do not conform with a contract of sale[25].

- There is a different meaning of 'delivery' under the Sale of Goods Act 1979[26] for a consumer than for a business. A consumer is to have a reasonable opportunity to examine goods which are delivered to them[27].

---

[23] For example, where a supplier is selling a computer monitor they could add wording such as:

'We shall supply to you the goods that you have ordered. You should note that certain types of monitors occasionally suffer from minor errors in the manufacturing process. In particular LCD monitors have one or two pixels which incorrectly appear ("pixel errors"). Such pixel errors are in accordance with industry standards for the manufacture of LCD monitors.

Monitors must be set up correctly using the instructions provided. In particular setting up a monitor with the wrong display resolution is likely to damage the monitor. Monitors must be cleaned only as described in the instructions provided. A monitor, because it contains electric and electronic parts, should never be cleaned with water or other liquids. Also, the use of abrasive cleaners or rough clothes is likely to damage the monitor's casing or display.

Also our website contains further information concerning the monitors which you should read; (www.xxxxyyyy.co.uk)

We will not take responsibility for damage to the goods you have ordered where you do not set up or use the goods in accordance with the instructions manuals provided or statements or information which is provided with the monitor.'

[24] Sale of Goods Act 1979 ss 13, 14 and 15; Unfair Contract Terms Act 1977 s 6. **See 6.5.21.1.**

[25] Sale of Goods Act 1979, ss 48A–4E and Supply of Goods and Services Act 1982, ss 11A–11R. These are additional rights to those found in the Sale of Goods Act 1979 (ss 13, 14 and 15) and the equivalent provisions of the Sale and Supply of Goods Act 1982. There is a presumption that during the period of six months following delivery, goods which do not conform to the contract of sale are taken not to have conformed with the contract of sale on delivery.

[26] Sale of Goods Act 1979, s 32(4).

[27] Sale of Goods Act 1979, s 35.

- Where a guarantee is offered, it is likely to have contractual effect[28].

- For contracts concluded through distance communications (email, internet, facsimiles, etc) the consumer has the right to cancel the contract within a limited period of time, and has the right to receive certain information[29].

- A business/trader must clearly state the price of goods[30].

- Where a contract is made during a visit by a trader to the consumer's home or place of work or during a visit made to some place other than the trader's business (and which is organised by the trader), then the consumer has a right to a cooling-off period and to cancel the contract[31].

- A trader cannot trade unfairly or engage in certain misleading and aggressive practices[32].

7.4   Some key differences between UCTA and the Regulations

Both UCTA and the Regulations cover similar points but there are also some key differences[33]. Below are key issues which often need consideration when drafting contracts where a consumer is a party:

7.4.1   Meaning of 'consumer'

UCTA

A person is a consumer where he or she does not make the contract in the course of business, or hold him- or herself out as doing so, and the other party makes the contract in the course of business and the goods are of a

---

[28] See Sale and Supply of Goods to Consumers Regulations 2002, SI 2002/3045, reg 15. This is in addition to the guarantee provisions in UCTA 1977, s 5.

[29] Consumer Protection (Distance Selling) Regulations 2000, SI 2000/2334. It is not possible to contract out of the requirements of these Regulations, reg 25.

[30] Price Marking Order 2004, SI 2004/102 and Consumer Protection (Distance Selling) Regulations 2000, SI 2000/2334, reg 7(1). The Price Marking Order does not apply to goods supplied in the course of a service, see reg 3(1)(a).

[31] Cancellation of Contracts Made in a Consumer's Home or Place of Work etc, Regulations 2008 (SI 2008/1816).

[32] Consumer Protection from Unfair Trading Regulations 2008 (SI 2008/1277).

[33] The Law Commission has suggested that these two measures are replaced by one to remove the differences (see Unfair Terms in Contract, Report 292, 2005). See also paras 2.5 and 2.6 as to the Commission's list of differences between the two measures.

type ordinarily supplied for private use or consumption[34]. The courts have held that the definition of consumer in UCTA can include a business (even a limited company) for the purposes of UCTA, s 6[35].

The Regulations

A consumer is a natural person who is acting for purposes outside their trade, business or profession (ie a company cannot be a consumer for the purposes of the Regulations).

7.4.2   Scope

UCTA

UCTA only covers some provisions of a contract (other than tort)—mainly those concerning the limitation and exclusion of liability (and indemnity clauses in consumer contracts).

The Regulations:

The Regulations can cover all provisions of a contract, except for those that deal with the definition of the main subject matter of the contract or the price (but only so long as they are drafted in plain intelligible English), or which are individually negotiated.

7.4.3   Contract terms

UCTA

UCTA can cover both contractual terms and non-contractual notices[36].

The Regulations

The Regulations only apply to unfair terms in contracts between a trader and a consumer[37].

---

[34]   Unfair Contract Terms Act 1977, s 12.

[35]   *R & B Customs Brokers Ltd v United Dimensions Trust Ltd (Sanders Abbott (1980) Ltd, third party)* [1988] 1 All ER 847. Section 6 deals with the sections from the Sale of Goods Act 1979 which cannot be excluded or restricted at all or in specified circumstances.

[36]   Unfair Contract Terms Act 1977, s 2. Any contract term or notice cannot restrict or exclude liability for personal injury or death. For other types of loss or damage, a notice restricting or excluding liability for negligence needs to satisfy the requirement for reasonableness.

[37]   Unfair Terms in Consumer Contracts Regulations, reg 4(1).

7.4.4   Areas of law

UCTA

UCTA excludes contracts of insurance, contracts so far as they relate to the creation or transfer of interests in land, some types of auction and contracts for the sale of goods where the buyer and seller are based in different countries and some other conditions are fulfilled[38].

The Regulations

The Regulations contain none of these restrictions.

7.4.5   Goods and services

UCTA and The Regulations

Both UCTA and the Regulations cover goods and services.

7.4.6   Type of provisions caught

UCTA

UCTA applies to both standard form contracts and those which are individually negotiated.

The Regulations

The Regulations only apply to terms which are not individually negotiated or which are core terms. A core term is one which is drafted in plain, intelligible language and covers the definition of the main subject matter of the contract or the adequacy of the price or remuneration and is not assessed for fairness.

7.4.7   Language

UCTA

No requirements regarding drafting style.

---

[38]   Unfair Contract Terms Act 1977, ss 12(2), 26 and Sch 1(1).

The Regulations

There is a requirement to use plain, intelligible language in written contracts. If there is any doubt as to the meaning, the meaning most favourable to the consumer will be used.

7.4.8   Burden

UCTA

There is a burden on the party relying on a clause to show it is reasonable.

The Regulations

There is a burden on the consumer to show that a clause is unfair.

7.4.9   Effect

UCTA

UCTA makes contractual provisions:

- ineffective if they concern a sale by description or sample or those which are implied concerning (satisfactory) quality or fitness (for a purpose) (ie they cannot be excluded or restricted by reference to a contract term)[39];

- relating to the exclusion and limitation of liability subject to a requirement of reasonableness (ie where a business in breach attempts to render a contractual performance different from that which is reasonably expected of the business or renders no performance at all)[40];

- which concern an indemnity subject to the requirement of reasonableness[41].

The Regulations

All provisions will survive as long as they are fair (unless they are individually negotiated or are core terms)[42].

---

[39]   Unfair Contract Terms Act 1977, ss 6(2), 7(2).

[40]   Unfair Contract Terms Act 1977, s 3.

[41]   Unfair Contract Terms Act 1977, s 4.

[42]   Here the Regulations can offer 'less' protection to a consumer than under the Unfair Contract Terms Act 1977. Under the Regulations, a clause in a consumer contract which restricts in some way the implied term as to quality or fitness of goods could come in for assessment as to whether it is fair, although it would be ineffective under UCTA. In the event of a dispute reaching court, it would depend on how a consumer framed their action as to whether such a clause would bind the consumer.

7.5   General points about the applicability of the Regulations (not otherwise dealt with in this chapter)

The following are some general points about the application of the Regulations:

- the supplier of goods or services needs to be acting for the purposes of its trade, business or profession;

- the supplier can be a natural or a legal person;

- public authorities, state organisations etc come within the meaning of a 'supplier' for the purposes of the Regulations, even where they are exercising a public function[43];

- a consumer must be a natural person;

- the Regulations apply to oral and written contracts[44];

- the Regulations apply to the provision of goods and services. Such provision is given a wide meaning, and would include contracts relating to land, leases, etc and financial services[45].

7.5.1   Who is a consumer?

A consumer for the Regulations:

- is a natural person; and

- is acting outside the consumer's trade, business or profession (if applicable)[46].

This meaning of a consumer will exclude any type of organisation or company[47]. The second part of the meaning is the requirement to act outside

---

[43]   *Khatun v London Borough of Newham* [2004] EWCA Civ 55. The local authority was fulfilling a (public, statutory) duty to house the homeless under the Housing Act 2006 and in doing so granted tenancies. The Regulations applied to the provisions of the tenancies.

[44]   The Regulations do not themselves state whether they apply to oral contracts, but the directive underlying the Regulations does so at recital 11.

[45]   See *Khatun v London Borough of Newham* [2004] EWCA Civ 55 for how the court interpreted the meaning of goods and services to include the granting of leases. The decision of *Barclays Bank Plc v Alfons Kufner* [1998] WLR 1035 is an illustration that the Regulations also apply to financial services and instruments (ie that the Regulations can apply to a guarantee, so long as the guarantor and principal debtor did so as natural persons and were not acting in the course of their trade or profession).

[46]   Unfair Contract Terms in Consumer Contracts Regulations 1999, reg 3(1).

[47]   Contrast the position with Unfair Contract Terms Act 1977, s 12. Where a business (of whatever type) can receive protection as a consumer for the purposes of 1977 Act if it is not acting in the course of its business. See *R&B Customs Brokers Co Ltd v United Dominions Trust Ltd* [1988] 1 All ER 847.

the consumer's trade, business or profession. The key test appears to be whether the consumer has the intention of furthering their business, trade or profession. If the consumer has another intention which incidentally furthers the consumer's business, this will not take the consumer outside the protection of the Regulations[48]. For example, if a business person working from home needs to buy a new boiler to heat their home, which is mostly used by the consumer's family but also heats a small part where the business is run from, this is likely to come with the protection of the Regulations.

7.5.2   Is the contract or some or all of its provisions individually negotiated?

The Regulations do not apply to any provision of a contract which is individually negotiated[49]. If provisions are individually negotiated, they cannot come in for assessment as being unfair under the Regulations. Contractual terms not individually negotiated will be unfair but only:

- if contrary to the requirement of good faith;

- if they cause a significant imbalance in the parties' rights and obligations under the contract to the detriment of the consumer[50].

It is for the trader to show that a contract or contract provision is individually negotiated[51].

A contract provision will not be individually negotiated where a trader provides it in advance *and* the consumer is unable to influence the substance of the provision. The Regulations do not indicate the amount of effort that a consumer needs to demonstrate in order to show that a contract provision

---

[48] *Heifer International Inc v Christiansen and Others* [2007] EWHC 3015 (TCC). In this case the consumers, through a company, purchased a house for renovation by architects. The judge found that the house was not purchased as an investment opportunity, but for the consumers to live in. In this case, a company was able to benefit from the provisions of the 1999 Regulations because of the Arbitration Act 1996, s 90 which specifically extends the 1999 Regulations to non-natural persons where the Arbitration Act 1996 is engaged. In other cases, a person who buys a property (or more than one property) as an investment has been able to come within the Regulations as long as the purpose of buying the property is not for the person's business. For example, a lawyer who buys a series of houses to fund their pension plan and then lets the houses to fund the mortgages would not likely be seen as a professional developer, a commercial landlord or having a business in making investments, see *Office of Fair Trading v Foxtons Ltd* [2009] EWHC 1681 (Ch).

[49] Unfair Terms in Consumer Contracts Regulations 2009, reg 5(1).

[50] Unfair Terms in Consumer Contracts Regulations, reg 5(1). In *Director General of Fair Trading v First National Bank Plc* [2001] UKHL 52, at para 36 these three elements were considered independent elements. The likely implication is that a clause which only satisfies one of these elements might still be fair. However, from the same paragraph, the judge believed that '[t]he twin requirements of good faith and significant imbalance will in practice be determinative'.

[51] Unfair Terms in Consumer Contracts Regulations 2009, reg 5(3).

has been individually negotiated or whether a contract provision has been expressed differently to what the trader originally proposed. For example, a trader may have a standard set of terms but is still willing to negotiate its wording or change it substantially. If the consumer fails to make any changes, this situation may be different from the situation where the trader merely offers to provide the provisions to the consumer for review but is unwilling to make any changes requested by the consumer[52].

If one provision is individually negotiated (or parts of that provision), the Regulations will apply to the rest of the contract as long as the rest is a 'pre-formulated standard contract'[53].

It is perhaps worth highlighting that simply because a clause is not individually negotiated does not mean it is unfair; the purpose of the Regulations is to deal with unfair provisions, not to deal with fair provisions which happen not to be individually negotiated[54].

7.5.3   Core terms

There cannot be any assessment of the fairness of a contract term which relates:

- 'to the definition of the main subject matter of the contract; or

- to the adequacy of the price or remuneration, as against the goods or services supplied in exchange'[55].

The aim is to exclude from evaluation the 'bargain' that is made between the parties, ie the exchange of a good or service for a payment (whatever the goods and services are or the amount that the consumer will pay). For example, the aim of the Regulations is not to control the price the consumer pays (ie that the consumer has to pay a 'fair' price), but rather to ensure that all the provisions of the contract concerning price are brought sufficiently to the attention of the consumer. If the consumer pays too much for a good or service but is fully aware of the amount they are paying and the terms and conditions on which they are contracting then the Regulations will not protect the consumer from making a bad bargain.

---

[52] See *Bryen & Langely Ltd v Boston* [2004] EWHC 2450 (TCC) and in the Court of Appeal, [2005] EWCA Civ 973. Although the Court of Appeal did not come to a decision on this point, the issue of having the chance of influencing a specific provision but not taking that opportunity may take that provision outside the protection of the Regulations, subject to all the circumstances.

[53] Unfair Terms in Consumer Contracts Regulations 2009, reg 5(3).

[54] See comments of the Court of Appeal in *Bryen & Langley Ltd v Boston* [2005] at para 44.

[55] Unfair Contract Terms in Consumer Contracts Regulations 1999, reg 6(2).

The core terms cannot be assessed as to whether they are fair if they are expressed in plain, intelligible language. The converse is that a court can assess these points for fairness if they are not expressed in plain intelligible language.

As far as the Office of Fair Trading is concerned, the positioning in a contract of a provision drafted in plain intelligible language may influence whether or not the provision will be actually considered as a core provision[56]. Naturally this is only the view of the OFT; and the courts have not passed judgment on whether this is a tenable proposition.

The meaning of what is a 'core' provision under the Regulations has come under considerable scrutiny by the courts. The issue is what in a particular contract qualifies as the main subject matter and the price or remuneration in exchange for the goods and services supplied? This is likely to be a question of fact in each case. With regard to price or remuneration, the leading case on this point[57] held that the charges a bank can make for the services it offers, regardless of whether they are used frequently or at all by a customer (but are at all times available to the customer), come within the definition of 'price or remuneration'[58].

The courts have clearly recognised that a trader may wish to classify all payments payable under a contract as core terms and therefore outside the scrutiny of the Regulations, such that what is a core term will be interpreted

---

[56] For example, if a core provision (or part of it) is placed at the end of a contact or among wording which is of less importance in a contract (eg a law and jurisdiction clause, waiver clause etc). Or where a contract term is not shown to a consumer until the moment they enter into the contract. A trader will often wish to state that a term is a core term so as to escape scrutiny under the Regulations.

[57] *Office of Fair Trading v Abbey National Plc and Others* [2009] UKSC 6, [2010] 2 All ER (Comm) 945. The case concerned whether certain payments in banks' terms and conditions were fair. Banks' terms and conditions came into consideration as to whether they were core terms because they were held to be drafted, with some exceptions, in plain intelligible language.

[58] Ibid, from the judgment of Lord Phillips at para 78: 'I can see no justification for excluding from the application of reg 6(2) price or remuneration on the ground that it is 'ancillary or incidental price [or] remuneration'. If it is possible to identify such price or remuneration as being paid in exchange for services, even if the services are fringe or optional extras, reg 6(2) will preclude an attack on the price or remuneration in question if it is based on the contention that it was excessive by comparison with the services for which it was exchanged. If, on analysis, the charges are not given in exchange for individual services but are part of a package of different ways of charging for a package of varied services, this does not mean that they are not price or remuneration for the purpose of reg 6(2).'

The case was distinguished from the earlier case of *Director General of Fair Trading v First National Bank Plc* [2001] UKHL 52. In the earlier case, the payment of interest was not a core provision because it arose from where a consumer was in default. In the latter case, the payment, among other things, of overdraft fees where the consumer went into overdraft without permission was a core term as it was not a breach of the most of the bank's terms and conditions to go in an unauthorised overdraft.

restrictively[59]. Or a trader may try to draft its terms and conditions so that the subject matter of the contract includes matters such as exclusion of liability or where the consumer is in breach.

Although there is limited guidance available from the law and the courts, the following are examples of core terms:

- for an insurance contract, the provisions which set out what is and what is not covered by the insurer and the insurer's liability (as they will form the basis of what exactly the consumer will pay for)[60];

- the 'normal' rate of interest chargeable on a bank loan (but an interest rate (and other charges) payable in the event of a default by the borrower are not core provisions)[61];

- the commission payable on a house sale within a certain period of time (but a higher specific rate payable after that period, and a provision that another rate of interest was payable were held not to be core terms)[62];

- various charges made by a bank for unpaid items, charges for exceeding an agreed overdraft limit, etc are core terms (as well as the interest the bank earned on having access to the customer's money)[63];

- a specific extra cost if a customer decided to not pay a telephone bill using direct debit[64];

7.5.4   Use of plain, intelligible language in written contracts

A trader must write its contract terms in 'plain, intelligible language'[65]. The consequence of which is that, where there is a dispute as to the meaning

---

[59]   *Office of Fair Trading v Abbey National Plc and Others* [2009] UKSC 6, [2010] 2 All ER (Comm) 945 at para 43; *Director General of Fair Trading v First National Bank Plc* [2001] UKHL 52, [2001] All ER (D) 355 (Oct) at para 34.

[60]   Directive 93/13/EEC, recital 19.

[61]   *Director General of Fair Trading v First National Bank Plc* [2002] 1 All ER 97. In relation to the provision held not to be a core term, the court found that it did not define the main subject matter of the contract, it did not in a realistic way concern the adequacy of the remuneration as it only dealt with the situation when the borrower was in default.

[62]   *Bairstow Eves London Central Ltd v Smith* [2004] EWHC 263 (QB).

[63]   *Office of Fair Trading v Abbey National Plc and Others* [2009] UKSC 6, [2010] 2 All ER (Comm) 945. It was held that all the charges were the price the customer of the bank agreed to pay for the package of services received, rather than those charges for when the customer was in breach of an obligation.

[64]   *Bond v British Telecommunications Plc* a decision of the Walsall County Court, 28 March 2008, quoted in Lawson, Exclusion Clauses and Unfair Contract terms (10th edn, Sweet and Maxwell, 2011) p 272.

[65]   Unfair Terms in Consumer Contracts Regulations 2009, reg 7(1).

of a term, the interpretation which is most favourable to the consumer will prevail[66].

This requirement to use 'plain, intelligible language':

- applies only to written contracts;

- does not carry a sanction but, if there is any doubt as to the meaning of a provision, the meaning most favourable to the consumer will be used.

Concerning the last point, the sanction for wording which is not in 'plain, intelligible language' does not mean that the consumer will not be bound by the term, such as would be the case if the wording is unfair[67], but merely that it will apply in the way least favourable to the trader.

It is possible to write a provision using very dense language, which is very difficult to understand but which will still have only one meaning and that meaning will not be unfair.

Suggestions are made above at **7.2.2** (Basic steps for writing the contract in 'plain intelligible language') about the methods that a contract drafter should use in the drafting a contract.

7.6   Words which should not appear in a consumer contract

The following 'legal' wording is unlikely to be acceptable in a contract with a consumer[68]:

Word or phrase to avoid	Suggested replacement word or phrase
assignment (or variations such as 'sold, assigned and transferred')	transfer
consideration	price
consequential	loss
force majeure	the business/trader will do whatever is the subject matter of the contract within a reasonable time
(not) sell or offer for sale, assign, mortgage or pledge ... or otherwise deal with	must not sell, rent or dispose of ... not give anyone any legal rights over ...

---

[66]   Unfair Terms in Consumer Contracts Regulations 2009, reg 7(2). This is modern example of the *contra proferentum* rule.

[67]   Unfair Contract Terms in Consumer Contracts Regulations 1999, reg 8(1).

[68]   These are largely drawn from the Annex to the OFT *Unfair contract terms guidance*.

Word or phrase to avoid	Suggested replacement word or phrase
determination (or determine)	end the agreement
distress or execution is levied against any of [the consumer's] goods	the consumer's belongings are taken away
indemnify	will pay for
joint and several	that each consumer to the contract is liable for the whole amount due for payment by the consumers, and not just a proportionate part
jurisdiction	if you wish to take legal action you must do so within [specify country]
lien	business/trader can hold some or all of the goods until the consumer has paid the business/trader's charges (even if they do not relate to the goods)
liquidated damages	compensation
merchantable quality	satisfactory quality
risk	the consumer will be responsible for the goods on delivery
pro-rata	adjusted in proportion
time of the essence	specify a period of notice when something will happen or not happen and state what will occur
statutory reference (a mere reference to the statutory legislation)	explain briefly what the legislation does, provides, takes away etc
tender	offer to pay
title (property)	retain or have ownership

Chapter 8

Legal Terms and Lawyers' Jargon

8.1   Introduction

This chapter considers a selection of words and phrases which:

- are commonly used by contract drafters, including useful 'legal terms of art' and unnecessary legal jargon; or

- are defined by statute as having a particular meaning when used in contracts and other situations; or

- the courts have considered in cases involving the interpretation of contracts.

The material in this chapter focuses on practical issues which the drafter or negotiator might wish to consider in relation to the use of these 'legal' terms. As already mentioned, it is possible to divide legal terms into the following categories.

- *Liability and litigation terms.* For example: negligence; tort; Contracts (Rights of Third Parties) Act 1999; arbitration; proceedings; legal action; the parties submit to the jurisdiction of the [English] courts; exclusive jurisdiction; non-exclusive jurisdiction; expert. Terms of this kind are commonly found in the 'boilerplate' language towards the end of the contract.

- *Terms relating to the transfer or termination of obligations.* For example: assignment and novation; indemnity; hold harmless; breach; material breach; insolvency; liquidators; receivers. Again, these terms are commonly found in boilerplate clauses.

- *Obligations with a particular legal meaning.* For example: time shall be of the essence; condition/condition precedent/condition subsequent; warranties; representations; covenants; undertakings; guarantees; with full title guarantee; with limited title guarantee; beneficial owner; subject to contract; without prejudice; delivery. It is important for the drafter to be aware of the meaning of such terms and, where needed, to use them in an appropriate way.

- *Expression of time.* For example: year; month; week; day; from and including; until; from time to time; for the time being; forthwith; immediately; at the end of. These expressions are often to be found in the main commercial provisions of the contract, for example, in clauses which state when a party is required to perform obligations.

- *Other terms defined by statute.* For example: person; firm; subsidiary; United Kingdom; European Union; power of attorney; month; delivery. It is important to be aware of the statutory meaning of such words, particularly in those relatively few cases where the statute provides that the statutory definition applies when the word is used in a contract.

- *Other terms interpreted by the courts.* For example: best; all reasonable and reasonable endeavours; due diligence; set-off; consent not to be unreasonably withheld; material; consult; penalty; nominal sum; subject to. It is important be aware of the case law on the meaning of some of these words, which are commonly used in contracts.

- *Unnecessary legal jargon.* Such as words which are commonly encountered in contracts but which add little if anything to the contract or which could be replaced by simpler or more modern language, for example, 'hereinafter'.

It is convenient to discuss terms defined by statute, and expressions of time separately before discussing various other terms in alphabetical order.

8.2   Terms defined by statute

In a few cases, statute law provides that certain words will have a particular meaning, when used in contracts and other instruments. In particular, the following:

- *Month, person, singular, masculine.* Section 61 of the Law of Property Act 1925[1] provides:

  'In all deeds, wills, orders and other instruments executed, made or coming into operation after the commencement of this Act [ie 1 January 1926], unless the context otherwise requires:
  (a) "Month" means calendar month;
  …
  (h) "Person" includes a corporation;
  …
  (c) The singular includes the plural and vice versa;
  …
  (d) The masculine includes the feminine and vice versa.'

- *Full title guarantee, limited title guarantee, beneficial owner.* Under the Law of Property (Miscellaneous Provisions) Act 1994, certain terms are implied into 'dispositions of property' which are expressed to be made 'with full title guarantee' or 'with limited title guarantee'[2].

---

[1] See also the equivalent provisions in ss 5 and 6 of, and Sch 1 to, the Interpretation Act 1978. Section 17(2)(a) of this Act is discussed at **8.4.3**.

[2] These provisions replace the former law, under s 76 of the Law of Property Act 1925, by which certain terms are implied into a 'conveyance' of property if the seller expressly conveys the property 'as beneficial owner'. As to the implied terms, see the extracts from the 1994 Act set out in Appendix 2. As to the effect of the 1994 Act on assignment of intellectual property see Anderson, *Technology Transfer* 2010 Bloomsbury Professional, at 8.1.

- *Infants and minors.* Under the Family Law Reform Act 1969[3], the age of majority was reduced from 21 years to 18 years, and 'infant', 'infancy', 'minor', 'minority' and similar expressions are to be understood as meaning someone of less than 18 years. This applies to contracts as well as other 'instruments', unless the context requires otherwise.

8.3   Expressions of time

8.3.1   Actions to be taken within a specified time period

Consider the following example of a clause in a commercial contract:

> X shall within 3 months of 11th May 2011 pay to Y the sum of Z.

The last date on which X can pay this sum without being in breach of contract would normally be 11 August 1998. (The counting of the three-month period would start from and include 12 May 2011, and X can usually make payment up to midnight at the end of 11 August.)

This seems simple enough. In reaching this conclusion it is necessary to consider an extensive amount of confusing case law, which is briefly summarised as follows:

- *Statutory meaning.* Section 61 of the Law of Property Act 1925 (quoted above) provides that month means 'calendar month' in agreements governed by English law. Section 61 does not limit such a meaning to agreements concerned with property. At common (non-statute) law, 'month' meant calendar month only in bills of exchange and other commercial documents. Otherwise it meant 'lunar month'[4].

- *What is a calendar month?* In the leading case the court held the following points as being well established under English law[5]:

  ○ In calculating the period that has elapsed after the occurrence of the specified event such as the giving of a notice, the day on which the event occurred is excluded from the reckoning.

---

[3]   Section 1(2).

[4]   *Hart v Middleton* (1845) 2 Car & Kir 9 at 10.

[5]   *Dodds v Walker* [1981] 2 All ER 689, HL. *Register of Companies v Radio-Tech Engineering Ltd* [2004] BCC 277 is a recent illustration of the application of the principles set out in *Dodds v Walker*. In this case, a company had to file accounts within ten months of the end of its accounting period (30 September) in accordance with Companies Act 1985, s 244(1)(a). The company filed its accounts on 31 July. The Registrar of Companies applied the corresponding date rule, so that the last day for the company to file its accounts was 30 July 2006. The court agreed with the Registrar of Companies. See also *Migotti v Colvill* (1879) 4 CPD 233: 'A "calendar month" is a legal and technical term; and in computing time by calendar months the time must be reckoned by looking at the calendar and not by counting days.'

- ○ When the relevant period is a month or a specified number of months after the giving of a notice, the general rule is that the period ends on the corresponding date in the appropriate subsequent month (ie the day of that month that bears the same number as the day of the earlier month on which the notice was given). Except in a small minority of cases (see next point), all that a person has to do is to mark in his or her diary the corresponding date in the appropriate subsequent month.

- The corresponding date rule does not apply where the period is calculated by using weeks as the calculating factor, as the period it covers (ie seven days) is certain[6].

- *Ends of months* In the few instances when there is no corresponding date in the subsequent month, the corresponding day will be the last day of the subsequent month. This is illustrated by the example from the case: a party gave four months' notice on 30 October 2011. Time would begin to run at midnight on 30/31 October and the notice would expire at midnight on 28 February/1 March (or 29 February/1 March on a leap year).

- *At what time does the period expire?* Normally, the period expires at midnight at the end of the last day of the period in question. Fractions of a day are usually excluded[7]. A person under an obligation to do a particular act on or before a particular date has the whole of that date to perform it[8]. But there is nothing to stop the parties to an agreement specifying the particular time for when an obligation has to be completed (eg the 'Supplier shall deliver the Goods on the Date but no later than 5pm').

- *Dates calculated 'from' and 'until', etc.* The same principles apply to time periods calculated 'from' or 'after' a date or event. Normally that date is excluded[9]. 'Beginning from' is treated in the same way as 'from'[10]. To reduce doubt as when the period starts, consider using special words such as 'commencing on' or 'beginning with'.

  If the period is 'X months from the date of this Agreement', it seems that the date set out at the head of the agreement will be used as the reference point, even if the parties have misstated the date of execution of the agreement[11]. Words such as 'by', 'from', 'until' and 'between' may

---

[6] *Okolo v Secretary of State for the Environment* [1997] 4 All ER 242.

[7] *Re Figgis, Roberts v MacLaren* [1969] 1 Ch 123.

[8] *Alfovos Shipping Co SA v Pagnan and Lli, The Afovos* [1983] 1 All ER 449, HL.

[9] *Hammond v Haigh Castle & Co Ltd* [1973] 2 All ER 289 and *Trow v Ind Coope (West Midlands) Ltd* [1967] 2 All ER 990, CA, considered in *RJB Mining (UK) Ltd v NUM* [1995] IRLR 556, CA.

[10] See *Hammond v Haigh Castle & Co Ltd* [1973] 2 All ER 289 and *Trow v Ind Coope (West Midlands) Ltd* [1967] 2 All ER 900, CA.

[11] *Styles v Wardle* (1825) 4 B & C 908.

be ambiguous and lead to uncertainty as to which dates are included. It may be better to use phrases such as 'on or before', 'from and excluding', 'from and including', 'to and including', etc, which specify which dates are to apply[12].

- *Days.* To avoid any uncertainty over the duration of months (including whether calendar or lunar months are intended), it may be better to state the time periods in days rather than months (eg instead of an agreement stating 'Party A shall perform the Services within 3 months of the date of this Agreement', rather 'Party A shall perform the Services within 90 days of the date of this Agreement'). Generally, to avoid arguments over whether the start or end date of a period is taken into account[13], it may be better to give a couple of extra days' notice. The word 'day' may mean either a calendar day (midnight to midnight) or a period of 24 consecutive hours, depending on the context[14]. A 'working day' is normally understood as a (complete) calendar day which is not a holiday, and not just the working hours of a day, whilst a 'conventional day' begins at a defined time and ends 24 hours later[15].

- *Years.* Similar problems may arise with expressions such as 'year of this Agreement'—is this a year from a specified date or the period 1 January to 31 December? To avoid any uncertainty, the expression 'year of this Agreement' is sometimes defined in the contract.

- *Quarters.* Sometimes contracts refer to quarters of a year, for example, if royalty payments are to be paid quarterly. The contract should state which quarterly periods are to be applied (eg 1 January to 31 March, 1 April to 30 June, etc, as required). If the periods are not stated, the court may construe the contract as referring to the traditional quarterly periods used in landlord and tenant law, which ended on a 'quarter day' or some other period[16]. The usual quarter days are 25 March (Lady Day), 24 June (Midsummer), 29 September (Michaelmas) and 25 December (Christmas).

---

[12] In some agreements drafted by US lawyers, the interpretation clause defines what is meant by expressions such as 'until'. Americans also use the term 'through' as in 'through March 1st', which means 'up to and including March 1st'.

[13] For example, see *Re Hector Whaling Ltd* [1936] Ch 208.

[14] See, eg, *Cornfoot v Royal Exchange Assurance Corpn* [1904] 1 KB 40, CA, distinguished in *Cartwright v MacCormack* [1963] 1 WLR 18, CA.

[15] *Reardon Smith Line Ltd v Ministry of Agriculture, Fisheries and Food* [1963] AC 691, HL. Where an agreement is with a financial institution (such as a bank), a 'day' (unless otherwise defined) will run until to the end of working hours *(Momm (t/a Delbrueck & Co) v Barclays Bank International Ltd* [1977] QB 790).

[16] For example, 'two quarters of a year' was construed in one case as meaning six calendar months, see *East v Pantiles (Plant Hire) Ltd* [1982] 2 EGLR 111, CA; *Samuel Properties (Developments) Ltd v Hayek* [1972] 1 WLR 1296, CA.

8.3.2   Actions to be taken 'forthwith' or 'immediately' or 'as soon as possible'

In one leading case[17], the court made the following comment on the meaning of the term 'forthwith', in the context of an obligation to file court documents 'forthwith':

> 'In many cases it may well be that unless the notice is filed the same day it cannot be said to be filed "forthwith", but it may be filed forthwith even though not filed the same day. Their Lordships do not propose to attempt to define "forthwith". The use of that word clearly connotes that the notice must be filed as soon as practicable, but what is practicable must depend on the circumstances of each case.'

Normally, forthwith means immediately[18], without any delay. Sometimes the courts are prepared to interpret forthwith less strictly, as meaning 'within a reasonable time' if no harm can result from this interpretation[19] or 'as soon as reasonably possible'[20].

The courts have also interpreted similar words such as 'immediately'[21], 'as soon as possible'[22], 'directly'[23] and 'promptly'[24]. However, not all of these cases were concerned with the interpretation of contracts.

In a case[25] which was concerned with the interpretation of a contract, the court was asked to rule on the meaning of an obligation to manufacture part of a gun 'as soon as possible'. The manufacturer delayed making the gun because he did not have a suitably qualified member of staff to make the part.

---

[17]   *Sameen v Abeyewickrema* [1963] AC 597, PC.

[18]   It appears that 'forthwith' will usually have the same meaning as 'immediately': 'There appears to be no material difference between the terms "immediately" and "forthwith". A provision to the effect that a thing must be done forthwith or immediately means that it must be done as soon as possible in the circumstances, the nature of the act to be done taken into account' 45 *Halsbury's Laws of England* (4th Edn Reissue) Vol 45, para 251.

[19]   *Hillingdon London Borough Council v Cutler* [1968] 1 QB 124, CA.

[20]   *R v Secretary of State for Social Services, ex p Child Poverty Action Group* [1990] 2 QB 540, CA.

[21]   As meaning 'with all reasonable speed' considering the circumstances of the case, see *R v Inspector of Taxes, ex p Clarke* [1974] QB 220, CA; and *Hughes (Inspector of Taxes) v Viner* [1985] 3 All ER 40.

[22]   As being stricter than 'as soon as reasonably practicable'—see *R v Board of Visitors of Dartmoor Prison, ex p Smith* [1986] 2 All ER 651 at 662, CA.

[23]   As meaning speedily or at least as soon as practicable, and not just within a reasonable time. But directly does not mean 'instantaneously'. See *Duncan v Topham* (1849) 8 CB 225.

[24]   See *R v Stratford-on-Avon District Council, ex p Jackson* [1986] 1 WLR 1319, CA; *Bank of Nova Scotia v Hellenic Mutual War Risks Association (Bermuda) Ltd, The Good Luck* [1992] 1 AC 233, HL; and see the comments of Lord Wilberforce in *Bremer Handelsgesellschaft mbH v Vanden Avenne-Izegum PVBA* [1978] 2 Lloyd's Rep 109 at 113, HL; and the words of Lord Hope in *R (Burket) v Hammersmith LBC* [2002] 3 All ER 97, HL, where 'promptly' meant the 'avoidance of undue delay' in the bringing an application for judicial review.

[25]   *Hydraulic Engineering Co Ltd v McHaffie Goslett & Co* (1878) 4 QBD 670 at 3, per Bramwell LJ, CA.

This was held to be a breach of the obligation. One of the Court of Appeal judges in that case stated in his judgment:

> '... to do a thing "as soon as possible" means to do it within a reasonable time, with an undertaking to do it in the shortest practicable time ... I quite agree that a manufacturer or tradesman is not bound to discard all other work for the occasion, in order to take in hand a thing which he promises to do "as soon as possible".'

However, another judge in that case stated that the manufacturers had undertaken:

> '[to] make the gun as quickly as it could be made within the largest establishment with the best appliances.'

Thus (with all of these expressions) it comes down to a matter of construction of the contract. To avoid uncertainty it is usually preferable to state any required time for performance specifically, rather than hope that the party under the obligation and then a court will interpret an obligation to perform the obligation 'forthwith' in the way that one intended.

8.3.3   'From time to time'; 'for the time being'

Contracts sometimes include these expressions, as in the following examples:

Example 1

The Project Director shall be such person as Party A nominates from time to time.

Example 2

If the parties are unable to agree upon an arbitrator, the arbitrator shall be appointed by the President for the time being of the Law Society of England and Wales.

In Example 1, the phrase 'from time to time' is intended to clarify that party A can nominate a person to be Project Director more than once during the life of the contract. In other words, there is an ongoing right to nominate. In Example 2, the phrase 'for the time being' means, in effect, 'at the relevant time', so that if the parties are unable to agree on an arbitrator in five years' time, they will refer to the President of the Law Society at that time, not the person who was President when the agreement was signed.

8.3.4   Other 'time' expressions sometimes encountered

The following expressions are sometimes encountered in commercial agreements. They may not be defined and sometimes their meaning may not be clear without further investigation:

- *Bank holiday.* In England and Wales the following are defined as bank holidays: Easter Monday, the last Monday in May, the last Monday in

August, 26 December (if it is not a Sunday) and 27 December (in a year where 25 or 26 December are on a Sunday)[26]. Note (at least for England and Wales), Christmas Day, Good Friday and New Year's Day are not bank holidays. A definition which only uses the words 'Bank Holiday' would not capture other dates which are commonly not worked.

- *Business day.* This is likely to mean Mondays to Fridays (but excluding bank holidays at least) are business days[27].

- *Business hours.* The times different organisations are open will obviously vary. If under an agreement, a task needs completing by the end of a business day then the agreement should clearly spell out what the business hours are for the purposes of the agreement. For example, a computer supplier is installing a computer system into a retailer's shops. The shops are open until 8pm but the head office of the retailer business hours are open until 5pm. Unless specified clearly there can be doubt as to what are the business hours of the retailer. Completion of the work at 8pm might be outside the retailer's 'business hours'[28].

- *Public holiday.* These words, although often appearing in statutes and contracts, appear not to have a defined meaning. One common meaning appears to be days which are holidays (such as Christmas Day and Good Friday) including bank holidays[29].

8.4   Other legal terms used in contracts

8.4.1   'Agreement' and 'contract'

The words 'agreement' and 'contract' are often used interchangeably. The word 'agreement' can have three meanings relevant in a commercial context:

---

[26]   Bank and Financial Dealings Act 1971, s 1(1) and Sch 1. Note that New Year's Eve in England and Wales is not a bank holiday. The bank holidays for Scotland and Northern Ireland are different. In Scotland the following are bank holidays: New Year's Day (if not a Sunday, but if it falls on a Sunday then 3 January), 2 January (if not a Sunday, but if it falls on a Sunday then 3 January), Good Friday, first Monday in May, first Monday in August and Christmas Day (if it is not a Sunday, but if it falls on a Sunday, then 26 December will be the bank holiday).

[27]   For the purposes of the National Debt (Stockholders Relief) Act 1892 a business day is any day other than Saturday, Sunday, Good Friday, Christmas Day and any day which is a bank holiday in the United Kingdom under the Banking and Financial Dealings Act 1971 (plus any other days that may be specified under the 1892 Act). A normal workng week from and including Monday to Friday is the conventional view, but will not apply to certain businesses which normally operate on the other days of the week (eg the retail sector where many shops are open seven days a week). Also many services now operate on the internet. Some or all of the services may be available on every day of the week (eg an insurance company may be open for people making a claim seven days a week, but not be open in relation to some 'back office operations'). Also the start of a conventional working week in England may be Monday, but in other countries, it may be a Sunday or Saturday.

[28]   See *Re Kent Coalfields Syndicate* (1898) 67 LJQB 503.

[29]   See Arbitration Act 1996, s 78, one of the few statutes to give a meaning to the words.

- the name of a document;
- the fact that parties have reached an understanding, which may or not be a legally binding;
- the fact that parties have entered into a legally binding contract.

Where the word is used to refer to a type of document or arrangement between two or more parties, the meaning of the word 'agreement' normally means 'contract'[30].

Where the parties are involved in a transaction, event or situation which needs to be referred to or is subject to a legislative provision, the exact meaning should be checked[31].

Similarly with EU competition law, an agreement can have a meaning where the parties have reached an understanding of a non-binding nature[32].

8.4.2 'and/or'

An agreement may require a party to fulfil an obligation in one of several ways or a party to come within one or more situations. For example, a party providing a service may have to produce a report at the end of the agreement and the agreement specifies various ways the party can provide the report to the other party, ie:

> The Consultant shall supply a final Report within 30 days of the termination of this agreement to the Client by post and/or email and/or facsimile and/or in person.

In this example, the Consultant can provide the report either:

- by post or email or facsimile or in person; or
- by post and email and facsimile and person.

That is, to fulfil the obligation, it is possible for the consultant to provide the report either conjunctively or disjunctively[33].

Having 'and/or' in a clause may have unintended consequences, particularly where a party is to do or provide something, as the 'and' part of 'and/or' may

---

[30] *Re Symon, Public Trustees v Symon* [1944] SASR 102, 110; *Goldsack v Shore* [1950] 1 KB 708 at 713, CA, per Evershed MR.

[31] Eg, Enterprise Act 2002, s 129, where agreement 'means any agreement or arrangement, in whatever way and whatever form it is made, and whether it is, or is intended to be, legally enforceable or not'.

[32] See *Electrical and Mechanical Carbon & Graphite Products* (Comp/E-2/38 . 359).

[33] This appears to be the default meaning as held by courts, see *Stanton v Richardson* 45 LJCP 82; *Gurney v Grimmer* (1932) 38 Com Cas 7.

entitle that party to fulfil the obligation in multiple instances or in ways that the other party does not wish to occur.

8.4.3   'As amended'

If the contract includes any references to legislation, it may be appropriate to refer to the legislation 'as amended from time to time', to take account of changes to the legislation during the life of the contract. Alternatively the parties may want to avoid having their contract changed as a result of changes in legislation (eg if they use a definition of 'subsidiary' set out in the Companies Act 2006)[34].

Under s 17(2)(a) of the Interpretation Act 1978, a reference to an enactment in a contract is to be understood as referring to an enactment which repeals and re-enacts the earlier enactment. Rather than rely on this section (which may be too narrow in some cases, and unacceptable in others), it is common to include wording along the following lines:

> 1. In this Agreement, subject to clause 2 below, any reference to any enactment includes a reference to it as amended (whether before or after the date of this Agreement) and to any other enactment which may, after the date of this Agreement, directly or indirectly replace it, with or without amendment.
>
> 2. The reference to section 1159 of the Companies Act 2006 in clause 3 of this Agreement shall be interpreted as meaning section 1159 in the form in which it is enacted as at the date of this Agreement, and without any subsequent amendments or re-enactment.

8.4.4   'Assignment' and 'novation'

The term 'assignment' is used in several senses, including:

- the transfer of title in property (ie ownership), for example, of intellectual property or land;

- the transfer of rights, for example, rights under an agreement (such as a right to be paid the price stated in the agreement).

The term 'assignment' should not refer to the transfer of obligations under an agreement, although in practice this is sometimes done. (A clause dealing

---

[34] However, there are dangers in not referring to statute where a defined word or clause is based on the statute, particularly if the statute is amended (perhaps adding further or different categories of some situation or event). An example of this would be where an agreement allows a party to terminate if another party becomes insolvent, and the wording in the clause uses the meanings of insolvency as defined in a statute (but makes no reference to the statute). If the statute changes and includes newer forms of insolvency, but the agreement is not explicitly amended, then if the other party becomes insolvent in one of the newer ways the first party will not be able to termiante for that new form of insolvency. See *William Hare Ltd and Another v Shepherd Construction Ltd* [2010] EWCA Civ 283, [2010] All ER (D) 168 (Mar) for an illustration of this point.

with the assignment of rights, the transfer of obligations and other matters is commonly called just the 'assignment clause'.) It is bad practice to refer to 'assigning an agreement' since this phrase does not make clear whether obligations, as well as rights, are to be transferred[35].

Generally, it is possible for one party to assign rights under a contract[36] unless the contract is one involving a personal relationship (eg agent or employee), or there is an express or implied term preventing assignment. Transferring obligations under an agreement requires the consent of the other contracting party. If the rights and obligations are transferred there is in effect a 'novation' of the contract, whereby the contract is, in effect, cancelled (with the agreement of the original parties) and replaced by a new one with different parties[37]. It is possible to 'novate' only some of the rights and obligations of an agreement[38]. For example, in an agreement where a supplier provides a range of services to a customer, the parties may decide that a third party will provide one of the services, and also that the third party will receive any payments for that service from the customer. In this situation, it is possible to novate just that one service.

8.4.5   'Best endeavours', all reasonable endeavours ,and 'reasonable endeavours' (as well as absolute obligations)

These phrases indicate the level of obligation (whether absolute or qualified) and the amount of effort that a party is required to put into put into fulfilling a specified obligation. See the discussion on these points at **5.5**.

8.4.6   'Boilerplate'

'Boilerplate clauses' are a set of clauses which are often found in commercial agreements almost irrespective of the subject matter of the agreements. They are often placed at the end of an agreement. Some 'boilerplate' is concerned with the operation of the agreement itself (such as notices, law and jurisdiction and interpretation clauses), whilst some deal with the rights and obligations of the parties (clauses such as assignment and subcontracting, entire agreement, waiver, *force majeure*, etc). There is no fixed list of what constitutes 'boilerplate',

---

[35]   See [Clause 8.3 in Precedent 1 in Appendix 1] for example wording. Although the heading of the clause is called 'Assignment', the actual wording of the clause, among other things, deals with assignment *and* transfer.

[36]   Unless there is express or implied prohibition, an assignment can be without the consent of the other party, *Caledonia North Sea Ltd v London Bridge Engineering Ltd* [2000] Lloyd's Rep IR 249.

[37]   See also *Linden Gardens Trust Ltd v Lenesta Sludge Disposals Ltd* [1994] 1 AC 85 at 103, per Lord Browne-Wilkinson.

[38]   *Telewest Communications Plc v Customs and Excise Commissioners* [2005] EWCA Civ 102, [2005] All ER (D) 143 (Feb).

and the classification of certain clauses as 'boilerplate' does not really turn on their importance[39]. As a general proposition, the longer the agreement the greater the amount of boilerplate is found—there are more clauses covering a greater amount of detail.

The authors classify boilerplate as the following—depending the complexity or importance of the agreement:

- *very simple/very unimportant agreement*: Clauses dealing with notices, law and jurisdiction and Contracts (Rights of Third Parties) Act 1999.

- *simple and short*: Clauses dealing with notices, law and jurisdiction and Contracts (Rights of Third Parties) Act 1999, (brief) interpretation provisions, (separate) definitions.

- *medium length/medium importance*: Clauses dealing with notices, law and jurisdiction and Contracts (Rights of Third Parties) Act 1999, (more extensive) interpretation provisions, (separate) definitions; entire agreement, amendment, assignment, waiver, (no) agency or partnership (particularly where the parties are working together on a project), further assurance (if there is a transfer of property), severance (if any provisions are thought to be problematic and not pass judicial scrutiny) and announcements.

- *Full-scale boilerplate: medium length/medium importance*: Clauses dealing with notices, law and jurisdiction and Contracts (Rights of Third Parties) Act 1999, (more extensive) interpretation provisions, (separate) definitions, entire agreement, amendment, assignment, waiver, (no) agency or partnership (particularly where the parties are working together on a project), further assurance (if there is a transfer of property), severance (if any provisions are thought to be problematic and not pass judicial scrutiny), announcements, costs and expenses (of negotiating and entering to the agreement), counterparts and duplicates, joint and several liability, priority of terms, retention of title (if not dealt with in a payments clause), set-off (if not dealt with in a payments clause), cumulative remedies, capacity (to enter into the contract), arbitration and meditation/ADR (if not in law and jurisdiction clause).

8.4.7   'Breach' and 'non-performance'

The word 'breach' could be considered as a technical term, not used in everyday speech. A few contracts use the more modern word 'break', as in 'if X breaks this contract', but this has not become a common practice.

---

[39] For example, the boilerplate section of an agreement usually contains an 'entire agreement' clause (see **6.5.5** and **6.5.22.10**). Such clauses have received considerable scrutiny by the courts in recent years.

Technically, there is (or some lawyers consider there to be) a difference between breach of a contract's terms and failure to perform obligations under the contract. However, it seems unlikely that a court would interpret a clause dealing with breach of contract as not covering non-performance, unless the contract refers elsewhere to non-performance and breach as being two separate things.

8.4.8   'Cash'

It is unlikely that many commercial agreements will require payment in actual notes or coins. 'Notes' and 'coins' is perhaps a common understanding of the meaning of 'cash'. If immediate payment is required (ie that the payor has immediately available funds to make payment), then the use of clear wording as to the type of funds available should be used, rather the use a term such as 'cash'[40] (eg that a supplier will consider that payment is made when it has received cleared funds in a specific bank account).

8.4.9   'Change of control'

A 'change of control' clause concerns what is to happen where there is a change in:

- the ownership of shareholding of a party; or

- in the directors (or others) who manage a party.

A change of control clause will specify what is to happen in the event of these situations occurring. For example, the party affected by such a change may have to notify the other party. The clause may then provide that certain actions can or will occur in consequence, such as the second party being able to terminate an agreement.

A change of control clause is commonly used where the issue of who owns and/or manages one party is of particular interest or importance to the other party. For example, a party (the licensor) might develop specialised software for accountancy work in a particular industry. It licenses the software to another party (the licensee). The licensee may not wish one of its competitors to own or control the licensor. This could, for a number of reasons, include the competitor acquiring access to confidential information of the licensee,

---

[40]   For example, in *Re Stonham, Lloyds Bank Ltd v Maynard* [1963] 1 WLR 238 the phrase 'cash … in bank' was held to mean, in the circumstances of the case, to mean money both in deposit and current accounts. Also under the meaning of cash in various statutes varies (eg in s 289(6) of the Proceeds of Crime Act 2002, including bearer bonds and bearer shares).

refusing to license the software (or new or improved versions) to the licensee, and so on.

Such a clause is often used in addition to an assignment clause[41]. The latter is concerned with the transfer of rights and obligations (including assets), but does not deal with the situation where there is no transfer of rights or obligations but the nature of the other party (whether through ownership or management) has fundamentally changed (such as a sale of large part or all of the shareholding in the party).

8.4.10   Competition and anti-trust

The main competition laws affecting English law agreements are domestic UK competition laws, including the Competition Act 1998, other UK statutes and the common law on restraint of trade, and EC competition laws, particularly Articles 101 and 102 of the EU Treaty.

In the United States, competition laws are known as anti-trust laws. This name derives from the late nineteenth century, when laws were introduced to deal with the anti-competitive activities of major commercial trusts in the steel industry. At that time, prior to the development (or widespread use) of limited liability companies, the trust was a common vehicle for commercial activities.

8.4.11   Comfort letter

A letter which contains statements by a party (or someone connected with a party). The statements are intended to re-assure another party, but they are usually not intended to be legally binding. See the discussion of comfort letters and letters of intent at **1.12**.

For example, a supplier of goods to a buyer might require, if the buyer is a subsidiary of another company (ie a holding company), the holding company to provide a comfort letter which indicates that the holding company normally meets the liabilities of its subsidiaries (even though not legally liable to do so). If the supplier's concerns are strong there are other ways of tackling them, such as requiring a guarantee from the holding company or making the holding company be a party to the contract.

8.4.12   'Completion' and 'closing'

'Completion' is a stage in a contract when the main purpose of the contract takes effect, for example, in a house sale, it will include the formal conveyance

---

[41]   See **8.4.4**.

of property[42]. The term is also often used in sale of business agreements. The term 'closing' is an equivalent expression used in the United States.

With some contracts it may not be clear what is the exact meaning of completion, ie the extent to which the contract obligations are fulfilled (by one or both parties), where the contract does not involve a house sale. For example, for some types of building contract, there can be completion of the building work although there may still be some minor items needing doing or attention ('snagging')[43]. In appropriate cases not involving specialist areas such as conveyancing or building contracts, what constitutes 'completion' may need specifying in detail to avoid (as far as possible) any disputes[44].

8.4.13   Consent

A party is sometimes required to obtain the consent of the other party or from a third party before carrying out an obligation under an agreement. For example, a software development agreement may require the developer to obtain consent before carrying a 'live' test on the data of the customer (so that the customer can make appropriate back-ups and take safety measures). A person will not normally give consent by remaining silent or being silently acquiescent[45].

Clear wording should always be used in such circumstances so that it is clear what is to happen at each stage in a contract and what is to happen if the party does not undertake an obligation or respond to a notice from the other party. In the above example, in some software development agreements where the software is being tested on live data, the customer is given a set number of days to respond and if they do not, then either the test is deemed accepted and the developer moves on to the next stage or the developer has the right to terminate the agreement or charge extra for any delay.

8.4.14   Consideration

See the discussion in Chapter 1.

---

[42]   If the word is specifically defined in an agreement, then it will mean the actual completion and not the date named for completion, *Richards v Pryse* [1927] 2 KB 76.

[43]   *Emson Eastern Ltd (in receivership) v E M E Developments* (1991) 55 BLR 114.

[44]   For example, a contract may provide that an agreement terminates automatically on 'completion of the Project'. The supplier of the goods or services may consider it has completed the project when it has delivered the goods and installed them, and considers the agreement terminated. However the customer/client may not because it considers completion to mean a period to allow the goods to operate after installation. If 'completion' is not defined as meaning a set of steps, then there is greater scope for a dispute between the parties.

[45]   *Macher v Foundling Hospital* (1813) 1 Ves & B 188.

8.4.15   Consult

An obligation to consult with someone is generally considered less onerous than an obligation to obtain that person's consent. There is case law on the meaning of this term in public law[46].

In contracts, it seems likely that an obligation on party A to consult with party B is not met until party A has properly considered party B's views on the matter on which he was consulted[47], and that party A must consider those views with a receptive mind[48].

8.4.16   Covenants

Traditionally, covenants were promises by deed[49] with a secondary meaning that it is possible to apply the word 'covenant' to any promise or stipulation whether under a seal or not[50]. In some forms of agreement the word 'covenant' is routinely used (eg 'restrictive covenants' in employment contracts). Generally, only in transactions relating to real property (land) will 'covenant' have a special meaning going beyond a mere contractual obligation.

Sometimes, this term is used indiscriminately for any undertaking, perhaps to make the undertaking sound more solemn and important, but adding nothing to the legal meaning.

8.4.17   'Deemed'

Contracts sometimes include a provision that an event is 'deemed' to take place if certain conditions are met, or if certain circumstances arise. For example, Party A might be 'deemed' to give consent if it fails to respond to a request for consent within a specified time period. Thus, the event (giving of consent) has not actually taken place but for the purposes of the contract it is considered to

---

[46] For example, see *R v Secretary of State for Social Services, ex p Association of Metropolitan Authorities* [1986] 1 All ER 164, 167; *R v Secretary of State for the Environment, ex p Brent London Borough Council* [1983] 3 All ER 321 at 352 onwards, per Ackner LJ; and *Slough Estates Plc v Welwyn Hatfield District Council* [1996] 2 PLR 50; *R v North and East Devon Health Authority, ex p Coughlan* [2001] QB 213 at 258, CA; and *R (Capenhurst) v Leicester City Council* [2004] EWHC 2124, [2004] All ER (D) 93 (Sep).

[47] By analogy with tender procedures—see *Blackpool and Fylde Aero Club v Blackpool Borough Council* [1990] 3 All ER 25, CA.

[48] *Agricultural, Horticultural and Forestry Industry Training Board v Aylesbury Mushrooms Ltd* [1972] 1 All ER 280 at 284.

[49] *Rank Xerox Ltd v Lane (Inspector of Taxes)* [1979] 3 All ER 657 at 663; *Hagee (London) Ltd v Co-operative Insurance Society Ltd* (1991) 63 P & CR 362.

[50] *Rank Xerox Ltd v Lane (Inspector of Taxes)* [1979] 3 All ER 657 at 663.

have taken place. Non-lawyers sometimes find this concept puzzling (and the concept may need explanation to a client), but it is commonly encountered in contracts.

8.4.18   'Delivery'

The meaning of the 'delivery' has a technical meaning to lawyers and is very different to how most non-lawyers would understand the word. A non-lawyer, who is not familiar with the detail of English contract law (and/or not experienced in negotiating commercial agreements under English law), might believe that delivery means the physical transportation of goods to the buyer. Such an assumption is wrong[51]. Delivery (unless the parties to a contract agree otherwise) takes place at the seller's place of business[52].

Where physical delivery to a particular place is required the parties will need to make such an obligation explicit in the wording of the agreement.

8.4.19   'Due diligence'

This term has two related meanings:

- as a shorthand for the investigations which the purchaser of a business makes into the state of the business (such as looking at the company's records, etc). This usage has come from the United States; and

- in a more general sense in contracts, as where a party undertakes to 'use all due diligence' to perform some obligation. Another way of saying this might be to say:

   X shall perform his obligations diligently.

   For example, such an obligation is sometimes found in senior employees' service agreements.

8.4.20   'Engrossments'

Originally an engrossment was a fair copy of a document (usually a deed) ready for signing. Now it usually means the final version of a document

---

[51]   For example, see *Kwei Tek Chao (t/a Zung Fu Co) v British Traders and Shippers Ltd* [1954] 2 QB 459.

[52]   Sale of Goods Act 1979, s 29(2). The 1979 Act provides a definition for 'delivery' as meaning the 'voluntary transfer of possession from one person to another'. Part IV of the Sale of Goods Act 1979 has a number of assumptions which are implied into contracts concerning delivery in different circumstances. A description of these is beyond the scope of this book, but for a summary of these see 'Commercial Contracts and Other Documents' in *The Encyclopaedia of Forms and Precedents* Butterworths, Vol 7(2), 101, [210]–[216]. Different assumptions are made by the 1979 Act where delivery takes place to a consumer.

which is ready for signature. The word is (English) lawyers' jargon, but in the absence of a better term ('final versions for signature' is more accurate but sounds clumsy), it is still used[53]. Although commercial parties (and lawyers who specialise in dealing with commercial parties only) are less likely to encounter or use the term[54].

8.4.21   'Escrow'

There are two common usages of this term:

- *Deeds.* Deeds do not take effect until delivery. Where a party executes a deed but it is only delivered on the fulfilment of a condition, it is held 'in escrow'. Delivery will only take place on the fulfilment of the condition (eg receipt of agreed payments into that party's bank account). The deed is often held by a party's solicitor or the other party's solicitors (or even the other party). Whoever holds the deed will do so on the condition that they can only use the deed when the condition is fulfilled. This is also sometimes done with agreements which are not deeds, although the legal effect may be less certain, as ordinary agreements do not need to be formally delivered.

- *Computer software source code.* A different usage of the term is encountered in relation to computer software agreements, between a software owner and a user (eg a licensee). If the software owner is willing to provide the source code of the software to the licensee (providing only an object code version), then the software owner may agree instead to deposit the source code with a third party (eg the National Computing Centre in Manchester). The third party agrees to hold the source code in confidence and to release it to the user only if certain conditions are met (eg the software owner becomes insolvent or fails to maintain the software). The terms on which the third party agrees to act are set out in an 'escrow agreement'.

8.4.22   'Exclusive', 'sole' and 'non-exclusive' licences

There are no definitions of these words which automatically apply to contracts. These words are usually encountered with regard to the appointment of agents and distributors and the licensing of intellectual property rights.

---

[53]   Equally, now that many documents are drafted, and exchanged electronically, such expressions as 'print-out' or 'hard-copy' are of limited assistance in determining the status or version of the document. Hard copy has a statutory meaning, see Finance Act 1995, Sch 28, para 9: 'In relation to information held electronically means a printed out version of that information.'

[54]   See also **2.16**.

The meaning of 'exclusive licence' is defined in the principal UK intellectual property legislation[55]. But these definitions are only for the purposes of that legislation. It is generally understood that the words have the following meanings:

- *Exclusive licence.* Under an exclusive licence the licensor agrees not to license anyone else within the scope of the licensee's licence and the licensor agrees not to exploit the licensed rights itself.

- *Sole licence.* Under a sole licence, the licensor agrees not to license anyone else but the licensor may exploit the licensed rights itself.

- *Non-exclusive licence.* Under a non-exclusive licence the licensor can grant similar rights to more than one person and is also able to exercise those itself.

Some lawyers hold that there is no clear distinction between the meanings of 'exclusive' and 'sole'. Also, sometimes agreements refer to the grant of 'sole and exclusive' rights which is confusing, but generally means 'exclusive' (as described above). To avoid any doubt, if any of the terms 'exclusive', 'sole' or 'non-exclusive' are used, their meanings should be defined or included in interpretation provision, for example, along the following lines:

> For the purposes of this Agreement, references to the grant of 'exclusive' rights shall mean that the person granting the rights shall neither grant the same rights to any other person, nor exercise those rights directly in the Field and in the Territory [to the extent that and for as long as the Licensed, Products are within subsisting claims of unexpired Patents, or the Know-how is not public knowledge in the relevant country].

8.4.23   'Exclusive' and 'non-exclusive jurisdiction'

See the discussion at **5.11**.

8.4.24   'Expiry'

If a contract provides for a fixed duration, it may (depending on how the contract is worded) automatically expire at the end of that period. To avoid any doubt over whether this would be a form of 'termination' of the contract (eg for the purposes of the clause dealing with consequences of termination), it may be desirable to include a clause stating that termination includes termination by expiry.

---

[55]   Patents Act 1977, s 130(1); Copyright, Designs and Patents Act 1998, s 92(1) and Trade Marks Act 1994, s 29. There is also a definition of 'exclusive licence' in Capital Allowances Act 2001, s 466.

8.4.25   'Execution' and 'executed'

These are lawyers' terms which cover a number of things but will normally mean, for an ordinary contract, that one or more of the parties signed the contract. For example:

This is to let you know Party A executed the contracted on 5 January 2007[56].

8.4.26   'FOB', 'ex works', 'CIF', etc

These expressions are used mainly in contracts for the supply of goods[57], to describe the allocation of responsibilities for delivery, insurance, risk, etc. It is best to use these terms in accordance with the definitions set out in the International Chamber of Commerce's 'Incoterms', which are updated periodically[58].

If the contract does not specify Incoterms definitions, the terms may be interpreted in accordance with local laws which may be significantly different to the position under Incoterms.

With an ex-works contract, for example, the purchaser is responsible for collecting the goods from the supplier's premises and bears the risk of loss or damage in transit to the purchaser's premises.

8.4.27   'Force majeure'

See the discussion at **5.12.2**.

8.4.

8.4.29   Further assurance

When a transaction is completed there are sometimes further actions one or more parties need to undertake. For example, an agreement may concern the sale of a business (including all its assets, including land and building). One step may be formal registration with the Land Registry to ensure that ownership of the land has passed from one party to another (although the parties may have already passed over possession and use of the land and buildings). A further assurance clause will specify what further steps the parties are obliged to undertake. Such further action is usually confined to the formal steps needed to complete the transaction, in particular signing

---

[56]   See also **2.12**.

[57]   The Incoterms, eg, do not extend to 'intangibles' such as computer software.

[58]   The current version is known as 'Incoterms 2001'. Consult http://www.iccwbo.org/incoterms/.

necessary documents, delivering such documents, co-operating with the other party to make applications to regulatory bodies and so on.

Such a provision is sometimes extended so that if one party refuses or is not available to undertake the necessary steps, the other party can sign documents in the name of the first party[59].

8.4.30   Good faith/agreements to negotiate

Under the laws of some countries, the parties to a contract are required to act in good faith. In England, it has traditionally been thought that there is no general requirement of good faith in contracts, except in certain special cases (eg the requirement for 'utmost good faith' in insurance contracts and good faith in consumer contract terms, ie not to show a significant imbalance in the rights and obligations of the parties to the detriment of the consumer).

Contracting parties sometimes include in their contract an obligation to negotiate the terms of a further agreement in good faith. The general position under English law is that an agreement to negotiate in good faith is not legally binding[60]. However an obligation not to negotiate with any other person for a specified period can be legally binding[61].

Similarly, an obligation to use best endeavours to agree something is not legally enforceable[62].

---

[59]   Where there is this type of provision, it is sometimes in the form of an irrevocable power of attorney. See power of attorney at **8.4.56** and Chapter 1, concerning the formalities for creating a deed.

[60]   See *Walford v Miles* [1992] 2 AC 128, HL. In this case on this subject Lord Ackner referred to an obligation to negotiate in good faith as follows: 'how is the vendor ever to know that he is entitled to withdraw from further negotiations? How is the Court to police such an agreement? A duty to negotiate in good faith is as unworkable in practice as it is inherently inconsistent with the position of a negotiating party; it is here that the uncertainty lies. In my judgment, while negotiations are in existence either party is entitled to withdraw from those negotiations, at any time and for any reason. There can be thus no obligation to continue to negotiate until there is a "proper reason" to withdraw. Accordingly a bare agreement to negotiate has no legal content.'

[61]   For example, undertakings not to enter into an agreement with a third party during the period of the negotiations can be enforced under English law, see *Walford v Miles* [1992] 2 AC 128 and *Pitt v PHH Asset Management Ltd* [1993] 4 All ER 961, CA. Even if this type of agreement contains no express duration provisions it may be enforceable as a contract terminable on reasonable notice, see *Global Container Lines Ltd v Black Sea Shipping Co* [1997] CLY 4535.

[62]   See comments of Millett LJ in *Little v Courage* (1994) 70 P & CR 469, CA: 'An undertaking to use one's best endeavours to obtain planning permission or an export licence is sufficiently certain and is capable of being enforced: an undertaking to use one's best endeavours to try to agree, however, is no different from an undertaking to agree, to try to agree, or to negotiate with a view to reaching agreement; all are equally uncertain and incapable of giving rise to an enforceable legal obligation.' This case was applied in *London and Regional Investments Ltd v TBI Plc* [2002] EWCA Civ 355, [2002] All ER (D) 360 (Mar).

The above points are different from what often occurs in modern commercial dealings: the parties may reach an agreement on the main points of a contract but leave some points for further discussion. However, they never get to discuss those points or agree a final position regarding them but the parties start work and make payments operating on the basis of what is agreed. In such cases and similar situations the courts may find that there is sufficient evidence to show that the parties intended to create legal relations, or the court may be prepared to fill in any gaps in a contract[63].

8.4.31 'Gross negligence'

The expression 'gross negligence' has a specific legal meaning under the laws of some countries, but not under English law[64]. International contracts sometimes include references to gross negligence (eg in liability or indemnity clauses), which are probably not appropriate to English law agreements.

8.4.32 Group companies

It is sometimes useful to include a definition of group companies or affiliates in a contract. This is commonly done by using the definitions of 'subsidiary' and 'holding company' set out in s 1159 of the Companies Act 2006. If a very broad definition is required, an alternative is to make use of the definition of 'group undertaking' set out in s 1162 of the Companies Act 2006.

8.4.33 Guarantees (and full title guarantee)

See **8.2**.

8.4.34 'Hereby'

See the comments at **6.5.9**.

---

[63]   See the comments of Rix LJ in *Mamidoil-Jetoil Greek Petroleum Co SA v Okta Crude Oil Refinery AD* [2001] EWCA Civ 406, [2001] 2 All ER (Comm) 193 at [70], reproduced at **1.10.1**.

[64]   There is apparently conflicting case law on this topic, see *Martin v London CC* [1947] KB 628 and *Pentecost v London District Auditors* [1951] 2 KB 759 where the expression was held not to have a definite meaning. In the latter case the use of the phrase was discouraged: 'The use of the expression "gross negligence" is always misleading. Except in the one case of when the law relating to manslaughter is being considered, the words "gross negligence" should never be used in connection with any matter to which the common law relates because negligence is a breach of duty, and, if there is a duty and there has been a breach of it which causes loss, it matters not whether it is a venial breach or a serious breach' (per Lord Goddard, CJ). While in an earlier case a meaning was assigned to 'gross negligence' as 'any negligence is gross in one who undertakes a duty and fails to perform it' (*Lord v Midland Rly Co* (1867) LR 2 CP 339, which appears to be of little assistance in distinguishing between 'ordinary' negligence and a more serious type).

8.4.35   'Hereinafter' and similar words

See the comments on archaic language at **3.6**.

8.4.36   'Including', 'Including without limitation'

See the discussion at **3.9.2**.

8.4.37   Indemnity

See the discussion at **5.8**.

8.4.38   Injunctions

There are two types of injunction: interim (previously known in English law as interlocutory) and final (or permanent). Injunctions normally require a person to do something or prohibit a person from doing something. Contracts sometimes mention injunctions, for example, a confidentiality clause may state that a party will be entitled to an injunction if the other party discloses confidential information. This is probably not appropriate in an English law contract, as injunctions are in the discretion of the court.

8.4.39   Instrument

It is possible for virtually any type of document to be an 'instrument' in writing which is to have a legal effect. The term is old-fashioned but is still used (but is unnecessary in many situations). It is defined in many Acts and its precise meaning varies from Act to Act. For example, an instrument can be a more formal type of document (such as a deed, a court order, etc)[65] or can be every type of written document (see s 122 of the Stamp Act 1891).

8.4.40   Intellectual property

There is no universally accepted meaning for the term 'intellectual property'. It is generally understood to refer to:

- patents (including supplementary protection certificates);

---

[65]   See, eg, **8.2** and s 61 of the Law of Property Act 1925.

- registered designs;

- the separate protection known as design rights;

- community registered and unregistered designs;

- copyright;

- database right;

- registered and unregistered trade marks;

- community trade marks;

- applications for registered intellectual property (principally patents and trade marks).

Know-how is sometimes treated as a type of intellectual property—it is commonly licensed and sold in the same way as the above types of intellectual property. However, it is not, strictly speaking, a form of property[66]; it may be more accurate to describe know-how as information (particularly technical information) which may be protected under the law of confidence.

'Intellectual property' is defined for specific purposes in certain statutes[67]. However, none of the definitions are comprehensive or entirely consistent among themselves; also most do not deal with the considerable EU-wide intellectual property rights. For example, the Companies Act 2006[68] defines intellectual property as: 'any patent, trade mark, registered design, copyright or design right … any licence under or in respect of such right'.

This definition seems to confuse types of intellectual property (patents, trade marks, etc) with licences under intellectual property[69]. This 'lumping together'

---

[66] Although it capable of being treated as an asset, see *Moriarty v Evans Medical Supplies* [1958] 1 WLR 66, *Rolls-Royce* v *Jeffrey; Rolls-Royce* v *IRC* [1962] 1 All ER 801, HL.

[67] Companies Act 1985, s 396(3A); Atomic Energy Authority Act 1998, s 8(2); Income and Corporation Taxes Act 1988, Sch 25, Pt II; Finance Act 2000, s 129(1); and Finance Act 2002, Sch 29, Part 1, para 2.

[68] See s 861(4A).

[69] A similar confusion arises in some other legislation, see, eg, Finance Act 2002, Sch 29, Part 1, para 2:

'References in this Schedule to an intangible asset include, in particular, any intellectual property.

For this purpose "intellectual property" means—

(a) any patent, trade mark, registered design, copyright or design right, plant breeders' rights or rights under section 7 of the Plant Varieties Act 1997 (c. 66),

(b) any right under the law of a country or territory outside the United Kingdom corresponding to, or similar to, a right within paragraph (a),

(c) any information or technique not protected by a right within paragraph (a) or (b) but having industrial, commercial or other economic value, or

(d) any licence or other right in respect of anything within paragraph (a), (b) or (c).'

The Income Tax Act 2007, s 195(6) covers the first two items but not items (c) and (d).

of intellectual property and rights in or under intellectual property is not uncommon in legislation which is not primarily concerned with intellectual property—reflecting perhaps the lack of specialist IP knowledge on the part of the drafters and the absence of a generally recognised definition.

None of the principal pieces of UK intellectual property legislation provides a definition of intellectual property[70]. The term industrial property is sometimes used, (although now largely superseded by the term intellectual property). Industrial property is sometimes understood to mean patents and industrial designs, but not copyright (or at least not copyright for non-industrial items, eg literary works)[71].

Note, there is no general cateogry of intellectual property law protection; instead it is necessary to consider the specific protection given for each type of property. Although UK intellectual property for different types of property was drafted at different times, the rules governing transactions in each type are not entirely uniform. The differences are now somewhat reduced with the implementation of EU directives and regulations intended to harmonise intellectual property within the EU[72]. Also there is the introduction of a number of EU-wide intellectual property rights (such as the community trade mark); these have further reduced the differences between transactions in various types of intellectual property.

8.4.41   Interpretation

It is conventional to include interpretation provisions in contracts in the boilerplate section of an agreement, for example, as follows. In the absence of such provisions, the provisions of s 61 of the Law of Property Act 1925 (see **8.2**) may apply.

Example:

In this Agreement:

(a)   the headings are used for convenience only and shall not affect its interpretation;[73] and

---

[70]   For example, Patents Act 1977, Copyright, Designs and Patents Act 1988 and the Trade Marks Act 1994.

[71]   For example, on the European Commission internal market website industrial property consists of inventions (ie patents), industrial designs (design right, registered designs) and trade marks. See [http://ec.europa.eu/internal_market/indprop/index_en.htm].

[72]   Such as the Registered Designs Act 1949 (heavily amended by the Regulatory Reform (Registered Designs) Order 2006, SI 2006/1974).

[73]   For judicial commentary on the effect of headings in legislation see *DPP v Schildkamp* [1971] AC 1, HL per Lords Reid and Upjohn.

(b)   references to persons shall include incorporated and unincorporated persons[74]; references to the singular include the plural[75] and vice versa; and references to the masculine include the feminine; and

(c)   references to clauses shall mean clauses of this Agreement.

8.4.42   'Joint venture'

The expression 'joint venture' has no specific legal meaning under English law (unlike the position in some countries). There is no English statute on joint ventures, comparable to the Companies Acts for companies[76]. In practice, joint ventures are often set up as partnerships or as companies in which each of the joint venturers is a shareholder. Sometimes each joint venturer will own 50% of the issued share capital of the company.

8.4.43   Law and jurisdiction

This covers two issues:

- *Law:* which country's law should deal with the interpretation of the provisions of an agreement and/or the disputes which arise from the agreement or its performance; and

- *Jurisdiction:* which country's courts should resolve issues arising from the agreement.

It is entirely possible for one country's courts to resolve a dispute between parties to an agreement but use another country's law. See the discussion at **5.11**. International conflict of laws is a complex subject on which specialist advice should be obtained.

8.4.44   Licence

A licence is a permission to do something[77]. In intellectual property agreements it is a right to do the things specified in the licence which would otherwise be

---

[74]   See discussion of 'persons' below.

[75]   However, wording of this kind should not be relied on if changing to the plural would alter the 'character' of the provision. Instead specific wording should be used in the relevant clause. See *Blue Metal Industries Ltd v Dilley* [1970] AC 827, PC; *Floor v Davis (Inspector of Taxes)* [1980] AC 695, HL (both cases concerned the interpretation of legislation).

[76]   Although the term does appear in tax legislation, eg Corporation Tax Act 2001, s 584, where the definition is in relation to certain property transactions.

[77]   For example, a licence 'is an authority to do something which would otherwise be wrongful or illegal or inoperative': per Latham CJ, *Federal Commissioner of Taxation v United Aircraft Corpn* (1943) 68 CLR 525.

an infringement of the intellectual property; while in real property law (land, houses, flats), a licence is different to a lease[78].

8.4.45   'Material' and 'substantial'

These terms are sometimes used in contracts, for example, a termination clause providing that a party can terminate for 'material breaches' or 'substantial breaches' by the other party, or a clause prohibiting a party from disposing of a 'substantial part' of its assets. These terms are often designed to exclude minor or trivial breaches[79], parts or whatever, but their precise meaning will often be unclear[80], and will be a matter for interpretation by the court in each case[81].

There is a body of case law on the meaning of 'substantial' in cases involving payment of rent under leases. In the particular circumstances of those cases it has been held that £14 was not a substantial proportion of £175 (ie 8%), nor £23 a substantial portion of £280[82] (ie 8.2%), £15 was not a substantial portion of £185[83] (ie 8.1%), £70 was not a substantial portion of £520 (ie 13.5%), although it was 'very near the borderline'[84] (this may suggest that a figure of around 15% is substantial). In another case, 9.12% of the rent was not considered to be a substantial part of the whole rent[85]. However, as Lord Scarman put it[86]:

---

[78] For example, *Street v Mountford* [1985] AC 809.

[79] For example, in one case it was held that the word 'material' could be derived from 'the normal dictionary definition of material as 'of serious or substantial import, of such consequence, important', see *DB Rare Books Ltd v Antiqbooks (a limited partnership)* [1995] 2 BCLC 306, CA, and in another case 'substantial' in the phrase 'substantial economic hardship' meant more than ordinary, everyday variations and difficulties arising in economic circumstances; it meant something weight or serious', see *Superior Overseas Development Corpn and Phillips Petroleum (UK) Co v British Gas Corpn* [1982] 1 Lloyd's Rep 262.

[80] See *Terry's Motors Ltd v Rinder* [1948] SASR 167.

[81] See *Dalkia Utilities Services Plc v Celltech International Ltd* [2006] EWHC 63 (Comm), [2006] All ER (D) 203 (Jan) for an analysis of recent case law on the meaning of 'material breach'. In this case some factors which were taken into consideration included the seriousness of the breach (such as the party missing three payments out of 174, and each missed payment was not trivial or minimal). Other factors to be taken into account included: (i) the circumstances surrounding the breach, including the provisions of the agreement as well as the nature and consequence of the breach; (ii) explanations as to why the breach had occurred (but the facts of the case indicated non-payment was not due to mistake or administrative error). A determining fact as to the seriousness was that if a payment was three days late that party not in breach had the right to require payment of the entire outstanding sum, and this indicated the importance placed on prompt payment.

[82] *Palser v Grinling* [1948] 1 All ER 1 at 11, HL.

[83] *Artillery Mansions Ltd v Macartney* [1949] 1 KB 164, CA.

[84] *Woodward v Docherty* [1974] 1 All ER 844, CA.

[85] *Mann v Cornella* (1980) 254 *Estates Gazette* 403, CA.

[86] See *Woodward v Docherty* [1974] 2 All ER 844, CA per Lord Scarman, cited in *Nelson Developments Ltd v Taboada* (1994) 24 HLR 462, CA.

'… arithmetic can help a lot; but even so it is not capable of answering the question—what is "substantial"? In applying the subsection, arithmetic is a handy tool, a useful check, but not, in my judgment, a determining factor.'

In particular cases, rather than relying on words such as 'material' or 'substantial' it may be better to specify what is to happen when a particular type of breach occurs.

8.4.46   'Merchantable quality'

This is no longer the correct phrase to use for goods bought or sold in England and Wales (although it is still used for goods bought and sold in the US). See the discussion of satisfactory quality at **8.4.62**.

8.4.47   'Mutatis mutandis'

This is a horrible Latin expression, which when it is used in contracts usually means something like 'making such changes as are necessary'. For example, under a contract party A gives a detailed undertaking to indemnify party B against losses arising from party A's negligence. At the end of the clause which sets out A's undertaking, there may be a sentence which reads:

> Party B shall indemnify party A in equivalent terms to the indemnity given by party A above, *mutatis mutandis*.

In most cases it will be preferable to state the obligation specifically rather than rely on this kind of lawyers' shorthand.

8.4.48   'Negligence'

In relation to exemption clauses, see the discussion at **6.5.22**.

8.4.49   'Negotiate'

Where a person or organisation has an obligation to negotiate the terms and conditions of a (further) agreement it might be unclear, unless expressly stated, what they are entitled to do. For example, a sales agent may be required to obtain sales and then negotiate the terms and conditions of that sale, or professional advisors (such as lawyers or accountants) will sometimes be instructed to settle some or all of the terms and conditions of a contract between their client and another party in a proposed deal. The issue is the extent of the power to negotiate and when that power to negotiate will terminate in the absence of clear instructions. In one case a power to negotiate was held to mean to settle all the terms and conditions including the price with the power ending when the consenting party gave its consent[87].

8.4.50   'Nominal sum'

Contracts sometimes provide for the payment by one party to the other of a nominal sum (eg £1), to ensure that consideration passes under the contract (as to which, see **1.9**)[88].

8.4.51   'Notarisation'

Notarisation usually covers one of the following situations:

- a person signing a document in the presence of a notary[89]; or

- the notary certifying a copy of an original document (and stating or not stating the original is genuine); or

- a notary making statements about facts or law[90].

Notaries do not have a role in England and Wales[91] but do have an important role in most other countries. For commercial matters a notary is often needed where there is a party based in England and:

- is entering into a transaction with a party based in another country (an agreement is being signed)[92]; or

- is giving authority to someone to act on its behalf in another country (such as the giving of a power of attorney); or

---

[87]   *Re Macgowan* [1891] 1 Ch 105.

[88]   In *Midland Bank Trust Co Ltd v Green* [1981] AC 513, HL, Lord Wilberforce commented: '"Nominal consideration" and a "nominal sum" in the law appear to me, as terms of art, to refer to a sum or consideration which can be mentioned as consideration but is not necessarily paid.'

[89]   Or notary public or public notary. They mean the same thing. Scrivener notaries are also encountered but their role is the same as 'ordinary' notaries in England and Wales.

[90]   For example, that the directors are entitled to sign a document on behalf of a company (implying that the notary has determined that the company exists and is validly constituted), the company has the power to enter into such a transaction, that the directors are in fact directors, and have the power to sign such documents on behalf of the company (implying that the company's records have been checked such as minute book); and/or that a document has been signed in accordance with English law.

[91]   Except two or three very minor instances which are unlikely to arise in commercial transactions. For more on notaries (including finding one) see http://www.thenotariessociety.org.uk/.

[92]   The signing of contracts before a notary is not a requirement of English law. Sometimes contracts entered into with parties based in other countries (or contracts made under the law of a country other than England) are required to be signed in the presence of a notary.

- is required to establish certain facts (eg an English company opening a foreign bank account may need to provide a notarised copy of its certificate of incorporation and memorandum and articles of association which the notary would obtain directly from the Registrar of Companies and then notarise); or

- is registering a transaction, a person or company, etc with a government department or agency in another country (such as filing an assignment of a patent).

Generally, an English party will only know that a notary is required when it is involved in a transaction or event in another country (or with a party in another country) and the English party is informed by the other party to a transaction or by their agent or adviser, that the use of a notary is necessary.

The formalities of using a notary are high, including checking the identities of persons signing the document and also, separately and in addition, checking the 'identities' of the organisations the persons signing work for or represent[93].

For most documents which need to go abroad there is a further step: legalisation (the validation of the signature and seal of a notary). For many countries this is done by the Foreign and Commonwealth Office[94]. Some countries do not require legalisation (mainly commonwealth countries and many states in the United States)[95].

8.4.52   *Notices*

See discussion at **5.12.1**.

8.4.53   *'Notwithstanding'*

This means 'despite', as in:

> Notwithstanding clause 4 above, X shall ...

---

[93]   Such as making checks with the Registrar of Companies (and often obtaining a 'certificate of good standing' from the Registrar) and examining the minutes book of a company registered or regulated by the Companies Act 2006. The level of formality required to get documents notarised is sometimes very unfamiliar to business people in England and Wales.

[94]   For countries which have signed the Hague Convention of 5 October 1961 abolishing the requirements of legalisation for foreign public documents. Most commercially significant countries are members of the convention (such as all EU countries, many countries in Latin America, India, New York and California (and a few other states) in the USA, but not China).

[95]   Such as most Commonwealth countries, including Australia, Canada and New Zealand. Nearly all Arab countries are not part of the Convention, therefore legalisation will take place directly with the country's embassy or consulate. New York and California are the two principal states in the United States which do require legalisation (through the FCO).

A client may find the word confusing, particularly one for whom English is not their first language, and in the authors' experience it has been misunderstood by clients as meaning 'subject to' (ie the exact opposite of the true meaning). If possible, it is suggested that this word be avoided—consider saying 'this clause overrides all other clauses'.

If 'notwithstanding' is used, it should be used sparingly; if several clauses begin 'notwithstanding any other provision of this Agreement', there may be a conflict between those clauses, which is not resolved by use of these words.

8.4.54   'Penalties' and 'liquidated damages'

Under English law a contractual clause which provides for a penalty if a contractual obligation is not met, will generally be void on public policy grounds. By contrast, a 'liquidated damages' clause is normally valid, as long as the amount to be paid by the party who breaches the contract represents a genuine pre-estimate of the other party's likely loss arising from that breach. There is a considerable amount of case law in this area[96].

8.4.55   'Person'

In law, a person may be

- a human being (known in law as an 'individual'[97]), or

- a legal person, for example, a limited company, a corporation incorporated by Royal Charter, a limited liability partnership, etc.

It is common in contracts to clarify (generally in an interpretation clause—see discussion and example above) that the word 'person' is being used in a broad sense, as including organisations such as partnerships (known in English law as 'firms'), companies and limited liability partnerships.

Sometimes very lengthy wording is included in such a clause, for example, stating that bodies such as joint ventures are included. There is a definition in the Interpretation Act 1978, which provides a broad meaning to 'person', but uses rather archaic in language: '"Person" includes a body of persons corporate or unincorporate.' This apparently includes joint ventures and committees[98]. An equivalent definition in slightly more modern language might be as follows:

---

[96]   See *Dunlop Pneumatic Tyre Co Ltd v New Garage & Motor Co Ltd* [1915] AC 79.

[97]   Although even an individual might, exceptionally, be construed as including a company—see *Société United Docks v Government of Mauritius* [1985] AC 585 at 601C, PC.

[98]   *R v Minister of Agriculture and Fisheries, ex p Graham* [1955] 2 QB 140.

'Person' includes both an incorporated and an unincorporated body of persons.

8.4.56   *Power of attorney*

A power of attorney is a type of agency document, where party A gives authority to party B so that party B can act on behalf of party A (and in party A's name). In most circumstances, there is no legal requirement that this type of permission must be in the form of a power of attorney. What distinguishes a power of attorney from another type of agency document is that it must comply with the formalities for the creation of a deed[99]. A power of attorney is sometimes used for the same reason that deeds are generally used[100], but also it is conventional in some transactions for a power of attorney to be included. For example, in an assignment of intellectual property a power of attorney is commonly coupled with a 'further assurance' clause which enables the assignee to sign documents and carry out certain other acts in the name of the assignor (if the assignor refuses or is unable to carry out those acts, such as sign a document which needs to be registered with a government office). Also where a person needs to authorise a person in another country what is usually expected is that the authorising document is called a 'power of attorney'.

8.4.57   *'Procure'*

This is typically used in contracts to mean 'ensure', as in:

> Party A shall procure that its employees comply with the provisions of this Agreement.

In everyday English it is rarely used, except in relation to certain unlawful activities. In contracts, the word 'ensure' will often be preferable.

8.4.58   *Provisos ('provided that …')*

Provisos are old-fashioned, but are sometimes useful. If used properly, a contractual obligation is followed by words such as 'provided that' and these words are followed by a qualification, condition or exception to the contractual obligation just stated.

---

[99]   And which must also comply with and be subject to the Powers of Attorney Act 1971. To use the language of the 1971 Act, the giver of a power of attorney is called the 'donor', and the agent is called the 'donee'. For deeds see **1.3**.

[100]   See **1.3** and following.

Sometimes provisos are used more loosely to tack on an additional provision (such as a separate obligation) to the same clause or sentence; this should be avoided. Nor should the proviso be broader in scope than the first part of the clause; the court may construe the proviso as being limited to the same subject area as the first part of the clause[101]. It will sometimes be preferable to state the proviso in a separate clause and make the first clause subject to it.

8.4.59   Real property

Real property is land and buildings. Everything else is personal property. Intellectual property (see above) is a type of personal property[102].

8.4.60   Reasonableness

The concept of reasonableness is a familiar one in English law, less so under some other countries' laws (where concepts such as good faith (see above) may be more common). In contracts, the most common example may be clauses which require a party not to do something without the other party's consent 'such consent not to be unreasonably withheld'. Ultimately it is for the court to decide what is reasonable or unreasonable conduct; if the parties wish to avoid the uncertainty that this brings, they may prefer to be more specific. For example, in the above example, the contract might specify the circumstances in which it would be unreasonable to withhold consent.

8.4.61   'Representations', 'warranties' and 'undertakings'

These terms have different meanings in different contexts. It is common to include a clause in which a party 'represents, warrants and undertakes' in relation to a list of matters. In this sense, a representation is a statement which predates the contract and induced the other party to enter into it; a warranty is a statement of a fact, forming part of the contract, which the party giving the warranty asserts to be true; whilst an undertaking is an obligation to do something. Thus one does not warrant that one will do something, nor does one undertake that something is true. However, it should be emphasised that the term 'warranty' is used in other senses, for example: (i) a manufacturer's guarantee, or (ii) a contractual promise that is less important than a 'condition'.

---

[101] See *Thompson v Dibdin* [1912] AC 533, HL, and for a case in which this was not done see *Stamp Duties Comr v Atwill* [1973] AC 558, PC.

[102] Patents Act 1977, s 30; Copyright, Designs and Patents Act 1988, s 90; and Trade Marks Act 1994, s 22.

8.4.62 'Satisfactory quality'

This statutory implied term replaced that of 'merchantable quality' in contracts for the sale of goods[103]. See further at **6.5.21.1**.

8.4.63 'Set-off' and 'retention'

Set-off means, in effect, 'deduction' as where a party deducts part of a sum it is due to pay to another party, in satisfaction of a debt owed by the other party to him[104].

Retention is sometimes used to mean 'holding back', as where a contract provides that a sum is not to be paid until the contract work is successfully completed, or that title to goods is retained by the seller until the price for those goods has been paid. Retention of title clauses are notoriously difficult to enforce[105].

The defence of set-off is available under English law. Where a defendant contends that it is entitled to money from the claimant, and relies on this as a defence to the whole or part of the claim, the contention may be included in the defence and set-off against the claim, whether or not it is also a counterclaim[106].

A discussion of the detailed circumstances in which set-off (and a related defence of 'abatement') is available under English law is beyond the scope of this book. Generally, the claim for set-off must in some way relate to the claim made by the claimant. Thus, if the two claims concern unrelated contracts, set-off may not be available.

Rather than rely on the general law of set-off, parties may prefer to agree specific terms in their contract, either:

(a) to exclude any right of set-off, for example, an undertaking to make payments under the contract without any discount, deduction, off-set or counterclaim whatsoever[107]; or

---

[103] 'Merchantable quality' is still encountered in US contracts.

[104] While there are obvious advantages for a party to a contract prohibiting set-off, such as where a seller of goods wishes to prohibit set-off by a buyer of those goods, there is case law which indicates that the requirement of reasonableness under the Unfair Contracts Terms Act 1977 is relevant to clauses which prohibit 'demand, deduction or set-off' (see *Stewart Gill Ltd v Horatio Myer & Co Ltd* [1992] QB 600; *Fastframe Ltd v Lohinski* 3 March 1993 (unreported), CA). Agreements which produce provisions which are too one-sided should be avoided.

[105] Complete books have been written on this subject. For a brief summary see M Anderson and V Warner, *A-Z Guide to Boilerplate and Commercial Clauses* 2006 Tottel Publishing, pp 408–410.

[106] See Civil Procedure Rules, r 16.6.

[107] In *Hongkong and Shanghai Banking Corpn v Kloeckner & Co AG* [1990] 2 QB 514, Hirst J held that such a clause was valid. This case was applied in *Coca-Cola Financial Corpn v Finsat International Ltd* [1996] 3 WLR 849, CA, but distinguished in *National Bank of Saudi Arabia v Skab* (23 November 1995, unreported) at first instance, per Longmore J.

(b) to extend the right of set-off to include all claims that one party may have against another (eg arising under an unrelated contract)[108].

If the right is to be extended, the clause will need careful drafting, for example, to address whether interest on a debt can be deducted, and whether contingent or unascertained debts are to be included, and if so how they are to be calculated. There is also a danger that if it is too broad, the clause may be construed as a penalty, in which case it will be unenforceable[109].

8.4.64   Severance

Parties sometimes provide that if their contract includes unlawful or unenforceable provisions, the unlawful part will be deleted from the contract, and the remaining provisions will remain in force. This may be useful, for example, in relation to anti-competitive provisions such as post-termination restrictions in employment contracts. The deletion of the offending provision is known as severance.

8.4.65   Signed and use of signatures

As indicated at **1.4** for most types of contract, there is no specific requirement that an agreement needs to be in writing, nor a requirement that the agreement is signed by a party to it. A different issue which non-lawyers frequently ask is what constitutes a signature when a party is intending to sign a contract. The following points are derived from case law over the centuries[110]:

- Generally where a signature is used it can consist of the person's name, some variation or abbreviation of it or simply a mark (such as 'X' if a party so wishes).

- A valid signature can also be the name of a party but signed by another person (with the authority or on behalf of the person, eg Jane Smith asks John Adams to sign a contract that Jane Smith is entering into, John Adams could validly sign the contract with the words 'Jane Smith')[111].

Generally a signature does not require physically writing onto a piece of paper. For example, the use of a facsimile (a document sent through a facsimile machine with the signature of a party), a stamp, a name typed on a computer in a word-processing program, etc)[112] can all amount to (and be acceptable

---

[108] Such a provision has been held to be valid: see, eg, *Watson v Mid Wales Rly Co* (1867) LR 2 CP 593 at 600; and *Newfoundland Government v Newfoundland Rly Co* (1888) 13 App Cas 199 at 210.

[109] See, eg, *Gilbert-Ash (Northern Ltd) v Modern Engineering (Bristol) Ltd* [1974] AC 689, HL, considered in *Linden Gardens Trust Ltd v Lenesta Sludge Disposals Ltd* [1994] 1 AC 85, HL.

[110] See, eg, *R v Kent Justices* (1873) LR 8 QB 305.

[111] See, eg, *Re Horne (a bankrupt)* [2000] 4 All ER 550, CA.

[112] *J Pereira Fernandes v Metha* [2006] EWHC 813 (Ch), [29].

as) a signature. However, a third, but distinct, issue is whether a document not signed in a conventional manner is acceptable to another party. A common example is the opening of a bank account. If not signed with a 'real' signature (but with a stamp or the application form is signed and then sent to the bank by facsimile) it may not be acceptable to the bank.

8.4.66   'Subject to'

One clause may be 'subject to' the provisions of another clause. For example, a clause stating the duration of the contract might be stated to be subject to the provisions for early termination (eg in the event of breach or insolvency) set out in another clause. In this sense, the first clause will not apply if it contradicts the other clause. Or, to put it in the words of one judge:

> 'In my judgment, the phrase "subject to" is a simple provision which merely subjects the provisions of the subject subsections to the provisions of the master subsections. When there is no clash the phrase does nothing: if there is a collision, the phrase shows what is to prevail. The phrase provides no warranty of universal collision.'

8.4.67   'Subject to contract'[113]

This phrase is often used in correspondence or draft agreements to state:

- that the provisions of the correspondence or draft agreement are not intended to be legally binding; and
- that legally binding obligations will arise only when a formal, written contract is signed by the parties or at some specific point agreed between the parties[114].

Conventionally documents relating to transactions relating to land are marked with this phrase[115].

If there is any doubt about the status of negotiations or about the wording of any documents exchanged between parties[116] (such as a document labelled 'heads of terms', etc), then at a minimum documents should be labelled 'subject to contract'[117] and also, in addition, the status of the document should be separately spelled out, for example, using the following wording:

---

[113] See also **1.12**.

[114] This phrase will usually prevent the creation of a binding agreement, see *Munton v Greater London Council* [1976] 1 WLR 649; *Cohen v Nessdale* [1982] 2 All ER 97; *Confetti Records (a firm) v Warner Music UK Ltd (trading as East West Records)* [2003] EWHC 1274 (Ch) (2003) *The Times*, 12 June 2003. Also see **1.12**.

[115] No longer necessary following the implementation of s 2 of the Law of Property (Miscellaneous Provisions) Act 1989.

[116] See *DMA Financial Solutions Ltd v BaaN UK Ltd* [2000] All ER (D) 411.

[117] Labelling a document 'heads of terms', 'heads of agreement' is unlikely to be determinative as whether it is to be binding or not, see *Beta Investment SA v Transmedia Europe Inc* [2003] EWHC 3066 (Ch), [2003] All ER (D) 133 (May).

This [*specify type of document*] is not intended to be legally binding, nor to create, evidence or imply any contract, obligation to enter into a contract or obligation to negotiate. Either party may withdraw from negotiations without incurring any liability to the other party, at any time prior to the execution by both parties of a[n] [formal][written] agreement.

However, what is critical is that the parties do nothing (starting or carrying out any work) which might lead to a contract (ie arising out of conduct).

8.4.68   'Such consent not to be unreasonably withheld'

Sometimes the contract provides that an action may only be taken with the consent of the other party (eg subcontracting the work to be done under the contract). In leases and other real property transactions, where a provision is included requiring the consent of another party, it is sometimes implied that the consent will not be unreasonably withheld. Such a term is not generally implied into ordinary commercial contracts[118], and so it should be stated that 'such consent shall not be unreasonably withheld' if this is intended. Similarly, if a party is to be required to give reasons for withholding his consent, this should also be stated in the contract.

It seems the courts may make a distinction between a matter requiring 'a general and unrestricted consent' and consents to very specific matters, for example, approving 'a title or plans which are free from any tenable objection'; in the latter case it seems the court may more readily imply a term that the consent will not be unreasonably withheld, if necessary to give business efficacy to the contract[119]. These principles were stated in cases involving real property transactions, and it is not clear whether the principles would extend to ordinary commercial contracts.

8.4.69   'Term' and 'determine'

Sometimes the word 'term' is used to mean the duration of the contract, whilst 'determine' is used to mean 'terminate'. These are likely to be confusing to many non-lawyers. It is best not to use them in agreements (particularly as there are good, understandable alternatives, as noted here).

---

[118] In *Price v Bouch* (1986) 53 P&CR 254, Millett J commented: 'There is no principle of law that, whenever a contract requires the consent of one party to be obtained by the other, there is an implied term that such consent is not to be unreasonably refused. It all depends on the circumstances.'

[119] This distinction was made by Megarry J in *Clerical Medical and General Life Assurance Society v Fanfare Properties Ltd* (1981, unreported) and approved by the Court of Appeal in *Cryer v Scott Bros (Sudbury) Ltd* (1986) 55 P & CR 183.

8.4.70   *Territory*

Within the United Kingdom. A contract can apply only to part of a country (eg a sales agent being responsible for obtaining sales only in Wales). The precise meaning of Great Britain as opposed to the United Kingdom might not be immediately obvious to an average business person who has not come across the issue before. The Interpretation Act 1978 defines various parts of the United Kingdom (although such meanings are not intended for use in contractual documents)[120]. If they are used without further definition, it is likely a court will apply the statutory meanings[121]. The principal definitions in the 1978 Act are:

- United Kingdom: Great Britain and Northern Ireland[122];

- Great Britain: England, Wales and Scotland[123];

- England, consisting of specific set of counties plus Greater London and the Isle of Scilly;

- Wales, consisting of a specific set of counties.

Outside of the United Kingdom. The issue of defining (and understanding the extent of) territory can equally apply overseas. For example, the European Union is continually expanding and since the first edition of this book, the number of countries which are members has risen from 12 to 15, to 25 and then to 27. Loose or imprecise definitions used in contracts may mean difficulties in interpreting the extent of any rights or obligations[124]. For example, an agreement entered into in 1999 permitting a person to sell a product in a defined territory of the 'European Union' could in 2011 easily lead to arguments as to whether the person can now sell to only the 15 countries who were members in 1999 or the current number (27) in 2011[125].

---

[120] The meanings noted here are intended to be used in other Acts, see s 22(1) of the Interpretation Act 1978.

[121] See *Navigators and General Insurance Co v Ringrose* [1962] 1 All ER 97, CA, a case where 'United Kingdom' was interpreted in a commercial contract. The judge in this case indicated that assigning 'a meaning to a word in Acts of Parliament does not necessarily mean that it has that meaning in commercial documents. Nevertheless, it is of some guidance in ascertaining their true construction'. In this case it was found that there was no evidence that there was a special meaning by custom to be given to the words 'United Kingdom' in commercial documents relating to insurance or of any other nature other that found in an earlier version of the Interpretation Act 1978 (or a passage in *Halsbury's Laws* based on the Act).

[122] Therefore the Channel Islands and the Isle of Man are not part of the United Kingdom, although both are part of the definition of British Isles in the Interpretation Act 1978.

[123] See Union with Scotland Act 1706, art 1 and Interpretation Act 1978, Sch 2, para 5(a).

[124] Some countries and regions are subject to political change and having their borders redefined. The former Yugoslavia and Czechoslovakia are just a couple of examples in recent times.

[125] Clear words in the agreement are desirable. Therefore a territory definition which is for the European Union might include wording to indicate whether it will be amended to allow for new members who join the EU after the date of the agreement.

Even worse is to use words like Europe, America, etc where it is not possible to derive a commercially sound meaning, except by explicit definition in the agreement. While some territory definitions are unlikely to change (eg the 'United States of America' has had a settled meaning for over 60 years), there are other states (or particularly groupings of states) other than the EU whose membership changes from time to time, such as the European Economic Area, or the European Free Trade Association. If the agreement is to define territory based on such groups, the relevant membership needs checking as well as consideration of what is to happen if there is a change in membership after the date of the agreement.

8.4.71   Time of the essence'

An obligation which is of the essence is a fundamental term. Breach of such a term will give the party not in breach the right to terminate the agreement.

This right to terminate when a provision is of the essence will apply even if the breach is trivial or technical. Obligations such as making a payment or delivering something by a certain date are often made 'of the essence', particularly where one party has a stronger bargaining position. For example, an obligation on a party to pay a sum by 5pm on a Monday expressed to be of the essence would be breached if the payment was made by 5.01pm and would give the other party a right to terminate, even if the difference in timing of the payment of one minute made no difference to the party not in breach.

Generally under English law a 'time of the essence' requirement is not implied into obligations[126]. However, time of the essence will be more readily implied in a mercantile contract[127] in appropriate circumstances, such as where there is a fixed date for undertaking an obligation or task and meeting that date is essential[128]. For non-mercantile contracts time will generally not be of the essence unless the parties expressly stipulate that a condition must

---

[126] For example, stipulation as to time of payment (Sales of Goods Act 1979, s 10(1)), other stipulations of time (s 10(2)), providing services within a reasonable time (Supply of Goods and Services Act 1982, s 14) and land (Law of Property Act 1925, s 41).

[127] A contract for the sale of goods, the sale of shares or a charterparty.

[128] See, eg, *Msas Global Logistics v Power Packaging Inc* [2003] EWHC 1393 (Ch); [2003] All ER (D) 211 (Jun), where a clause in an agreement concerning the time for completion of the sale of the entire share capital of a business was found to be of the essence. The key issues are the subject matter of the contract and/or the surrounding circumstances. If a product deteriorates almost immediately then it will be more easy to work out whether time is of the essence. But if the goods are not of this type, then it will be difficult without clear wording in the agreement to make time of the essence. If it is not clear from the wording in the agreement then it will be for a court to work out the solution. The best course is clear wording, such as 'Time is to be of the essence in clause (no) of this agreement' and also separate wording to deal with the consequence of a failure of party under such an obligation (termination, and also outlining the financial consequences for the party not in default).

be strictly adhered to or the subject matter of the contract or its surrounding circumstances indicate that time is of the essence[129].

Although a contract obligation may not be of the essence when the contract is made, it is possible for time to be made of the essence subsequently. If a party is subject to unreasonable delay, and that party then gives notice to the party in breach with the notice making time of the essence[130].

8.4.72   'To the intent that'

This is a very old-fashioned phrase, and is often confused with 'to the extent that'. It is sometimes used to introduce an explanation of the purpose of a provision. It is not recommended for modern contracts.

8.4.73   'Unless the context requires otherwise'

In definitions sections it is sometimes provided that the definitions set out below will apply 'unless the context requires otherwise'. This reflects the practice in the definitions sections of some Acts of Parliament. These words provide a 'safety valve' in case the definition is inappropriate to the usage of a term in a particular clause. Even if not stated, this may be implied[131]. The courts have considered the effect of 'unless the context requires otherwise' type language in legislation[132] and in a company's articles of association[133].

8.4.74   Waiver

If a party is in breach of contract, the other party may choose to ignore the breach or take a long time to react to it. As a matter of general law, if a party wishes to terminate on account of the other party's breach, he should do so without undue delay in a reasonable period of time. Waiver clauses generally

---

[129] See *United Scientific Holdings v Burnley Borough Council* [1978] AC 904. For recent examples where time was not held to be of the essence in non-mercantile: *Lancecrest Ltd v Asiwaju* [2005] EWCA Civ 117, [2005] 1 EGLR 40; *Allardyce v Roebuck* [2004] EWHC 1538 (Ch), [2004] 3 All ER 754.

[130] *Hartley v Hymans* [1920] 3 KB 475; *Charles Rickards Ltd v Oppenheim* [1950] 1 KB 616, [1950] 1 All ER 420. Generally, the notice making time of the essence must allow the party in breach reasonable time to complete, *Green v Sevin* (1879) 13 ChD 589; *Crawford v Toogood* (1879) 13 ChD 153.

[131] See *Meux v Jacobs* (1875) LR 7 HL 481 at 493, per Lord Selborne

[132] *Beswick v Beswick* [1968] AC 58, HL. This case concerned the interpretation of the Law of Property Act 1925.

[133] *Guinness Plc v Saunders* [1990] 2 AC 663, HL.

state that failure to take action in respect of one breach does not amount to a waiver of a party's rights to take action in respect of that current breach or subsequent breaches.

8.4.75   'Whatsoever'

See the comments on this word at **6.5.9**.

8.4.76   'Without prejudice to the generality of the foregoing'

These words are generally used to introduce a specific obligation which may be thought unnecessary in the light of a more general obligation stated earlier. To avoid the general obligation being interpreted in a narrow sense in the light of the specific obligation (ie under the *ejusdem generis* rule at **6.5.17**) words such as 'without prejudice to the generality of the foregoing' are used. The meaning is similar to, but not quite the same as 'including without limitation'.

8.4.77   'Without prejudice'

The words 'without prejudice' when used in communications between parties has quite a different meaning to that given immediately above. Where the phrase is used in negotiations to settle a dispute between parties, then the contents of those negotiations will not normally be revealed to a court[134]. Both oral and written communications can be covered by the 'without prejudice' privilege.

---

[134] See Civil Procedure Rules, r 2.2 and glossary. See *Cutts v Head* [1984] Ch 290 at 306: 'The rule applies to exclude all negotiations genuinely aimed at settlement whether oral or in writing from being given in evidence. A competent solicitor will always head any negotiating correspondence "without prejudice" to make clear beyond doubt that in the event of negotiations being unsuccessful they are not to be referred to at the subsequent trial. However, the application of the rule is not dependent upon the use of the phrase "without prejudice" and if it is clear from the surrounding circumstances that the parties were seeking to compromise the action, evidence of the content of those negotiations will, as a general rule, not be admissible at the trial and cannot be used to establish an admission or partial admission ... the question has to be looked at more broadly and resolved by balancing two different public interests namely the public interest in promoting settlements and the public interest in full discovery between parties to litigation.' Approved in *Rush & Tompkins Ltd v Greater London Council* [1989] 1 AC 1280 at 1299. There are similar statements in *Unilever Plc v Procter & Gamble Co* [2001] 1 All ER 783, [2000] 1 WLR 2436 and most recently *Ofulue v Bossert* [2009] UKHL 16, [2009] 3 All ER 93, [2009] AC 990 and most latterly in *Oceanbulk Shipping and Trading SA v TMT Asia Ltd and Others* [2010] UKSC 44; [2011] 1 All ER (Comm) 1. This latest case provides the most up-to-date statement of the without prejudice rule and the exceptions to it.

Communications which are not made for the purpose of settling a dispute will not have the 'without prejudice' privilege[135].

For example, party A agrees to sell some goods to party B, and party B agrees to pay £100 for those goods. Party B does not pay for the goods. Party A writes a letter to party B which states that party A will accept £90 to settle the matter. If later party B still does not pay and then party A sues party B for the price of the goods, £100, party B could introduce the letter as evidence that party A has gone back on its rights to claim £100. However, if the letter is marked 'without prejudice' then the letter will not normally be admissible in any litigation and party B will not be able to rely on its contents.

It is best to mark correspondence (in whatever form) to negotiate the settlement of a dispute with the words 'without prejudice'[136].

A party may wish to write to another, partly about settling a dispute and partly about other matters (which the party does not mind being shown to a court if the dispute does result in litigation). Those latter matters should normally be put in a separate document (often called 'open' communication).

---

[135] *Standrin v Yenton Minster Homes Ltd* (1991) *The Times*, 22 July 1991, CA. There are some exceptions to the 'without prejudice' privilege, see *Unilever Plc v Proctor & Gamble Co* [2000] FSR 344 at 353–354, CA for a list of some of them. The exceptions to the rule develops from case to case. Although most are fairly limited, new categories are added from time to time.

[136] Although it is usual for correspondence to have the words 'without prejudice', the privilege may still apply if it is clear that the correspondence or other communication was made with the intention of settling a dispute. If it was held that where one letter is written with the words 'without prejudice', the 'without prejudice' privilege will cover all subsequent communications even though they do not have those words (until there is a clear break in the communications), see, eg, *India Rubber, Gutta Percha and Telegraph Works Ltd v Chapman* (1926) 20 BWCC 184, CA. On the later point see also *Unilever Plc v Proctor & Gamble Co* [2000] FSR 344, CA, where it was held that a court should not 'dissect out identifiable admissions and withhold protection from the rest of without prejudice communications (except for a special reason) would not only create huge practical difficulties but would be contrary to the underlying objective of giving protection to the parties, in the words of Lord Griffiths in *Rush & Tompkins Ltd v Greater London Council* [1988] 3 All ER 737 at 740, [1989] AC 1280 at 1300: "to speak freely about all issues in the litigation both factual and legal when seeking compromise and, for the purpose of establishing a basis of compromise, admitting certain facts." Parties cannot speak freely at a without prejudice meeting if they must constantly monitor every sentence, with lawyers or patent agents sitting at their shoulders as minders.'

Chapter 9

Techniques for checking contracts before signing them[1]

9.1　Introduction

This chapter focuses on how to progress from the end of negotiating and drafting an agreement to the point when it is signed. It covers the practical steps that the contract drafter can take to minimise or remove the mistakes, errors or omissions left in the agreement.

Everyone will agree that an agreement needs checking before it is signed. The problem is having the time and the people to do so.

For those involved in the production of large numbers of routine documents/ contracts, having a checking procedure built in can be part of the process of dealing with such documents. Sometimes only a few provisions may change, and consequently, the amount to be checked is reduced[2].

However for individual, bigger contracts or where negotiations carry on right up to the deadline for signing, the time necessary to check an agreement may simply not be available or if available, only within severe time limits. There is no easy answer, and sometimes there is *no* answer, to this problem. Part of the purpose of this chapter is to provide not only suggestions as to the checking that needs to take place but also to make readers aware of potential issues to enable them to decide on what to concentrate.

It is possible to divide the checks required in an agreement into three broad categories:

- *factual information* (correct parties named, correct pricing, correct start and end dates, and so on);

---

[1]　This chapter is intended to be entirely practical. Some of the ways of checking, cleaning up or changing documents involve steps to follow in a word processing program. Microsoft Word is chosen, primarily because it is the most widely used word program. Version 2010 is used as the basis for the examples (although version 2007 has most of the capabilities described). The steps involved for some of the examples are illustrated via the use of keystrokes. Where there is the instruction for 'Alt', press down that key and release it. All other major word processing programs can carry out the functions described, including WordPerfect, OpenOffice, LibreOffice.

[2]　In such cases, often the terms and conditions of an agreement are fixed and only deal-specific information, such as the name of the other party, stated quantities of specific products etc, is required.

- *proofing and formatting* (such as cross-referencing pointing to the right places, definitions correctly applied (ie use of capitals), removal of metadata, removal of version/draft data, making sure the right changes/amendments are applied, checking for typos);

- *commercial issues* (that the agreement as a whole correctly expresses the commercial intentions of the parties rather than being a series of individually negotiated and drafted clauses).

This chapter covers these three areas, as well as dealing with:

1   a 'top-ten' list of priorities that a contract drafter should always check, even if pushed for time;

2   some common-sense suggestions for helping with the process of checking agreements;

3   some issues with using Microsoft Words revision marks function (track changes).

9.1.1   *Obviousness and a step back in time*

Some (or much of) what follows may seem obvious or lead to the response 'Of course I know I have to do this'. However, in a pressured environment sometimes obvious things are missed (because they were just assumed to be right all along or it was correct the last time it was checked). Another point is that in many trades or professions there is a requirement for a written procedure or policy covering how they operate, part of which includes a list of items that need checking. These checklists often prove useful in reducing obvious mistakes or obvious items being overlooked[3].

The use of computer technology to write, amend and exchange agreements has resulted in the reduction of the amount of people involved in an agreement. Before everyone had personal computers (and virtually instant communications with others), the method of preparing an agreement was much more time (and people) consuming:

1   the contract drafter would prepare a draft (whether in writing or dictate it);

2   the draft would be provided to the secretarial staff to type;

---

[3]   For example, the World Health Organisation developed a checklist for use in medical surgery, part of which includes checking the identity of the patient prior to commencing the surgery. This might be rather an obvious thing to do but the introduction of a checklist in operating theatres has reduced the number of errors (eg basic errors, such as not checking the identity of the patient). See http://www.who.int/patientsafety/safesurgery/tools_resources/SSSL_Manual_finalJun08.pdf.

3   after typing the draft agreement the secretarial staff would return it to the contract drafter for checking;

4   the contract drafter would then send the draft agreement to their manager for approval;

5   there might possibly be several iterations of the above procedures before the other side to the deal even received the draft agreement.

Apart from the first step (obviously with the contract drafter typing the agreement, or amending an existing agreement), all the other steps are often omitted.

9.2   Top ten essential things to do (when you are right up against a deadline)

If negotiations have run right up to a deadline, there may not be the time or resources to carry out a full review of an agreement. Even with limited time available, it is still possible to check essential parts of an agreement where most often errors occur[4]:

1   Are the right companies/persons made parties to the agreement?

2   Are the start and end dates correct?

3   Are the price and other payment provisions (timing and method of payment) correctly stated?

4   Does the notices clause contain the right contact details and persons for each party?

5   Have all references to the agreement being a draft, subject to contract or having a version number been removed?[5]

6   Do all cross-references to other clauses, schedules, documents etc point to the correct destinations?

7   Has all metadata been removed?[6]

8   Are all documents referred to in the agreement (such as schedules, other agreements due for execution at the same time, etc) available?

---

[4]   The ten points here are the authors' selection as to what is most important to check. It is possible to create a very (hopefully not completely) different selection on what is important to a client or the particular deal.

[5]   This information is often included in a header or footer.

[6]   Most agreements which go through one or more rounds often use a word processing feature (either built in or as an add-on) to indicate what changes are made.

9   Are there any approvals or decisions contingent on the signature of the agreement (such as a board resolution approving the signing of the agreement or other agreements needing signing signed)?

10   Is the person who is to sign the agreement available to sign at the right time?[7]

9.3   Things to do when there is time

If there are no significant time restrictions on checking an agreement then the following are the matters which need consideration in order to carry out a fuller review of an agreement. To check an agreement 'properly', particularly in the case of longer agreements, it can take many hours and may involve many people. What follows are suggestions (with explanatory comments) of what is possible to check in an agreement; of course, not all points will be relevant for every agreement.

9.3.1   Process steps

Here are some practical steps to help with the process of checking an agreement:

1   Stop looking at the agreement (put it aside and take a break from looking at the document over and over again).

2   Do you want to read the agreement on screen? If so:

(a) use the zoom function to make the text bigger or use other reading aids available in modern word processors[8];

(b) do you work in a room/office with poor overhead lighting/fluorescent lighting, or does the screen you are using face a window? All of these will tire your eyes and reduce your concentration.

---

[7] In some organisations, agreements of particular types can only be signed by certain persons. Beyond mere authority to sign, some organisations also require a particular procedure before the right person will/can sign. For example, when an agreement is ready for signature, there may be a requirement that a 'signing note' is prepared, outlining the main commercial points, how the draft agreement accords (or not) with the standard template the organisation has, and so on.

[8] For example in Microsoft Word 2010 consider the full-screen reading function (Alt, W (view), F (Full Screen Reading)). Other methods: increase the type size (quick way in Microsoft Word (after making a copy of the file): (Control+A (select the whole document), then Alt, H (Home ribbon), FS (select type size on that ribbon), enter new type size, press enter or return key).

3   Print the agreement out on paper (old-fashioned nowadays, but looking at an agreement in another medium can sometimes help in checking it)[9].

4   Whether you read on-screen or on paper, do not read the agreement from the start to finish, but either (or both):

   (a) read it in small sections (with intervals in between or start at the end); or

   (b) select a logical section of provisions and read only those at any one time (eg payment provisions, termination provisions, etc).

5   Have someone else look at the agreement. If you can do this:

   (a) brief them on wording or issues which have changed the most (to concentrate their efforts on what is important);

   (b) where a clause has undergone most revision, read it aloud to them[10].

6   For wording which is difficult to understand either read it aloud (to yourself, or if someone is available and willing to participate, to them). Does it make sense? Are commas in the right place? Do you run out of breath midway or towards the end of a sentence (a sign that a sentence is too long)?

7   For longer clauses (or clauses which contain several parts or sub-clauses) break the clause down into its parts. Does each part make sense?

8   Draw up a list of key issues which need careful checking.

9   Gather together (either on paper or in a computer folder) all the relevant documents relating to the negotiations and preparations for entering into the agreement (including saving emails to file)[11].

---

[9]   If the agreement is formatted so that the text is in a small typeface, make a copy of the file, in the copy select all the text and make the text size larger (at least 12pt) and then print that version onto paper.

[10]   At first sight this may sound a bizarre suggestion, but in the authors' experience reading a clause aloud can often reveal things which reading silently cannot (or which appear fine). For example, reading a long sentence aloud can sometimes reveal that its meaning is not clear.

[11]   Nowadays, such information is also found in text messages and voice mail messages left on mobile telephones, both of which can be extracted from the telephone and often contain key commercial information or points of agreement. For example, if the parties were discussing the price that one party should pay for the goods of another, the senior executives might negotiate over the telephone, with the one executive agreeing to communicate their decision on the other party's proposal at a later stage. That executive might communicate their decision via text message in the minute or two available between meetings as the quickest way of doing so. It might be the only permanent record of what was agreed as to the price. Having a more tangible record of that decision may be important in the event of a dispute later on.

9.4   Factual information

This section provides common factual issues that need checking to ensure they are correct (or need to be present when the signing of the agreement takes place).

9.4.1   Parties[12]

1   Is each party correctly identified?[13]

2   Are their names spelt accurately?

3   Is the correct legal status of each party stated (Limited, PLC, LLP, etc)?

4   If a party is an individual, is their 'proper' name used (eg if the person's name is 'Robert Allan Smith' is this used rather than variations such 'RA Smith', 'Bob Smith', 'R Allan Smith' or 'Al Smith')?

5   Is the official address (and where relevant, the principal business address) stated?

6   If the party has an official number, is it correctly stated?

9.4.2   Pricing and payment terms

1   Are the amounts payable correctly stated?

2   If several payments are envisaged, are the periods and amounts of each correct?[14]

3   Are the timings of the payments accurate?

4   Are the amounts exclusive or inclusive of VAT and is this clear?[15]

5   Is the method of payment correctly stated?

---

[12]   For more on parties see **2.5**. For obtaining 'official' information for companies registered in the UK use the webcheck page of the Registrar of Companies website: http://www. companieshouse.gov.uk/. For non-UK companies, see the list of links maintained by the Registrar of Companies (see http://www.companieshouse.gov.uk/links/introduction. shtml#reg).

[13]   A party may be part of a large group of companies. The representative of a party dealing with preparing the final version of the agreement may have been dealing with a representative of another party but that other party may not be the contracting party.

[14]   For example, a party may make a payment on signing the agreement, and then various staged payments dependent on when certain activities under the agreement occur. When certain activities occur, any attendant payments are often the subject of intense commercial negotiations and subject to change.

[15]   For most business-to-business transactions, prices are normally always stated as exclusive of VAT; for consumer transactions as inclusive.

6   Are the correct banking details stated (including the right account number, sort code, BIC and IBAN numbers)?[16]

7   Are any payment reference numbers correctly stated, if obtained?

8   For the supply of goods, is the point when the risk and the property pass correctly stated?

9   If the pricing and/or payment terms were the subject of (extensive) commercial negotiations, is there a (permanent and file) record of what was agreed?

10 Are there any internal financial or accounting controls or approvals that need dealing with, so it is possible for the making of payments (or for the receipt of payments so that party's accounting system correctly allocates them) at the right time(s)?

11 If a payment needs making on signature of the agreement are the funds available to do so?

9.4.3   *References to official bodies, regulations, etc*

- Are there references to International Chamber of Commerce terms such as CIF, EXW, FOB etc. If so, are the correct terms and the correct version used (eg Incoterms 2010, Incoterms 2000)?[17]

- Is there reference to an official body, association or regulatory body? Is its full (ie spelt-out) official name used?

- Is there reference to a particular statute, regulation or legislative measure? Is it properly stated?[18]

- Where there is a reference to a statute etc, will the particular clause in which the reference to the statute is located also apply where the statute etc is amended or replaced? If so, is there appropriate wording to deal with this?[19]

---

[16] Many banks nowadays will not deal with payments unless the BIC and IBAN numbers are provided.

[17] It is possible to check the basic meaning of each term at http://www.iccwbo.org/incoterms/.

[18] For English law it is possible to find the most recent Acts of Parliament and statutory instruments, in their amended versions, at http://www.legislation.gov.uk/.

[19] The wording for this is often contained in an 'interpretation' clause which deals with a number of 'meaning' issues, such as references to the masculine also refers to the feminine. Wording which addresses the point specifically is usually along the lines of: 'Any reference in this agreement to any statute or statutory provision shall be construed as referring to that statute or statutory provision as the same may from time to time be amended, modified, extended, re-enacted or replaced (whether before or after the date of this agreement) and including all subordinate legislation made under it from time to time'.

9.4.4   *Notices clauses*

- If a specific person is named is it the correct person?[20]

- Is an accurate role title used (managing director, project director)?

- Are the address and other contact details correctly stated?[21]

- Are the correct methods of providing notices included (eg whether email is permitted, the number of days allowed for a notice to be deemed as received?)

9.4.5   *Start and termination dates (and other periods of time)*

- Is the correct start date used (such as in a definition of 'Commencement Date')?

- If there is a fixed termination date, is this the correct date (such as in a clause dealing with termination of an agreement or a clause dealing with main contractual obligations of a party)?

- If a party needs to make payments on certain dates or by certain times are these accurate?

- If a party needs to make a payment or carry out a certain activity within a specific period, are these correctly stated?

- If there are any post-termination time periods, are these correctly stated?[22]

---

[20]   It is not always appropriate to name a particular individual. In some roles, there may be a high turnover of staff, or the industry may be subject to re-organisation. If it is possible to send a notice by email and the email address is that of a particular person and they leave, then the email may not be forwarded to the right person (eg if no-one instructs IT support to set up forwarding of emails for those that leave).

[21]   If the registered address is used, does mail get forwarded to its intended destination in a timely manner? Some companies may frequently undergo restructuring and other organisational changes with a particular division or department changing from one location to another. In larger organisations those at the registered office may not have all the latest information as to where persons, departments etc are located. In such cases, a notice sent to the registered office may take time to reach the right person. There is a similar issue with the use of emails. If an email address is given which is the name of a specific person, and that person moves on, then any emails (after a time or at all) may not be forwarded appropriately. These points are likely to be relevant only where the party sending a notice does no more than is formally required by the notices clause (and does not contact the other party in any other way to indicate that a formal notice is on its way).

[22]   For example, a licensee may have a trade mark or other intellectual property licence from a licensor. There may be post-termination provisions in the agreement, which may include time periods in which the licensee can sell off any remaining stock, pay any royalties on stock sold prior to the date of termination, or dispose of any stock or (confidential) documents.

- If there is a period stated for how long information is to remain confidential, is the correct length of time included?[23]

9.4.6   Timing

- Have the start and/or end dates changed? Have the changes been made in the agreement?

- Are there changes in the contract which will have a knock-on effect on other clauses concerning timing of activities or termination of some or all of the contract? For example:

  ○ in a contract which provides for defined stages each with a specific period of time for completion, if one or more of the stages are changed then any dates or periods of time or termination date may no longer be achievable or accurate;

  ○ if the specification for the goods or services is changed, any change may affect when parts of the contract take place, such as when certain tasks are carried out, the timing of payments (as well as the amount of payments) etc.

9.4.7   Consequences of termination

- Are any cross-references to other clauses which are to survive termination correct?[24]

- Have any specific provisions which are to survive termination been checked for accuracy?

- Is there a clause which states that other than those clauses which survive termination, the parties are under no further obligation to each other?

---

[23] The length will depend very much on the time of information as well as the nature of the agreement. For example, an agreement might be for the design of a new product and one of the parties may be providing technical specifications of the new product to a designer. Before launch of the product the technical specification may need protection as confidential information but after it would not make any sense to bind the designer to confidentiality obligations if the technical specification becomes public knowledge on launch of the product.

[24] Often the clause that indicates which clauses survive termination does not receive sufficient attention; particularly, if clauses are added and removed during negotiations and any cross-referencing is not updated to take account of such changes. As a practical point, in many agreements clauses which typically survive termination deal with issues of confidentiality, payment provisions, maintenance of records (if relevant), continuation or expiry of (intellectual property) licences, and issues concerning warranties and indemnity. Obviously what will need including will depend on the nature of the agreement, as well as the drafting technique of the party preparing the agreement.

9.4.8   Third parties

- Will the agreement allow any third party directly to enforce one or more provisions? If so, does the third parties clause identify which clause(s) allows for this?[25]

- If there is a provision which is intended to allow a third party directly to enforce it, is the wording used sufficiently clear to identify the party and to indicate that the contracting parties intended for the third party to benefit under the agreement?[26]

9.4.9   Law and jurisdiction

- Does the agreement involve parties from more than one country? Is so:
- Has the correct law that applies to the agreement been used?
- Has the jurisdiction of the correct country's courts been chosen?
- Is the jurisdiction to be exclusive or non-exclusive?

9.5   Proofing and formatting

This section concentrates on the elements which concern the formatting of an agreement.

9.5.1   Removal of version draft data

If an agreement goes through multiple stages of drafting and exchange between the parties, a party (or its lawyers) may have a policy to mark all agreements with the fact that it is a draft, the number of the draft and the date (plus sometimes other information). The party who is responsible for producing the final version for signature should normally remove this information.

Typically such information is stored in a header[27] or in the properties section[28] of a word processing program.

---

[25]   This assumes that there is the 'standard' type of clause found in most agreements nowadays which expressly disclaims the provisions of the Contracts (Rights of Third Parties) Act 1999 Act (such as found in clause 8.13 of Precedent 1 in the Appendix).

[26]   There is recent case law which indicates that the parties have to intend to benefit a third party as one of the purposes of the agreement. Obviously, the clearer the wording the less likely there will be any doubt on this point.

[27]   To completely remove a header in Microsoft Word: Alt, N (Insert Tab), H (Header), R (Remove Header).

[28]   To display the properties section of a Microsoft Word document: Alt-F, I.

9.5.2   *Figures and words*

If a party wants to use both words and figures, such as

> Fixed amounts: In consideration for the Services, the Company shall pay to the Consultant the following amounts on the following dates:
>
> (a)   £123,750 (one hundred and twenty three thousand and seven hundred and fifty pounds sterling) within 30 days of the date of this Agreement; and
>
> (b)   £100,000 (one hundred thousand pounds sterling) within 30 days of the first anniversary of the Commencement Date.'

the words need checking against the figures. Although there is no legal requirement to state both (at least in England) some parties like this style of drafting (perhaps as a safety check)[29].

9.5.3   *Cross referencing*

An agreement will often include clauses which:

- make reference to other clauses (what is to happen to them, or how they are to operate in a particular circumstance); or

- are subject to a clause in another part of the agreement (such as the other clause coming into force or expiring or operating on the occurrence of a particular event); or

- need reading together with another clause or wording within the same clause.

There is nothing remarkable in cross-referring to other clauses in an agreement. The problem is that when agreements are drafted, (sub-)clauses can be added and/or deleted such that any existing cross-referencing is no longer accurate.

Tip: All modern word processors include a cross-referencing feature. This will generate an automatic cross reference to either a clause number or page, together with an optional hyperlink. In the event of an addition or deletion, the word processor will adjust the cross reference number (with user intervention).

Danger: While using the cross-referencing feature of a modern word processor can make it easy to add one, the danger is to make sure the cross-references are updated after every revision[30].

---

[29]   There is a presumption, where there is a difference between the amounts in words and figures that the former is used (See **3.11**).

[30]   For example, in Microsoft Word, the way to make all cross-references up to date (assuming that they are in use) is to select the whole document (Control+A) then press the F9 key.

9.5.4   *Definitions*

The use of definitions can cause a number of problems, including:

- If the definition contains a reference to a clause or schedule, are the references correct?[31]

- Is the styling of a definition applied consistently in the agreement? For example, in England, the usual way of notifying a user of an agreement that a definition is being used is by capitalising the defined words (eg Intellectual Property, Net Sales Value).

- Are there any uses of defined words which are not styled as definitions? Is this intended?[32]

- Does the definitions clause include 'unless the context provides otherwise' or similar wording? If the agreement contains such wording is it relevant to the agreement?[33]

Other points about definitions:

- *Order of definitions:* If they are to appear in alphabetical order, but some definitions are added, have all the definitions been sorted into alphabetical order?[34]

- *Definitions appearing other than in the definitions clause:* Does the agreement contain definitions contained within clauses of the agreement other than

---

[31]   As the negotiating and drafting progresses, schedules are sometimes added, moved in the order in which they appear, or broken down into separate schedules; all of which might lead to the number assigned to a particular definition no longer being accurate.

[32]   With modern word processors it is possible to do case-sensitive searches. An ordinary search for 'intellectual property' will find all instances of these words, including 'intellectual property', 'Intellectual property', 'intellectual Property' and 'Intellectual Property'. While a case-sensitive search of 'Intellectual Property' will find only those words with initial capitals, it is possible to search for any instances where the words are not capitalised (if the definition appears frequently in a longer document or series of documents), but ignoring those words which are capitalised. For example, to search for lower case 'intellectual property' and ignore any capitalised 'Intellectual Property', undertake a search for 'intellectual property' and check the 'match case' in Microsoft Word (Alt, H (Home Tab), FD (Find), A (Advanced)) to open the find and replace window.

[33]   There is recent case law on how a court will look at a definition which does not make sense when used in a clause. Although a court will be reluctant to depart from the meaning as stated in the definition, it appears that the use of 'unless the context requires otherwise' may provide a slightly more open door for a court to do so.

[34]   Modern word processors can automatically sort paragraphs or rows of tables. Often definitions are set out in two column tables (the first column containing the defined word, the second containing its meaning). However it is not necessary to use a table in Microsoft Word to sort words or paragraphs (each separated by the enter/return key). To sort lists in Microsoft Word: First select the text/list for sorting, then Alt, H (Home Tab), SO (Sort Text) and choose 'paragraph' under Sort By (if not sorting within a table).

the definitions clause (typically clause 1)? If this is the case, should the definitions clause contain a cross reference to this definition?

9.5.5   Schedules

Where an agreement contains schedules, the following are the likely issues that may occur:

- Where there is reference to a schedule in the agreement, is the correct reference used at each point? For example, if a clause refers to 'schedule 2' is schedule 2 in the agreement? For some agreements schedules are added or removed and the number in the agreement may need changing.

- Does the agreement use the same term to refer to a schedule (ie is it a 'schedule', an 'annex' or an 'appendix')?

- Is there a boilerplate clause which states that the schedules are part of the agreement? ie 'The schedules to this Agreement are and shall be construed as being part of this Agreement.'

- Is the schedule placed before or after the signature block? This is a matter purely of convention, but the practice in US agreements is for the signature block to appear after the schedule, while in UK agreements they usually appear before.

9.5.6   Spell checking

This is so obvious, why mention it? Most modern word processors will show under each word whether it is spelt correctly or not. What is not often checked is whether the correct document language is used or 'spelling check as you type' is turned off altogether. In either case, mistyped words will not show, and unless a spell check is run then the misspelt words may remain in the agreement.

The authors recommend that any use of spell-checking should *not* be delegated to a secretary or administrator. We have seen mistakes introduced into an agreement through incorrect acceptance of alternatives suggested by the spell-check, eg 'inure' being changed to 'insure'.

9.5.7   Clearing the document of metadata

See Chapter 10 for the meaning of metadata. The issue here is how to remove it in such a way that if the agreement is then circulated amongst the parties (or third parties) there is no, or very little, chance of the metadata being recovered or seen at some subsequent point. A party may have added comments or used revision marks to add internal comments not intended for sight by anyone. Sometimes a party may add different commercial information (such as pricing information) which is intended for internal review. Sometimes this information may amount to confidential information or provide valuable insight into how a party operates.

Frequently, particularly in larger organisations, a document may be sent from person to person for internal review, all of whom might add comments etc, but there is no one person who is responsible for dealing with the issue of information contained within the document before it is sent out to the other party[35].

The removal of metadata is an issue not only for the final version of an agreement, but at any stage when a version of an electronic document is exchanged with another party (or their representative). Consider the following common example: a company enters into an agreement for the supply of a product and the terms and conditions are negotiated over a period and changes are made and incorporated using Microsoft Word revision marks. The final version of the agreement is prepared but rather than accepting or rejecting all revision marks and the removal of any comments they are simply turned off (ie hidden from view on the screen or when printed out). The company then wishes to enter into another agreement on the same terms and conditions. The contract negotiator for the company may simply make a copy of the document containing the terms and conditions, but not otherwise change the document (such as the removal of the metadata being the revision marks or comments which are 'hidden' from view). In such a case, the company may provide details about a previous deal to a new party it is hoping to enter into contract with.

If Microsoft Word is used then the most likely metadata which needs removing from a document are:

- revision marks (track changes);
- comments;
- annotations;
- headers and footers; and
- (file) properties.

In recent versions of Microsoft Word, it is possible simultaneously to remove all of this information using the Document Inspector function[36]. This will search

---

[35]   In the authors' experience, the level of training of many users of the advanced features of Microsoft Word is minimal, and the consequences of using some of these features.

[36]   In Microsoft Word 2010: Alt, F, I (Info), I (Prepare for Sharing), I (Check for Issues), choose what you wish Document Inspector to check for (in the Document Inspector window that appears), then I (Inspect). Then choose the metadata that needs removing.

for and optionally remove this metadata. However there are limitations (ie it only permits the removal of all revision marks, comments and annotations together; you cannot select which of these you wish to keep or remove).

Even with the removal of metadata, some parties are still unhappy about sending documents to other parties and will either wish to password protect a Microsoft Word file against editing, send the file in PDF or text format or print onto paper. Such an approach, while attractive in principle, is unlikely to be conducive to relations as it imposes extra burdens on the recipient of an agreement presented in this way to comment on it. Most parties nowadays expect to receive documents in a format which permits editing and the use of Microsoft Word's set of tools to do so.

9.6   Catching the cheats, the use of revision marks and lesser crimes

A problem than can sometimes occur where an agreement is sent from one party to a second party for review is that the changes made by that second party are not highlighted, mentioned or shown. The usual way nowadays in most cases is to mark changes using Microsoft Word's revision marks (track changes) function. However, there is nothing to stop a party receiving a document:

- turning off the track changes feature at any particular point;

- making a change;

- turning the track changes feature back on; and

- returning the document back to the first party but without notifying that party of the change made.

No doubt the second party engaging in such a practice will hope that the first party will not notice the change, relying on the assumption that the first party will only be looking for changes marked with track changes. The second party will probably be relying also on the further assumption that the first party will not have the time (let alone the inclination) to do a manual line-by-line comparison.

Such 'cheating' shows the utmost bad faith particularly if the second party knows that the first will not have time to check. Whether a party can avoid a contract (or one of the other contractual remedies to get out of a contract) is not the subject matter of this chapter. However, particularly where commercial parties are involved, it is unlikely that a party who has signed a contract will be able to avoid it because another party has a made a change which the first party did not spot.

9.6.1   How to deal with a 'cheat'

There is no simple remedy; the response will in part depend on whether a party is sufficiently aware of the risk and also the extent that they trust the other side[37]. Here are some suggested solutions:

1   *Short-term fix:* Most at risk are the following provisions: key commercial obligations, payments and timing, meaning of definitions as well as provisions which deal with the allocation of risk and liability among the parties (such as warranties and indemnities).

2   *Medium-term fix:* Carry out a file comparison using the feature available in modern word processors between the version of the agreement sent for review and the version of the agreement returned[38]. The aim is to show all the changes made by the second party, not only those which they have selected to show.

3   *Heavy-duty fix:* In the worst cases, the agreement will require a word-by-word comparison between versions. This is obviously the most time consuming and laborious method.

9.6.2   Not all 'mis-use' of revision marks is cheating

An acceptable, one-style-in-all-circumstances, use of revision marks is not possible. Consider the following example. A party receives an agreement marked with revision marks. Its policy is to go through the agreement, and to mark the change as accepted if it likes it and delete those changes it does not like. It then returns the agreement to the other side, but otherwise does not indicate what it has accepted. The onus is on the other side going through the agreement to determine what is agreed, as simply looking at document will not indicate this. The other side will have to carry out a comparison (whether electronically or manually) to work this out. In this example, the party adopting the practice indicated does not have the intention to mislead the other side;

---

[37]   If a party has suspicions that another party engages in this type of 'cheating' then, other than pulling out of the deal, the only realistic option is to provide the resources to handle the extra checking necessary.

[38]   For example in Microsoft Word (after making copies of the files involved): (1) open each file and accept the track changes (optional) and save the changes; (2) Alt, R (Review Tab), M (Compare), C (Compare), (3) then in the Compare Documents window, enter for 'Original document' type in the file name of the file sent for review, for the 'Revised Document' type in the file name of the file returned, (4) Microsoft Word will state that all that track changes will be accepted. If you choose to see a separate window you will see a window with the document in a compared form (showing changes over the one you sent) together with separate windows showing the file as sent and the file as returned (but neither showing track changes).

The Microsoft Word file compare is adequate for relatively simple documents without extensive changes. Note, if there are several rounds or revisions, or revisions from more than one source, use Word's combine function.

it just has a particular method of using the tool available in Microsoft Word. Ultimately, the practice of using revision marks is a matter of etiquette, and a party may wish to indicate to the other how it uses this Microsoft Word function or provide a summary of the changes made. This will relieve the party who made the initial changes from going through a document to check how each change it made has been handled by the other side.

9.6.3   The settings

Irrespective of what a party may do (or how it uses the revision marks function), either party may set up Microsoft Word in different ways as to what is shown on their screen and therefore changes, deletions or additions might be hidden.

9.7   Commercial issues

Which commercial issues need checking will depend, to an extent, on the deal. It is also possible to describe some of the points above as commercial points. For example, the details of the amounts to be paid or received and when this is to happen is both a commercial issue (as to whether they are in the interests of the party at all) and also a factual issue (as to whether the information entered into the agreement is correct).

The point under this heading which needs addressing is the 'bigger picture'— to look at the agreement overall, rather than as a series of negotiations and drafting on individual points (which junior staff may carry out after the main points of the deal are discussed by senior management). A change in one clause will need consideration against others.

For routine agreements or agreements where a party will only accept minor changes (because it can impose its terms and conditions unchanged) this type of consideration may not be a factor. In other agreements, carrying out a 'bigger picture' review may help focus on whether the deal is worth doing at all on the terms being offered.

In carrying out a review the following points can help:

- Gather together material used during the course of negotiations (such as heads of terms, agendas for meetings, notes of meetings, exchanges of emails (sometimes even text messages)). These can provide a useful checkpoint against which the current version of an agreement (or a clause) might be checked.

- Have any discussions taken place with the relevant departments of a party about whether what is being provided is achievable at all or within the timescales negotiated?

- Have the discussions about when payments are to be made (or the amounts to be paid) been checked with a party's finance/accounts department as to whether the funds are available at all or at the times required? In more complex cases, a party may need to raise funds (short term or long term) and this may involve agreements with the provider of such funds.

- If a party is being asked to provide warranties in an agreement which are outside of the 'normal' types of warranties it provides, has that party carried out any internal due diligence to see whether it can give the warranty at all or subject to limits on its knowledge?[39]

- If a party is asked to reduce its exclusion or limitation of liability provisions (including its liability for direct and consequential loss, or the amount payable in the event of a breach) have such changes been considered against the provisions of any insurance it carries (or checked with its insurer broker)?[40]

9.7.1   Other methods of considering commercial points

First suggestion: Another method of handling commercial issues is for a party to develop a series of policies on key commercial issues or contractual wording and, for each area, provide:

- a default position that the party will normally expect to see in a contract;

- acceptable variations from the default position;

- unacceptable variations from the default position (with example wording);

- a listing of acceptable and unacceptable wording (with example wording); and

- action required where wording comes within one of the above categories (ie an acceptable variation, if proposed, may need approval at a lower level of management, but an unacceptable variation would need consideration at senior management level).

These points are likely to be most relevant where a party is entering into a number of contracts relating to its normal activities. For example if it is selling

---

[39]   When negotiating a contract, a party may need to provide extra or more detailed warranties in order to negotiate a better price or better specification for the goods or services. For example, a licensor of software may need to provide the potential licensee with more detailed and specific warranties as to the rights it has to the intellectual property it owns and uses in order to achieve a better royalty rate.

[40]   Any insurance a party may hold to cover its business liability may be provided on the premise that it may be able to trade on the basis that it will only accept certain liabilities and then only up to a certain extent.

a particular product or licensing a standard item of intellectual property then it would normally expect to trade on standard terms and conditions.

Another suggestion: At important stages, prepare a note that summarises the key points of the deal which includes the changes that have occurred from the initial draft. This document may be for internal circulation only, or may be sent to the other parties depending on the stage negotiations have reached.

9.8   What to do when there is an error and the document has been signed?

If all the parties to the agreement agree that there is an error and they also agree as to what needs changing then there is not normally a problem. However, the issue then is how to fix the error. There are various options (moving from non-binding to binding on the parties):

- the parties ignore the error (ie make no reference to it in any documentation);

- the parties' representatives have an exchange of emails/letters which notes both the error and the position;

- the parties enter into an amending agreement which sets out what in the underlying agreement is incorrect and replaces that wording with the correct wording;

- the underlying agreement is cancelled and a new, error-free version is signed by the parties.

The various options move from very informal (and not binding) to very formal and binding. Which option to choose will partly depend on the nature of the error and the importance of the agreement.

Chapter 10

Drafting, exchanging and protecting documents electronically

10.1   Introduction

Since 1997 (when the first edition of this book was published) it has become commonplace for the majority of commercial lawyers and their clients to draft, review, edit and exchange drafts of agreements using computers[1]. The use of word processing and e-mail can involve a number of legal, technical and practical issues. This chapter considers some of them, including:

- whether drafters and users of agreements should send agreements electronically;

- the dangers of leaving metadata in a document;

- what constitutes an electronic signature and whether they are used in signing commercial agreements; and

- policies for sending e-mail communications.

This chapter does not aim to describe in substantial or technical detail the various methods by which documents can be edited and reviewed. It concentrates on setting out some of the more practical points in the use of these methods[2].

10.2   Exchanging documents electronically

One of the great benefits of using word-processing software and e-mail is the ease with which drafts of agreements can be prepared, revised and exchanged between parties (and/or their legal advisers).

10.2.1   The problem

There are a number of potential issues where a draft of an agreement is exchanged between parties and either party is able to alter the draft, including:

---

[1]   This comment is made in relation to most lawyers working in the area of commercial law, but some law firms in some non-commercial areas of law still follow the old system where the lawyer's assistant/secretary does all his/her typing and document generation.

[2]   Undoubtedly, technically sophisticated users of this book will be familiar with many of the features and issues described in this chapter. However, in the authors' experience, many lawyers and non-lawyers they deal with are unfamiliar at any level with most of the issues contained in this chapter, often because they lack training in the use of Microsoft Word, the primary tool used nowadays in the creation and amendment of documents.

- when one party makes changes to a draft of an agreement but does not inform the other party, whether in the document or otherwise, about the changes made; and

- whether the party receiving a document changed by another party has the time, and sufficient resources, to check the document in case there are any non-identified changes.

- Examples of how (and why) this might occur are found in Chapter 9— Techniques for checking contracts before signing them at **9.6**.

10.2.2   *What to do about the problem*

Whether the parties to an agreement trust each other (both in terms of integrity and accuracy in use of revision marks (track changes and the other tools available in modern word processors) is key to whether each party will allow the other to make changes to drafts of an agreement provided electronically. Where one party does not allow the other party to make changes to an agreement, this may be perceived by the other party as an indication that they are not trusted in some way. Such an approach may not assist ongoing negotiations or foster a spirit of give and take. Also, perhaps even more importantly, given the reduced timescales within which people now operate, such an approach may simply be unrealistic, irrespective of any views one or more of the parties may have as to whether other parties are trustworthy.

In former times documents were typed on manual typewriters and changes were usually made by only one party—by convention, this would be the party putting forward the draft. All the amendments, additions, deletions, etc would be provided to that party. In the authors' experience it is rare for one commercial party to insist that only it will make any changes to a document.

If drafts of agreements can be amended by both parties, then it is suggested that each party should consider doing the following on receipt of a new draft from the other party:

- run file-comparison software or utilities that will show any changes between a version of the document previously provided to the other party, and the version returned by the other party[3]; *and/or*

- read through the whole document comparing it with the previous version sent to the other party.

---

[3]   Users of Microsoft Word can use the built-in file comparison function, see **9.6**. Catching the cheats, the use of revision marks and lesser crimes. However, there are more robust and sophisticated third-party programs, including Workshare (http;//www.workshare.com), Change-Pro (http://www.change-pro.com/), DiffDoc (http://www.softinterface.com/index. htm), iRedline (http://www.softinterface.com/index.htm), plus several others.

Although these suggestions appear to be a counsel of perfection and are time-consuming there is no other way of guaranteeing the integrity of the text.

10.2.3   Should drafts of agreements be exchanged electronically at all—and how should this be done?

There is no ideal solution to this. The choice is between security and usability running on a continuum from:

- *maximum security*—either not exchanging documents electronically at all or exchanging documents electronically but allowing only one party to make changes, to

- *maximum usability*—allowing each party to change a document.

There are a number of possible ways to handle the exchange of documents nowadays, for example:

- *Providing the document only as a printed document (or facsimile).* While possible (and the most secure) this method is unlikely to be acceptable to most commercial clients or their lawyers (or between lawyers for that matter).

- *Providing the document in portable document format (PDF)*[4]. In the US, some law firms will only[5] provide their documents in PDF. Although it is not impossible to 'edit' a PDF in the same way as in a word-processing program[6], such editing is only suitable for small changes.

- *Password protection.* Most word processors and programs which allow for the creation of PDFs allow for the saving of documents with a password. For example, the latest versions of Microsoft Word permit the protection of documents in a number of ways. The main advantage of this method is to restrict who can actually see the document.

- *Restricting what can be changed.* This method means setting up the electronic document so that only certain parts can be altered[7], through the use of

---

[4]   In Adobe Acrobat format. There are also now many software publishers who provide software to print to PDF files. Most modern word processors provide this functionality as standard. Third-party suppliers also provide programs to create PDF files, such as PDF Factory (http://www.fineprint.com), BullZip PDFPrinter (and PDF-Xchange (http://www.tracker-software.com).

[5]   Particularly with a full version of the Adobe Acrobat or with PDF-Xchange. These allow a user of the PDF to add comments, but not change the text of the document itself. The full version of Adobe Acrobat and other programs (such as Corel PDF Fusion (http://www.corel.com and some others)) do permit the user to change individual lines. This functionality is however far from allowing the editing of text in the same way as a word processing program

[6]   See **10.6** below.

[7]   For example, Microsoft Word, OpenOffice, LibreOffice and Adobe Acrobat all allow for the addition of fields. Only within the defined fields can information be added or choices made from a list.

fields. Other parts of the document cannot be edited. This method is only suitable for standard-form agreements where virtually all the terms and conditions will not change but only the particular facts concerning the deal need entering (such as the price, quantity, dates, etc).

- *Using external methods to restrict access.* There are number of methods available, including:

  o copying one or more files into a zip file (which reduces the space that they occupy) and adding a password to the zip file and then providing the zip file to another party[8];

  o copying one or more files into an encrypted container and providing the encrypted container[9];

  o sending the file(s) by encrypted e-mail so that the file(s) are protected in their transit from the sender to the recipient[10].

- *Not placing any restrictions on the document at all.* Of course a drafter of an agreement can send it electronically without any of the restrictions identified immediately above (eg just as a normal Microsoft Word document). In this case the receiving party will be free to amend the document as it wishes even if the sending party says it will not accept changed documents back.

---

[8]   For example, there are programs which are file-copying utilities which contain zip features (which are much more powerful replacements for Windows Explorer, the program which allows a user to manage files (copy, delete, view files) and is built into Microsoft Windows). These include: Directory Opus (http://www.gpsoft.com.au/), Total Commander (http://www.ghisler.com/) plus many others. Standalone zip programs include: WinZip (http://www.winzip.com/win/en/index.htm) and PKZIP (http://www.pkware.com/). Some of these programs can password protect the zip file while others also allow for the encryption of files (with the use of a digital signature). Recent versions of Windows Explorer (such as Windows 7) can open zip files, including password protected (but not encrypted) zip files.

[9]   There are a number of possible ways of doing this. The principal way considered here is to create a disk within a file (with encryption software), which is then loaded using the encryption software and becomes another disk drive available in Windows. It is then possible to copy files to and from it. Once it is unloaded the disk appears to be just another file in Windows and it is possible to copy it. There are other ways of encrypting data, including encrypting the whole of a computer disk/partition prior to or after the booting of Microsoft Windows. The former methods will not allow for the copying of word-processing files in a secure fashion. The latter methods are designed to protect the whole of the data stored on a computer if the computer is lost or stolen. Software which performs encryption of data or disks include: TrueCrypt (http://www.truecrypt.org/) and Symantec http://www.symantec.com/business/ whole-disk-encryption (http://www.symantec.com/business/whole-disk-encryption).

[10]   This is principally through obtaining a digital signature, installing it in an e-mail program and then choosing (at the time an e-mail is sent) whether the e-mail (and any attachments) are encrypted. It is also possible digitally to sign an e-mail (with its attachment) so that the e-mail is not encrypted; but if the contents are changed then the fact that the e-mail or any attachment are changed will be become apparent. Microsoft Outlook provides for the installation of a digital signature at the following place: Alt, F (file), T (options), scroll down to Trust Center, Alt-T (Trust Center Settings, scroll down to E-mail Security, Alt-G (Get a Digital ID), which will direct you to a Microsoft web page with providers of digital signatures.

Whatever method is used, the recipient of the document can (with the right tools) create a version of the document and provide a revised version back to the sender[11]. This will still leave the sender with the problem of which version of the document to use.

10.3   Metadata

There is no precise definition as to the meaning of 'metadata', other than it is 'data about data'[12]. Such a definition is of no real help in understanding what it is and why it raises important issues concerning electronic documents. For the purpose of this section it means data whose content is normally not seen by the person working on a document.

10.3.1   What kind of information does metadata consist of?

A modern word-processing document, created or edited in a word processor such as Microsoft Word may contain[13]:

- personal details (name of the user of the computer, initials of that user, company or organisation name);

- details about the computer (computer name, name of network server or hard disk where document saved);

- file properties for the file (eg name of the author of the document, the name of the manager, company name, and any other added in the available fields found in the property window)[14];

- document revision marks ('track changes', eg indicating who made specific revisions to the document, when they were made and the contents of text which is amended or deleted)[15];

---

[11]   For example, a document provided in hard copy can be scanned and then turned into text with optical character recognition software. Or text in a document provided as a PDF can be copied and then reformatted. There is also software available which will extract the text and the formatting from a PDF. This recreation process can be time-consuming, however.

[12]   For readers who are interested in such technical matters, see http://en.wikipedia.org/wiki/Metadata. The location of material on wikipedia sometimes changes.

[13]   Some metadata is generated automatically on creating or editing a document. Metadata is also obtained from the computer system on which the document and word processer are located, in addition to that created by the users of the computer and the word-processing software.

[14]   Available at Alt, F (File), I (Info) and then on the right-hand part of the Info window click on the option needing changing. To look at more options (and display as a separate window): Alt, F (File), I (Info), QS (Properties button), then scroll down to Advanced Properties.

[15]   Revision marks (track changes) which are accepted are generally not recoverable, if the file which contains/contained them is then saved.

- comments (indicating who made the comment and of course the text of the comment itself)[16];

- ink annotations[17];

- hidden text (ie text that is formatted as 'hidden' and is not shown as such in a document)[18];

- details of the last person who worked on the document;

- macros;

- hyperlinks;

- routing information (ie information which is embedded in a document if it is sent via e-mail, showing in simple terms the path the document has taken).

10.3.2   Why is metadata important?

There are several potential consequences of not removing metadata from a document, including the following:

- revealing personal data or information about the organisation or party who created or edited the document;

- revealing information which might be in breach of client confidentiality (if the document is created or edited by lawyers or others working under professional rules);

- revealing data or information which is commercially sensitive, confidential or simply embarrassing if revealed to the other side or a third party.

Not all metadata is damaging to a party or should not be revealed to other parties. For example, a law firm, in creating an agreement for a client, would normally record in the file properties window details concerning the firm (such as its name, contact details, etc). There would normally be no problem with that information being revealed. But the same document might also contain revision marks, comments or hidden text which was made between

---

[16]   Available at Alt, R (Review), C (Comment). Like revision marks, it is possible to delete them, and then if the file which contains/contained them is saved they are not generally recoverable. However, it is also possible to hide them from view. This cannot be controlled by the sender of a file but by the recipient.

[17]   These are made with persons using a tablet PC (able to write on the screen of a computer).

[18]   Hidden text as the name indicates hides the text on screen and when the is document printed. This option needs to be understood. If the word 'continuing' in the following phrase 'the continuing failure of the law to protect' is hidden, then the phrase will appear as 'the failure of the law to protect'. (How to hide text: select text then Alt, H (Home tab), FN (Font dialog box), then under Effects choose Hidden.) Unless the following option is chosen then it will not normally be apparent that there is hidden text in a document. The Show/Hide button (Alt, H (Home tab), 8 (Show/Hide). This will display all the material which does not display.

the lawyer and the client that had not been properly deleted before sending the document to another party. To take a couple of examples:

- The client's representative inserts a comment in the draft agreement as a memo to herself that she should check whether the pricing information in the draft agreement should be the stated figure or a different amount which is charged to another customer of the client. The draft agreement is returned to the lawyer who is normally diligent in checking for all changes. However by accident the 'display comments' functionality is turned off[19]. As only track changes are displayed, it is assumed that there are no comments in the document[20]. The draft agreement is sent to the other party. The other party will be able to see the comment and potentially gain a negotiating advantage through knowing that the client is prepared to accept a different price.

- The client wishes the lawyer to prepare a draft agreement for a new contract. The lawyer's firm does not have a precedent library (or someone responsible for preparing previously used agreements for re-use). However the lawyer has been provided with an agreement used in another transaction which contains a number of observations using the comments feature of the word processor, but these have not been removed before sending the document to the other side. If they are of a personal nature then they might be embarrassing if revealed.

An equally serious issue concerns the breaching of client confidentiality or breaches of the Data Protection Act 1998 where lawyers are involved. This will commonly arise where an existing agreement is reused for a new deal but the relevant metadata is not deleted from it. If any litigation results from an agreement, the discovery process in litigation may nowadays involve electronic searching and production of data held on computers by a party involved in the litigation which can include mining metadata[21].

The authors' law firm regularly receives agreements from clients or the other side in a transaction that contain clear references to parties and matters relating to another transaction. There is no single method which will avoid this occurring other than a clear policy in every organisation on the creation, amending and exchange of documents. This could involve, as a relatively low-cost starting

---

[19] For example by typing Alt, R (Review Tab), TM (Show Markup), C (Comments).

[20] In this example the lawyer also fails to run a file comparison, which if run would reveal any comments as well as any hidden text.

[21] The implication being that if metadata is removed it would not normally be available for recovery during the discovery process in litigation. However, this is subject to the metadata not being removed at a time when litigation is threatened or actually taking place. Balanced against the desire to remove metadata are reasons why a party would wish to retain some of it. For example, notes made in a document (via the use, eg, of the Comments function in Microsoft Word) of the pre-contract negotiations are unlikely ever to be useable as evidence in a court case. But, a note which indicates an assumption or a fact that the parties were working from might.

point, training all users of the issues involved in electronic documents, some of which are set out in this chapter[22]. A further step would be for agreement drafters to have clear rules on the creation of new agreements, including:

- forbidding the creation of new agreements from previously used ones (unless they are cleansed of all transaction-specific metadata);

- creating agreements only from a documented precedent/template database (preferably with usage notes)[23];

- making a specific person responsible for implementing, adding to and maintaining the precedent database and for cleansing documents of metadata which are for use as templates.

The use of a precedent bank of standard agreements is a method commonly used by firms of lawyers as the starting point for new agreements[22].

10.3.3   How to remove metadata

There are a number of methods which are possible:

- *Copy content of an existing document to a new document.* This will remove some but not of all the metadata—principally it will remove revision marks (track changes)[24].

- *Print the document to PDF.* This process removes *most* but not all metadata (potentially that which could be most damaging), but does not allow the other party to edit the document[25].

- *Follow the instructions of the supplier of the word processor on removing metadata.* The main suppliers of word-processing software all provide a function to remove most forms of metadata. The steps involved in doing this in Microsoft Word are detailed in Chapter 9[26].

---

[22]   Which is likely to involve some understanding of what is metadata in a word-processing program, and the key features of the word-processing program which generate, store or constitute metadata.

[23]   There are many ways of accomplishing this from a full-blown document management system (integrating e-mail, file management and time recording), to document/agreement automation software, to a simple list of templates/precedents available via an intranet web page or in a word processed document. There are many document-management system software programs available, often tailored to particular industries and professions, including the legal profession (see http://www.venables.co.uk/software.htm for a starting point as to UK suppliers of such software). For automation of document creation, again there are many programs to help with this such as: Agreement Assistant and Forms Assistance from the Payne Group (http://www.payneconsulting.com/), HotDocs (http://www.hotdocs.com/), RapidDocs (http://www.epoq.co.uk/ep/rapidocs.cfm).

[24]   For example (in Microsoft Word), Ctrl+A (to select all), Ctrl+C (to copy), Ctrl+N (to create a new document), Ctrl+V (to paste the contents of the new document).

[25]   Although it appears some track changes and comments information may be retained where a document is printed to PDF.

[26]   At **9.5.7**—Clearing the document of metadata.

- *Use third-party software to remove metadata.* There are several providers of software which aim to remove metadata in a more automated and thorough way than is available with word processors themselves[27].

10.3.4   Should a lawyer look at the metadata in a document received from another party?

Surprisingly there appears to be no guidance (let alone a professional rule) concerning this issue for lawyers operating in England and Wales. In the US, the right of a lawyer to look at the metadata in a document varies from state to state, with some allowing it, others not allowing it and the remainder not taking a stance at all. The national American Bar Association does not forbid this at present[28].

10.4   Electronic signatures

An electronic signature performs essentially the same function as a 'traditional' signature[29]. It is a method for a person or organisation to identify itself and:

- to authenticate the electronic data; or
- to agree to or approve the contents of electronic data,

to which the electronic signature is attached. Electronic signatures (and electronic communications) are now recognised in law[30].

Every day millions of electronic signatures are created. The following are some examples:

- a person typing their name in an e-mail;
- a signature written in hand but scanned into a computer, saved as a graphic, and that graphic is inserted into word-processing documents and e-mails;

---

[27]   Such as Metadata Assistant from the Payne Consulting Group (http://www.payneconsulting. com); iScrub (http://esqinc.com/); Doc Scrubber (http://www.javacoolsoftware.com/ docscrubber.html#Principles) (Doc Scrubber). Meta*dact* (http://www.litera.com/metadact. aspx).

[28]   http://www.americanbar.org/groups/departments_offices/legal_technology_resources/ resources/charts_fyis/metadatachart.html.

[29]   Ie one written by hand (or with the use of a stamp). See **2.12**.For readers interested in knowing about the functions of signatures generally, consult M Anderson and V Warner, *Execution of Documents—A Practical Guide*, 2nd edition, 2008 Law Society Publishing.

[30]   Following the implementation of Electronics Signatures Directive (Directive 1999/93/ EEC) and Electronic Commerce Directive (Directive 2000/31/EC), into English law by the Electronic Communications Act 2000 and the Electronic Signatures Regulations 2002, SI 2002/318. The book mentioned in the previous footnote includes an outline of this law at chapter 25.

- a person 'clicking' on various buttons on an internet site, such as when placing an order;

- a digital signature,

- let alone the many millions of electronic and digital 'signatures' used when people order goods and services online or agree to receive information.

However, when it comes to the signing of commercial agreements, the use of electronic signatures is not common. In the authors' experience most commercial agreements which involve an element of negotiation and revision are signed in the traditional way, by a person writing their name in ink on a printed document (or, more rarely, using a rubber stamp containing their signature), even where parties are located in different countries[31]. There are several reasons for this, including:

- many types of electronic signature are inherently insecure and easy to 'forge', for example, if an unauthorised person 'clicks' on an internet site, claiming to be someone else, or an unauthorised person gains access to someone else's e-mail account and sends e-mails that purport to be from and signed by that other person. The most secure type of electronic signature is a *digital signature* which can be obtained from third-party provider; however, in many industries digital signatures are not (yet) widely accepted or regularly used by commercial parties for entering into commercial (one-off) agreements; and/or

- where the transaction is regarded as significant by one or both of the parties involved, they often require the extra 'formality' of getting an authorised signatory physically to sign a piece of paper with the signature block of the agreement to reflect its importance.

In the event of a dispute as to whether, for example, the managing director of a particular company has signed an agreement[32], it is much easier to show that a physical signature on a paper version of an agreement is that of an individual than to prove that an electronic or digital signature on an electronic document is similarly that of an individual and to demonstrate that the electronic document, in its travels through various computer systems around the world, has not been altered or that the data has not been tampered with by a third party. Even in the case of the most secure kinds of digital signature, their use depends on use of a password (to which others might be given or

---

[31]   Although sometimes, where parties are located in different countries, one party will send a scanned copy of the whole document or sometimes just the signature page of an agreement to the other party, to indicate that they have accepted the agreement.

[32]   By comparing the signed document against other documents signed by the individual whose signatures it purports to be. Although, nowadays, it will be almost unique for a case to turn on whether a document has been signed by the right person (ie that the signature showing the name Jane Smith has been signed by Jane Smith).

unlawfully obtain access) and it may be more difficult to establish a forgery than in the case of an idiosyncratic physical signature.

In the authors' experience none of their commercial clients has asked for an important, one-off agreement to be signed with an electronic signature.

10.5   E-mail policies

The use of e-mail, while allowing speed and ease of communication, does make it easier for other persons in an organisation to be 'cut out of the loop' in the negotiation process, whether deliberately or by chance. It is entirely possible for a junior member of staff of one party to engage in negotiations via the use of e-mail with another party and not inform their manager. The result is that they might make a representation or make a 'collateral' agreement which is not reflected in the main agreement. Although many commercial agreements include clauses designed to avoid such eventualities[33] the courts have held that the wording used in such clauses is not always effective in making such representations ineffectual[34].

The problem is a technical one, in that it is difficult to prevent a person who can send e-mails from doing so unless the approval of another is first obtained. Consequently, as e-mails are part of the process of negotiations and the main form of communications used by organisations, there is a need to have clear policies regarding their use, including:

- *generally* that employees receive training on how their organisation carries out negotiations, information on reporting structures, as well as the practicalities of dealing with the types of issues that need the approval or consideration by more senior staff and those that do not.

- *more specifically*:

  o that e-mails sent or received by a particular individual are copied to relevant other persons in the organisation[35];

  o that e-mails and any attachments (particularly drafts of agreements) are filed on the organisation's computer systems so that others can

---

[33] Normally called 'entire agreement' clauses. See **6.5.22.10** for a brief outline of the problems involved with entire agreement clauses.

[34] Particularly so where there is a complex sequence of negotiations or where the deal is complex. More information and examples of entire agreement clauses can be found in the *A-Z Guide to Boilerplate and Commercial Clauses*, 2nd edition, 2006, Bloomsbury Professional Publishing.

[35] The other side of the coin is that more people than necessary are copied in on e-mails. A person who is tangentially linked to a negotiation or whose involvement should be limited to serious matters, may be copied in on every e-mail—even the most mundane and routine ones. In such situations, a person may receive a deluge of e-mails and, due to the number received, may overlook the very e-mail that requires their immediate attention.

access them (and so that they do not get deleted by the e-mail's archiving or deletion feature)[36].

10.6   Security of files[37]

Exchanging documents is easy, but their contents are also easy to view without additional protection. There are two particular issues here:

- whether an individual document needs protection; and
- whether where the document is (electronically) located and from where it is sent also need protection.

10.6.1   *Protection of individual documents*

The protection of the contents of documents depends, naturally, on whether such contents contain sensitive, commercial, confidential or technical data which is valuable. In the authors' experience, across a wide range of commercial and non-commercial organisations and among many law firms (from specialist, niche law firms to large law firms in the UK and abroad, particularly the US) the protection of documents *themselves* usually does not take place[38]—perhaps because the exchange of documents is normally between those who are intended to use them. The other issue, perhaps, is that users of documents expect to be able to comment on them, and imposing restrictions makes this process difficult and raises the irritation level of those who encounter such restrictions[39].

The following are some suggestions where a user does wish to protect a document.

---

[36]   Document-management system software can deal with this issue by automatically filing all e-mails sent and received (or by creating a record in the software) with other related items (subject always to the user setting up the software correctly and using it as it is intended on a systematic basis). However, the cost involved in purchasing such software and the time needed to tailor it to the needs of the particular organisation and implementing it (as well as training employees in using it) is substantial.

[37]   This chapter does not deal with the merits of the different technologies in terms of their strength in stopping someone from overcoming that particular technology's protection.

[38]   This is separate to the issue of whether the computer on which a document is stored is secure. Some issues on this point are dealt with below.

[39]   For example, if a password is added to a word-processing file then the sender of the document has to tell the recipient what the password is. If the password is enclosed within an e-mail then if the e-mail is seen by someone other than the intended recipient, the document is no more secure than without a password. Also, if the recipient needs to pass the document on to others, s/he will hardly wish to tell each recipient the password verbally. This is the 'irritation' factor mentioned earlier in this chapter.

Preventing unauthorised changes in Microsoft Word

Microsoft Word provides a number of options to prevent unauthorised changes:

- *opening otherwise unprotected documents, in 'read-only' mode.* This offers the user opening a document the option of opening in a read-only mode or in 'normal' editing mode. This is no more than warning signal.

- *requiring a password to make changes to a document.* The user can open the document without entering a password. But to make changes which the recipient wishes to keep, the user will need to save the document under a different file name (the document under the new file name will lose the protection). This is only useful where the sender wishes to be sure that the file s/he has sent if returned is not changed[40].

- *preventing 'hidden' changes to the text of a document but allowing comments or revision marks.* Microsoft Word also can restrict, via a password, changes to a document so that it is only possible to add comments to the document or (separately) any changes made are marked as revision marks (whether displayed on screen or not). Allowing only the making of comments will not permit the changing of the text in a document. Only permitting revision marks will allow changes to the text but they are always marked as revisions. Neither will stop the copy of the text into a new document[41].

Other methods:

- *Printing the document to PDF.* This method, while stopping direct changes to the text contained in the PDF will not stop the contents being copied and the copied version being used outside the PDF as the basis of the version sent back by the recipient[42]

- *Controlling access to the document with a password.* If the sender of a document wishes to control access to the contents of the document then use of a

---

[40]   There appears to be a flaw, as opening a Microsoft Word file with this type of protection directly from Outlook does enable the recipient to add text and save the document under its existing file name. However a subsequent opening of the file, outside of Microsoft Outlook, will indicate that the file is read only.

[41]   Via the Restrict Editing function which, once implemented, is controlled by a password (ie the function cannot be turned off by the recipient if s/he does not have the password). Where the restriction relates to track changes, it allows the recipient of the document only to make track changes or only to make comments (ie it is not possible to add text to the document without track changes being switched on). If the restriction relates to comments, it is not possible to alter the existing text at all, but only to add comments. To locate this function: Alt, R (Review Tab), PE (Restrict Editing), choose the type of editing restriction required in the window/side bar that appears and click on 'Yes, Start Enforcing Protection' and enter password.

[42]   It is also possible at least with some programs which create PDFs to configure the software so that the contents of the resulting PDF cannot be copied.

password is the only realistic option[43]. Microsoft Word does provide this feature, and in so doing encrypts the file[44].

- *Restricting access to the document with third-party encryption and other software*[45]. This is most probably suitable where there are a number of documents and the sender does not wish to set a password (or other restricting means) for each document.

10.6.2   Protection of computer on which documents reside

The above methods are aimed at controlling access to a document after it leaves the sender's computer. The other factor is controlling or restricting access to the document on the sender's computer. The importance of this has grown, as many users of computers now use laptops and other mobile devices to work away from a specific location. Also the amount of information stored only increases, so that the storer/sender of a document may not only have confidential, commercial or technical information from his/her own organisation but also that of the other party in a transaction, as well as from third parties. With virtually no restrictions as to the amount of information that it is now possible to store on such devices, there is little incentive for many users to remove information.

For users concerned about this there are several methods of securing a device; primarily through the encryption of the whole, or parts of, the device[46]. However, whichever means are used, they are only as good as the weakest point—which is normally the point where a user leaves the machine on but not locked (so that anyone coming by can just start typing), or the use of simple, easy to guess passwords.

10.7   And finally…

As this chapter primarily involves the use of electronic methods of dealing with documents, the following are two electronic methods to help the drafter draft a better agreement:

---

[43]   In Microsoft Word: Alt, F (File), S (Save) *or* A (Save As), click on 'Tools' icon (or Alt+L then down arrow), G (General Options), then type password for 'Password to open', etc.

[44]   Encryption prevents anyone using other programs from seeing the text of the document. It is possible to open a normal Microsoft Word in a text editor (such as Notepad, NotePad++ and many others) and extract the text. Encryption prevents this.

[45]   See *Using external methods to restrict access* under 10.2.3—Should drafts of agreements be exchanged electronically at all—and how should it be done? above.

[46]   See footnote 8 for tools which can accomplish this.

- *Checking for consistency in an agreement.* It is possible to carry out a comparison of a version of an agreement with a different version, but none of the features in any word processor (or third-party file comparison software) will proof read the document (ie to check such things as whether there is any missing punctuation, whether an opening bracket—'('—is followed by a closing bracket—')', whether a defined term is used properly in an agreement or whether a word which is shown as being a defined term actually has an accompanying definition). This is the traditional task of a proof reader. In reality such a task requires careful (and laborious) reading of the document. As far as the authors are aware there is only one software program which provides a proof-reading function[47].

- *Writing simpler, clearer English.* In Chapter 3 there is a description of several techniques on how it is possible to draft agreements more clearly and simply. These depend at least in part on an understanding of the rules of grammar. Nothing can replace learning these and learning how to use them over time[48] and no electronic tools can realistically replace such knowledge. Microsoft Word does come with a grammar checker but the quality of its checking (let alone understanding its results) is open to debate[49]. For best use it needs configuration and understanding in detail what it can do and what it cannot pick up in a document. It is not designed to assist drafting, although such programs do exist[50].

---

[47] Deal Proof (http://accelus.thomsonreuters.com/solutions/business-law/dealproof/).

[48] Such as studying such guides as Ernest Gowers, *The Complete Plain Words, 2004,* 3rd edition, Penguin; Martin Cutts, *Oxford Guide to Plain English,* 3rd edition, 2009, Oxford University Press, plus many others.

[49] In the authors' view, the quality of Microsoft Word's grammar checker is best expressed in the following way: 'As a result of my testing, I am convinced that this feature works well for good writers and not for bad ones. Good writers follow most of the rules and this feature can help them on the margins. If you are a bad writer with a poor understanding of the rules, this feature will not help you at all' (from the website of Professor Sandeep Krishnamurthy, http://faculty.washington.edu/sandeep/check/). There are also third-party programs which carry out grammar checking independent of Microsoft Word.

[50] For example, StyleWriter (http://www.editorsoftware.com/) plus several others.

Appendix

Sample agreements

These sample agreements are included to illustrate the layout, spacing, etc of agreements, and types of clauses to be included. They are not for use in 'real life'. In the first precedent, reference is made to places in this book where further information is available on individual clauses or words. For further explanation or examples of alternative wording, users should consult the sister publication to this book, *A–Z Guide to Boilerplate and Commercial Clauses*.

Precedent 1—Specimen contract—in the form of an agreement

CONSULTANCY AGREEMENT[1]

THIS AGREEMENT *dated_____201[ ] is made by and between[2]:*

1) **ABC LIMITED**, a company incorporated in England and Wales under company number 0123456789, and whose registered office is at Townhouse, 1 Status Street, Rightshire, OP99 1LD (the 'Company'); and

2) **ANDERSON CONSULTANTS ZLC**, a zero liability corporation, incorporated in the Republic of St Kilda, whose principal place of business is at the Puff Inn, Village Bay, Hirta, Republic of St Kilda (the 'Consultant')[3].

RECITALS[4]:

A   The Company is considering an investment in a new business venture, more fully described in the Business Plan (which is attached to this Agreement as Schedule 1).

B   The Consultant is experienced in the provision of business consultancy services.

C   The Company wishes to commission the Consultant to investigate the potential market for the products described in the Business Plan and to prepare a report and recommendations, as are more fully described in the Specification, and the Consultant is willing to provide such services subject to the provisions of this Agreement.

---

[1]   For information on titles of agreements, see Chapter 2, **3**.
[2]   For more information on the date of an agreement see Chapter 2, **2.4**.
[3]   For more information on the date of an agreement see Chapter 2, **2.5**.
[4]   For more information on the date of an agreement see Chapter 2, **2.6**.

THE PARTIES AGREE AS FOLLOWS[5]:

1   Definitions[6]

In this Agreement, the following words have the following meanings:

Business Plan	The document attached to this Agreement as Schedule 1, as amended from time to time by agreement between the Parties.
Commencement Date	1st January 2012.
Compliance Letter	The letter set out in Schedule 3 to this Agreement.
Net Sales Value	The invoiced price of Products sold by the Company in arm's length transactions exclusively for money or, where the sale is not at arm's length exclusively for money, the price that would have been so invoiced if it had been at arm's length exclusively for money, after deduction of normal trade discounts actually granted and any credits actually given, any costs of packaging, insurance, carriage and freight, any value added tax or other sales tax, and any import duties or similar applicable government levies.
Parties	The Consultant and the Company, and 'Party' shall mean either of them.
Products	Any and all of the products described in the Business Plan.
Services	The services and other obligations to be performed by the Consultant as described in the Specification.
Specification	The document attached to this Agreement as Schedule 2, as amended from time to time by agreement between the Parties.

2   Condition precedent[7]

It is a condition precedent to the coming into effect of this Agreement that the Consultant shall have signed and delivered to the Company no later than [*date*] the Compliance Letter in the form set out in Schedule 3. If that condition is not met by that date, this Agreement shall not come into effect.

3   Services

3.1   The Consultant shall provide the Services to the Company from the Commencement Date.

---

[5]   For information on introductory wording to the operative provisions of the agreement see Chapter 2, **2.7**.

[6]   For more information on definitions see Chapter 2, **2.8**. See also Chapter 3, **3.9**.

[7]   For information on conditions precedent (and conditions subsequent) see Chapter 2, **2.9**.

3.2   The Consultant shall use its best endeavours[8] to complete the Services, including delivery of a final report to the Company, by 1 January 2013.

3.3   The Consultant shall provide the Services in such places as the Company may reasonably specify. Whenever the Consultant or the Consultant's staff work on Company's premises, the Consultant shall ensure their compliance with the Company's fire, health and safety rules and procedures.

4   Payments[9]

4.1   *Fixed amounts*: In consideration[10] for the Services, the Company shall pay to the Consultant the following amounts on the following dates:

   (a)   £100,000 (one hundred thousand pounds sterling) within 30 days of the date of this Agreement; and

   (b)   £100,000 (one hundred thousand pounds sterling) within 30 days of the first anniversary of the Commencement Date,

4.2   *Royalty*: In further consideration for the Services, the Consultant shall pay to the Company a royalty of 5% (five per cent) of the Net Sales Value of all Products sold by the Company during the period of 10 years from the Commencement Date.

4.3   *Payment terms*

   (a)   Royalties due under this Agreement shall be paid within 60 days of the end of each quarter ending on 31 March, 30 June, 30 September and 31 December, in respect of sales of Products made during such quarter, and within 60 days of the termination of this Agreement.

   (b)   All sums due under this Agreement:

      (1)   are exclusive of Value Added Tax which where applicable will be paid by the Company to the Consultant in addition;

      (2)   shall be paid in pounds sterling by cheque made payable to 'AZLC Offshore Account', and in the case of sales income received by the Company in a currency other than pounds sterling, the royalty shall be calculated in the other currency and then converted into equivalent pounds sterling at the buying rate of such other currency as quoted by National

---

[8]   For information on best endeavours, reasonable endeavours and all reasonable endeavours see Chapter 5, **5.5**.

[9]   For information on payments Chapter 5, **5.6**. See also Chapter 8, **8.4.8**, **8.4.50**, **8.4.63**, **8.4.71**. For information on the use of amounts (as numbers or written out) and formulas see Chapter 3, **3.12**, **3.13**.

[10]   For information on consideration see Chapter 1, **1.3**, **1.10**.

Westminster Bank plc as at the close of business on the last business day of the quarterly period with respect to which the payment is made; and

(3)   shall be made without deduction of income tax or other taxes charges or duties that may be imposed, except insofar as the Company is required to deduct the same to comply with applicable laws.

4.4   *Royalty statements*: The Company shall send to the Consultant at the same time as each royalty payment is made in accordance with Clause 4.3(a) a statement setting out, in respect of each territory or region in which Products are sold, the types of Product sold, the quantity of each type sold, and the total Net Sales Value in respect of each type, expressed both in local currency and pounds sterling and showing the conversion rates used, during the period to which the royalty payment relates.

4.5   *Records*

(a)   The Company shall keep at its normal place of business detailed and up to date records and accounts showing the quantity, description and value of Products sold by it on a country by country basis, and being sufficient to ascertain the royalties due under this Agreement.

(b)   The Company shall make such records and accounts available, on reasonable notice, for inspection during business hours by an independent chartered accountant nominated by the Consultant for the purpose of verifying the accuracy of any statement or report given by the Company to the Consultant under this Clause 4. The accountant shall be required to keep confidential all information learnt during any such inspection, and to disclose to the Consultant only such details as may be necessary to report on the accuracy of the Company's statement or report. The Consultant shall be responsible for the accountant's charges unless the accountant certifies that there is an inaccuracy of more than 5 per cent in any royalty statement, in which case the Company shall pay his charges in respect of that inspection.

5   Warranties, liability and indemnities[11]

5.1   Each of the Parties warrants that it has power to enter into this Agreement [and has obtained all necessary approvals to do so].

---

[11]   For information on warranties see Chapter 5, **5.7** and concerning liability and indemnities see Chapter 5, **5.8**. See also Chapter 8, **8.4.61**.

5.2   Each of the Parties acknowledges that, in entering into this Agreement, it does not do so in reliance on any representation, warranty or other provision except as expressly provided in this Agreement, and any conditions, warranties or other terms implied by statute or common law are excluded from this Agreement to the fullest extent permitted by law.

5.3   Except in the case of death or personal injury caused by the Consultant's negligence, the Consultant's liability under or in connection with this Agreement, whether arising in contract, tort, negligence, breach of statutory duty or otherwise howsoever, shall not exceed the sum of £1,000,000 (one million pounds sterling) in aggregate.

5.4   Neither Party shall be liable to the other Party in contract, tort, negligence, breach of statutory duty or otherwise for any loss, damage, costs or expenses of any nature whatsoever incurred or suffered by that other Party that (a) are of an indirect or consequential nature or (b) consist of any economic loss or loss of turnover, profits, business or goodwill.

6   Confidentiality[12]

6.1   Each Party shall:

(a)   maintain in confidence any information provided to it directly or indirectly by the other Party under, or in anticipation of, this Agreement, taking such reasonable security measures as it takes to protect its own confidential information and trade secrets;

(b)   use such information only for the purposes of performing its obligations under this Agreement; and

(c)   not disclose such information to any other person, other than to employees and consultants who (in each case) have accepted obligations of confidentiality and non-use equivalent to the provisions of this Clause 6 and who need to have access to such information in connection with the performance of this Agreement.

6.2   The obligations set out in Clause 6.1 shall not apply to any information which the Party receiving the information ('Receiving Party') can prove by written records:

(a)   was already lawfully in its possession prior to receiving it from the other Party;

(b)   was already in the public domain when it was provided by the other Party;

---

[12]   For information on confidentiality see Chapter 5, **5.9**.

(c) subsequently enters the public domain through no fault of the Receiving Party;

(d) is received from a third party who has the lawful right to provide it to the Receiving Party without imposing obligations of confidentiality; or

(e) is required to be disclosed by an order of any court of competent jurisdiction or governmental authority, or by the requirements of any stock exchange on which the shares of the Receiving Party are listed or are to be listed, provided that reasonable efforts shall be used by the Receiving Party to secure a protective order or equivalent over such information and provided further that the other Party shall be informed as soon as possible and be given an opportunity, if time permits, to make appropriate representations to such court, authority or stock exchange to attempt to secure that the information is kept confidential.

7   Duration and termination[13]

7.1 *Commencement and Termination by Expiry:* Subject to Clause 2, this Agreement shall come into effect on the Commencement Date and, unless terminated earlier in accordance with this Clause 7, shall continue in force until all obligations on either Party under this Agreement have been fulfilled.

7.2 *Early termination*

(a) The Company may terminate this Agreement at any time on 90 days' notice in writing to the Consultant.

(b) Without prejudice to any other right or remedy it may have, either Party may terminate this Agreement at any time by notice in writing to the other Party ('Other Party'), such notice to take effect as specified in the notice:

(1) if the Other Party is in [material] [substantial][14] breach of this Agreement and, in the case of a breach capable of remedy within 90 days, the breach is not remedied within 90 days of the Other Party receiving notice specifying the breach and requiring its remedy; or

(2) if the Other Party becomes insolvent, or if an order is made or a resolution is passed for the winding up of the Other

---

[13] For information on commencement and duration see Chapter 5, **5.3**. For information on termination and consequences of termination see Chapter 5, **5.10**.

[14] For information on the meaning of 'material' and 'substantial' see Chapter 8, **8.4.45**.

Party (other than voluntarily for the purpose of solvent amalgamation or reconstruction), or if an administrator, administrative receiver or receiver is appointed in respect of the whole or any part of the Other Party's assets or business, or if the Other Party makes any composition with its creditors or takes or suffers any similar or analogous action in consequence of debt.

7.3 *Consequences of termination:* Upon termination of this Agreement for any reason:

(a) the provisions of Clauses 4 and 6 shall continue in force;

(b) each Party shall return to the other Party any documents in its possession or control which contain or record any of the confidential information of the other Party; and

(c) subject as provided in this Clause 7.3, and except in respect of any accrued rights, neither Party shall be under any further obligation to the other.

8 General[15]

8.1 *Force majeure:* Neither Party shall have any liability or be deemed to be in breach of this Agreement for any delays or failures in performance of this Agreement which result from circumstances beyond the reasonable control of that Party, including without limitation labour disputes involving that Party. The Party affected by such circumstances shall promptly notify the other Party in writing when such circumstances cause a delay or failure in performance and when they cease to do so[16].

8.2 *Amendment:* This Agreement may only be amended in writing signed by duly authorised representatives of the Company and the Consultant.

8.3 *Assignment:* Neither Party shall assign, mortgage, charge or otherwise transfer any rights or obligations under this Agreement without the prior written consent of the other Party. However, either Party may assign and transfer all its rights and obligations under this Agreement to any company to which it transfers all or [substantially all] [any part] of its assets or business, provided that the assignee undertakes to the other Party to be bound by and perform the obligations of the assignor under this Agreement[17].

---

[15] For information on 'boilerplate' see Chapter 5, **5.12**, Chapter 8, **8.4.4**.

[16] For information on *force majeure* clauses see Chapter 5, **5.12.2**.

[17] For information on (non) assignment clauses see Chapter 5, **5.12.4**. For information on (non) assignment clauses see Chapter 5, **5.12.4**; Chapter 8, **8.4.6**.

8.4   *Waiver:* No failure or delay on the part of either Party to exercise any right or remedy under this Agreement shall be construed or operate as a waiver thereof, nor shall any single or partial exercise of any right or remedy preclude the further exercise of such right or remedy.

8.5   *Invalid clauses:* If any provision or part of this Agreement is held to be invalid, amendments to this Agreement may be made by the addition or deletion of wording as appropriate to remove the invalid part or provision but otherwise retain the provision and the other provisions of this Agreement to the maximum extent permissible under applicable law.

8.6   *No Agency:* Neither Party shall act or describe itself as the agent of the other, nor shall it make or represent that it has authority to make any commitments on the other's behalf.

8.7   *Interpretation:* In this Agreement:

    (a)   the headings are used for convenience only and shall not affect its interpretation; and

    (b)   references to persons shall include incorporated and unincorporated persons; references to the singular include the plural and vice versa; and references to the masculine include the feminine; and

    (c)   the Schedules to this Agreement shall form part of this Agreement as if set out here.

8.8   *Notices:*

    (a)   Any notice to be given under this Agreement shall be in writing and shall be sent by first class mail or air mail, or by fax (confirmed by first class mail or air mail) to the address of the relevant Party set out at the head of this Agreement, or to the relevant fax number set out below, or such other address or fax number as that Party may from time to time notify to the other Party in accordance with this Clause 8.8. The fax numbers of the Parties are as follows: Company—01234 567 890; Consultant—09876 543 210.

    (b)   Notices sent as above shall be deemed to have been received three working days after the day of posting (in the case of inland first class mail), or seven working days after the date of posting (in the case of air mail), or on the next working day after transmission (in the case of fax messages, but only if a transmission report is generated by the sender's fax machine recording a message from the recipient's fax machine, confirming that the fax was sent to the number indicated above and confirming that all pages were successfully transmitted)[18].

8.9 *Further action:* Each Party agrees to execute, acknowledge and deliver such further instruments, and do all further similar acts, as may be necessary or appropriate to carry out the purposes and intent of this Agreement.

8.10 *Announcements:* Neither Party shall make any press or other public announcement concerning any aspect of this Agreement, or make any use of the name of the other Party in connection with or in consequence of this Agreement, without the prior written consent of the other Party[19].

8.11 *Entire agreement:* This Agreement, including its Schedules, sets out the entire agreement between the Parties and supersedes all prior oral or written agreements, arrangements or understandings between them. The Parties acknowledge that they are not relying on any representation, agreement, term or condition which is not set out in this Agreement. Without limiting the generality of the foregoing, neither party shall have any remedy in respect of any untrue statement made to it upon which it may have relied in entering into this Agreement, and a Party's only remedy is for breach of contract. However, nothing in this Agreement purports to exclude liability for any fraudulent statement or act[20].

8.12 *Law and Jurisdiction:* The validity, construction and performance of this Agreement shall be governed by English law and shall be subject to the exclusive jurisdiction of the English courts to which the parties hereby submit, except that a Party may seek an interim injunction in any court of competent jurisdiction[21].

8.13 *Third parties:* This Agreement does not create any right enforceable by any person who is not a party to it under the Contracts (Rights of Third Parties) Act 1999[22].

---

[18]   For information on notices clauses see Chapter 5, **5.12.1**.

[19]   For information on assignment clauses see Chapter 5, **5.12.4**.

[20]   For information on entire agreement clauses see Chapter 6, **6.5.5**, **6.5.22.10**.

[21]   For information on law and jurisdiction clauses see Chapter 5, **5.11**.

[22]   For information on Contracts (Rights of Third Parties) Act 1999 clauses see Chapter 5, **5.2**, **5.12.5**.

AGREED *by the Parties through their authorised signatories*[23]*:*

For, and on behalf of **ABC LIMITED**

_____

Signature:

_____

print name:

_____

job title:

_____

date:

For, and on behalf of **ANDERSON CONSULTANTS ZLC**

_____

signature:

_____

print name:

_____

job title:

_____

date:

---

[23]   For information on execution clauses see Chapter 2, **2.11**. See also Chapter 8, **8.4.65**.

Schedule 1[24]

Business Plan

Schedule 2

The Specification

Schedule 3

The Compliance Letter

Precedent 2—Specimen contract—in the form of a letter[25]

[name of company, its contact details or printed letterhead]

[name of consultant]

[contact details of consultant]

Dear [ ]

Consultancy Agreement

I have pleasure in confirming the following terms and conditions under which you will provide consultancy services as described below and in the attached Schedule 1 (the 'Services') to [name of company] (the 'Company').

1   This Agreement will commence as of [date] and you will complete the Services by [date] or such later date as we may agree in writing.

2   During the consultancy you will give the Company advice and information, carry out studies and make reports as specified in Schedule 1 and in accordance with any reasonable instructions of the Company. The Company's representative(s) for the purpose of giving any instructions and approvals under this Agreement shall be me and such other persons as I may nominate in writing.

3   In consideration of the Services the Company will pay you the fees described in Schedule 1.

4   All reasonable expenses properly and necessarily incurred by you in the proper performance of the Services will be reimbursed by the Company

---

[24]   For information on schedules see Chapter 2, **2.10**.
[25]   For information on alternative agreement formats see Chapter 2, **2.16**.

provided that all air travel will be undertaken at [the most economic rates reasonably available] and in any event any item of expense which may exceed £[ ] will be agreed with the Company in advance.

5   You will raise invoices on the Company (and send them to the above address marked for my attention) showing the fees due and expenses claimed with documentary evidence of such expenses.

6   You will be responsible for the payment of any income tax, insurance contributions or other taxes, revenues or duties arising as a result of the performance of the Services or otherwise under this Agreement. For the avoidance of doubt neither you nor any person engaged by you in the performance of the Services will be an employee of the Company in performing the Services.

7   You will promptly communicate in confidence to the Company all ideas generated, work done, results produced and inventions made in the performance of the Services ('Results'). You will not, without the written consent of the Company, use or disclose to any other person or organisation either during or after termination of this Agreement any confidential information of the Company which may come into your possession. For this purpose all Results shall be treated as the confidential information of the Company.

8   On any termination of this Agreement you will return to the Company all documents, records (on any media) and other property belonging to the Company which are in your possession and are capable of delivery and you will retain no copies thereof in any form.

9   You undertake that all copyright, design right, rights to apply for patents, patents and other intellectual property in the Results shall belong to the Company. In consideration of the fees payable under this Agreement, you agree on demand to assign forthwith to the Company all intellectual property in the Results at any time after their coming into existence. At the Company's request and expense (but without further payment to you) you will use all reasonable endeavours to enable the Company at its discretion to make formal application anywhere in the world to obtain and maintain intellectual property in the Results.

10   Without prejudice to any other right or remedy, if you commit any serious breach of, or fail to comply with, any of your obligations under this Agreement, become bankrupt or any judgment is made against you and remains unsatisfied for seven days, the Company shall be entitled to terminate this Agreement forthwith on written notice to you.

11   This Agreement is personal to you and may not be assigned by you. This Agreement does not give you any authority to act as agent of the Company.

12   For the purpose of ensuring compliance with your obligations under this Agreement the Company shall have access to and the right to inspect any work being carried out by you under this Agreement.

13   This Agreement is made under English law and the parties submit to the non-exclusive jurisdiction of the English courts.

14   This Agreement does not create any right enforceable by any person who is not a party to it ('Third Party') under the Contracts (Rights of Third Parties) Act 1999, but this Clause does not affect any right or remedy of a Third Party which exists or is available apart from that Act.

I should be obliged if you would indicate your agreement to the provisions of this Agreement by signing and returning to me the enclosed copy of this letter.

Yours [faithfully][sincerely],

For, and on behalf of, [*insert name of company offering consultancy work*]

_____

[*Name of signer*]

[*Position*]

Acknowledged and agreed to by [insert name of the consultant]

_____

signed

_____

print name

_____

job title

_____

date

Schedule 1

Services

[ ]

Fees

[ ]

Regulation 5(5)

SCHEDULE 2   INDICATIVE AND NON-EXHAUSTIVE LIST OF TERMS WHICH MAY BE REGARDED AS UNFAIR

1   Terms which have the object or effect of –

(a)   excluding or limiting the legal liability of a seller or supplier in the event of the death of a consumer or personal injury to the latter resulting from an act or omission of that seller or supplier;

(b)   inappropriately excluding or limiting the legal rights of the consumer vis-à-vis the seller or supplier or another party in the event of total or partial non-performance or inadequate performance by the seller or supplier of any of the contractual obligations, including the option of offsetting a debt owed to the seller or supplier against any claim which the consumer may have against him;

(c)   making an agreement binding on the consumer whereas provision of services by the seller or supplier is subject to a condition whose realisation depends on his own will alone;

(d)   permitting the seller or supplier to retain sums paid by the consumer where the latter decides not to conclude or perform the contract, without providing for the consumer to receive compensation of an equivalent amount from the seller or supplier where the latter is the party cancelling the contract;

(e)   requiring any consumer who fails to fulfil his obligation to pay a disproportionately high sum in compensation;

(f)   authorising the seller or supplier to dissolve the contract on a discretionary basis where the same facility is not granted to the consumer, or permitting the seller or supplier to retain the sums paid for services not yet supplied by him where it is the seller or supplier himself who dissolves the contract;

(g)   enabling the seller or supplier to terminate a contract of indeterminate duration without reasonable notice except where there are serious grounds for doing so;

(h)   automatically extending a contract of fixed duration where the consumer does not indicate otherwise, when the deadline fixed for the consumer to express his desire not to extend the contract is unreasonably early;

(i)   irrevocably binding the consumer to terms with which he had no real opportunity of becoming acquainted before the conclusion of the contract;

(j)   enabling the seller or supplier to alter the terms of the contract unilaterally without a valid reason which is specified in the contract;

(k) enabling the seller or supplier to alter unilaterally without a valid reason any characteristics of the product or service to be provided;

(l) providing for the price of goods to be determined at the time of delivery or allowing a seller of goods or supplier of services to increase their price without in both cases giving the consumer the corresponding right to cancel the contract if the final price is too high in relation to the price agreed when the contract was concluded;

(m) giving the seller or supplier the right to determine whether the goods or services supplied are in conformity with the contract, or giving him the exclusive right to interpret any term of the contract;

(n) limiting the seller's or supplier's obligation to respect commitments undertaken by his agents or making his commitments subject to compliance with a particular formality;

(o) obliging the consumer to fulfil all his obligations where the seller or supplier does not perform his;

(p) giving the seller or supplier the possibility of transferring his rights and obligations under the contract, where this may serve to reduce the guarantees for the consumer, without the latter's agreement;

(q) excluding or hindering the consumer's right to take legal action or exercise any other legal remedy, particularly by requiring the consumer to take disputes exclusively to arbitration not covered by legal provisions, unduly restricting the evidence available to him or imposing on him a burden of proof which, according to the applicable law, should lie with another party to the contract.

2. Scope of paragraphs 1(g), (j) and (l)

(a) Paragraph 1(g) is without hindrance to terms by which a supplier of financial services reserves the right to terminate unilaterally a contract of indeterminate duration without notice where there is a valid reason, provided that the supplier is required to inform the other contracting party or parties thereof immediately.

(b) Paragraph 1(j) is without hindrance to terms under which a supplier of financial services reserves the right to alter the rate of interest payable by the consumer or due to the latter, or the amount of other charges for financial services without notice where there is a valid reason, provided that the supplier is required to inform the other contracting party or parties thereof at the earliest opportunity and that the latter are free to dissolve the contract immediately.

Paragraph 1(j) is also without hindrance to terms under which a seller or supplier reserves the right to alter unilaterally the conditions of a contract of indeterminate duration, provided that he is required to inform the consumer with reasonable notice and that the consumer is free to dissolve the contract.

(c)   Paragraphs 1(g), (j) and (l) do not apply to:

- transactions in transferable securities, financial instruments and other products or services where the price is linked to fluctuations in a stock exchange quotation or index or a financial market rate that the seller or supplier does not control;

- contracts for the purchase or sale of foreign currency, traveller's cheques or international money orders denominated in foreign currency;

(d)   Paragraph 1(l) is without hindrance to price indexation clauses, where lawful, provided that the method by which prices vary is explicitly described.

Index

[all references are to paragraph number]